CHAOS OR COVENANT?

Chaos or Covenant?

A Short Theological Introduction to the Pentateuch

⚛

MICHAEL S. MOORE

WIPF & STOCK · Eugene, Oregon

CHAOS OR COVENANT?
A Short Theological Introduction to the Pentateuch

Copyright © 2024 Michael S. Moore. All rights reserved. Except for brief quotations in critical publications or reviews, no part of this book may be reproduced in any manner without prior written permission from the publisher. Write: Permissions, Wipf and Stock Publishers, 199 W. 8th Ave., Suite 3, Eugene, OR 97401.

Wipf & Stock
An Imprint of Wipf and Stock Publishers
199 W. 8th Ave., Suite 3
Eugene, OR 97401

www.wipfandstock.com

PAPERBACK ISBN: 978-1-6667-8079-6
HARDCOVER ISBN: 978-1-6667-8080-2
EBOOK ISBN: 978-1-6667-8081-9

VERSION NUMBER 04/26/24

Contents

Abbreviations | vii

Introductory Remarks | 1

1　Genesis: Chaos or Creation? | 13
2　Exodus: Slavery or Freedom? | 51
3　Leviticus: Defilement or Holiness? | 67
4　Numbers: Wilderness or Homeland? | 76
5　Deuteronomy: Conflict or Covenant? | 113

Concluding Remarks | 129

Bibliography | 131
Subject Index | 161
Author Index | 163

Abbreviations

The abbreviations below complement those listed in *The SBL Handbook of Style*.

1 En.	1 Enoch
1QapGen	The Genesis Aprocryphon from Qumran Cave 1
1QH^a	The Hodayot scroll from Qumran Cave 1
1QM	The War Scroll from Qumran Cave 1
Abr.	*De Abrahamo*
AEL	*Ancient Egyptian Literature*. Miriam Lichtheim. 3 vols. Berkeley: University of California Press, 1971–80
Ag.	*Agamemnon*
AIL	Ancient Israel and Its Literature
A.J.	*Antiquitates judaicae*
AJEC	Ancient Judaism and Early Christianity
AJES	*American Journal of Economics and Sociology*
AJSL	*American Journal of Semitic Languages and Literatures*
AJSR	*Association for Jewish Studies Review*
Akk	Akkadian
Anab.	*Anabasis*
AnBib	*Analecta Biblica*
Andr.	*Andromache*
ANE	Ancient Near East

ANEM	Ancient Near Eastern Monographs
ANET	*Ancient Near Eastern Texts Relating to the Old Testament*. Edited by J. B. Pritchard. 3rd ed. Princeton: Princeton University Press, 1969
AOAT	Alter Orient und Altes Testament
AP	Advanced Placement
Apoc. Ab.	Apocalypse of Abraham
Arab	Arabic
AS	*Aramaic Studies*
Atr	Atrahasis
AYBC	Anchor Yale Bible Commentaries
AYBD	*Anchor Yale Bible Dictionary*. Edited by D. N. Freedman. 6 vols. 1992. Repr., New Haven: Yale University Press, 2008
AYBRL	Anchor Yale Bible Reference Library
b.	Babylonian Talmud
BA	*Biblical Archaeologist*
BBR	*Bulletin for Biblical Research*
BBRSup	*Bulletin for Biblical Research, Supplements*
BCBC	Believers Church Bible Commentary
BCOT	Baker Commentary on the Old Testament
BETL	Bibliotheca Ephemeridum Theologicarum Lovaniensium
BHT	Beiträge zur historischen Theologie
Bib	*Biblica*
BibEnc	Biblical Encyclopedia
BibInt	Biblical Interpretation Series
BibOr	Biblica et Orientalia
B.J.	*Bella judaicum*
BJS	Brown Judaic Studies
BM	British Museum
BR	*Biblical Research*
BRev	*Bible Review*
BZ	*Biblische Zeitschrift*
BZABR	Beihefte zur Zeitschrift für altorientalische und biblische Rechtsgeschichte
BZAW	Beihefte zur Zeitschrift für die alttestamentliche Wissenschaft

CA	*Current Anthropology*
CAD	*The Assyrian Dictionary of the Oriental Institute of the University of Chicago.* Chicago: The Oriental Institute of the University of Chicago, 1956–2006
CANE	*Civilizations of the Ancient Near East.* Edited by Jack M. Sasson. 4 vols. New York, 1995. Repr. in 2 vols. Peabody, MA: Hendrickson, 2006
CAT	*The Cuneiform Alphabetic Texts from Ugarit, Ras Ibn Hani, and Other Places.* Edited by M. Dietrich et al. Münster: Ugarit, 1995
CBC	Cambridge Bible Commentary
CBQ	*Catholic Biblical Quarterly*
CBQMS	Catholic Biblical Quarterly Monograph Series
CC	Covenant Code (Exod 21–23)
CD	Damascus Document
CDME	*A Concise Dictionary of Middle Egyptian.* Edited by Raymond O. Faulkner. Oxford: Griffith Institute, 1962
CH	Codex Hammurabi
CHANE	Culture and History of the Ancient Near East
Cho.	*Choephori*
CI	*Critical Inquiry*
CJ	*Classical Journal*
CJA	Christianity and Judaism in Antiquity
CMHE	*Canaanite Myth and Hebrew Epic: Essays in the History of the Religion of Israel.* Frank Moore Cross. Cambridge, MA: Harvard University Press, 1973
Con	*Concordia Journal*
COS	*The Context of Scripture.* Edited by William W. Hallo. 3 vols. Leiden: Brill, 1997–2002
CT	*Christianity Today*
CV	*Communio Viatorum*
D	Intensive form of the Semitic verb
DA	Deir ʿAllā texts
DDD	*Dictionary of Deities and Demons in the Bible.* Edited by Karel van der Toorn et al. Leiden: Brill, 1995. 2nd rev. ed. Grand Rapids: Eerdmans, 1999
DH	Deuteronomistic History (Joshua–Kings)

DI	Descent of Ishtar
DILA	Dialogue of Ipu-Wer and the Lord of All
DNWSI	*Dictionary of the North-West Semitic Inscriptions.* Jacob Hoftijzer and Karen Jongeling. 2 vols. Leiden: Brill, 1995
DocH	Documentary Hypothesis
DOTP	*Dictionary of the Old Testament: Pentateuch.* Edited by T. Desmond Alexander and David W. Baker. IVP Bible Dictionary. Downers Grove, IL: Intervarsity, 2003
DOTPr	*Dictionary of the Old Testament: Prophets.* Edited by Mark J. Boda and J. Gordon McConville. IVP Bible Dictionary. Downers Grove, IL: InterVarsity, 2012
DRM	Die Religionen der Menschheit
DSD	*Dead Sea Discoveries*
DSS	Dead Sea Scrolls
DSSSE	*The Dead Sea Scrolls Study Edition.* Edited by Florentino García Martínez and Eibert J. C. Tigchelaar. 2 vols. Leiden: Brill, 1997
Dtr	Deuteronomistic ideas and features in Deut-Kings
EA	El-Amarna tablets. According to the edition of Jørgen A. Knudtzon. *Die el-Amarna-Tafeln.* Leipzig: Hinrichs, 1908–15. Repr., Aalen: Zeller, 1964. Continued in Anson F. Rainey, *El-Amarna Tablets,* 359–79. 2nd rev. ed. Kevelaer: Butzon & Bercker, 1978)
Ebib	*Études bibliques*
ECC	Eerdmans Critical Commentary
EDSS	*Encyclopedia of the Dead Sea Scrolls.* Edited by Lawrence H. Schiffman and James C. VanderKam. 2 vols. New York: Oxford University Press, 2000
Ee	Enūma eliš
Eg	Egyptian
EHJ	*The Routledge Encyclopedia of the Historical Jesus.* Edited by Craig A. Evans. New York: Routledge, 2008
EN	Enki and Ninmaḫ (ETCSL 1.1.2)
Enc	*Encounter*
EncJud	*Encyclopedia Judaica.* Edited by Fred Skolnik and Michael Berenbaum. 2nd ed. 22 vols. Detroit: Macmillan Reference USA, 2007

ER	*Encyclopedia of Religion*. Edited by Lindsay Jones. 2nd ed. 15 vols. Detroit: Macmillan Reference USA, 2005
ET	English translation
ETCSL	The Electronic Text Corpus of Sumerian Literature (https://etcsl.orinst.ox.ac.uk/)
Eum.	*Eumenides*
FAT	Forschungen zum Alten Testament
FB	Forschung zur Bibel
FEC	*From Epic to Canon: History and Literature in Ancient Israel*. Frank Moore Cross. Baltimore: Johns Hopkins University Press, 1998
FOTL	Forms of the Old Testament Literature
FRLANT	Forschungen zur Religion und Literatur des Alten und Neuen Tetstaments
G	Grundstamm (basic stem, the simple form of the Semitic verb)
GE	Gilgamesh Epic
GEP	Great Empires of the Past
Gk	Greek
GNT	Greek New Testament
HBM	Hebrew Bible Monographs
HBR	*Harvard Business Review*
HBT	*Horizons in Biblical Theology*
HdO	Handbuch der Orientalistik
Hist. an.	*Historia Animalium*
HSM	Harvard Semitic Monographs
HTR	*Harvard Theological Review*
HTS	Harvard Theological Studies
IBC	Interpretation: A Bible Commentary for Teaching and Preaching
IBT	Interpreting Biblical Texts
ICC	International Critical Commentary
ID	Inanna's Descent
IDB	*The Interpreter's Dictionary of the Bible*. Edited by George A. Buttrick. 4 vols. New York: Abingdon, 1962
IECOT	International Exegetical Commentary on the Old Testament
IJST	*International Journal of Systematic Theology*

Il.	*Iliad*
Int	*Interpretation*
JAEI	*Journal of Ancient Egyptian Interconnections*
JAJSup	*Journal of Ancient Judaism Supplements*
JAOS	*Journal of the American Oriental Society*
JBL	*Journal of Biblical Literature*
JBQ	*Jewish Bible Quarterly*
JCS	*Journal of Cuneiform Studies*
JCT	*Jewish and Christian Texts*
JEDP	Yahwist, Elohist, Deuteronomic, and Priestly "source documents"
JETS	*Journal of the Evangelical Theological Society*
JJS	*Journal of Jewish Studies*
JNES	*Journal of Near Eastern Studies*
JQR	*Jewish Quarterly Review*
JR	*Journal of Religion*
JRE	*Journal of Religious Ethics*
JRJ	*Journal of Reform Judaism*
JSNT	*Journal for the Study of the New Testament*
JSNTSup	*Journal for the Study of the New Testament Supplement Series*
JSOT	*Journal for the Study of the Old Testament*
JSOTSup	*Journal for the Study of the Old Testament Supplement Series*
JSS	*Journal of Semitic Studies*
JTI	*Journal of Theological Interpretation*
JTISup	*Journal for Theological Interpretation Supplements*
JTS	*Journal of Theological Studies*
KAI	*Kanaanäische und aramäischen Inschriften.* Herbert Donner and Wolfgang Röllig. 5th ed. Wiesbaden: Harrassowitz, 2002
KBo	*Keilschrifttexte aus Boghazköi.* Leipzig: Hinrichs, 1916–23; Berlin: Gebr. Mann, 1954–
KR	*The Kenyon Review*
Lane	Lane, Edward W. *An Arabic-English Lexicon.* 8 vols. London: Williams & Norgate, 1863. Repr., Beirut: Libr. du Liban, 1980
LB	*Linguistica Biblica*
LCBI	Literary Currents in Biblical Interpretation

Let. Aris.	Letter of Aristeas
LF	*Lutheran Forum*
LGRB	Lives of Great Religious Books
LHBOTS	The Library of Hebrew Bible/Old Testament Studies
LNTS	The Library of New Testament Studies
m.	Mishnah
Marc.	*Adversus Marcionem*
MBS	Message of Biblical Spirituality
MC	Mesopotamian Civilizations
MIO	*Mitteilungen des Instituts für Orientforschung*
Mos. 1, 2	*De vita Mosis I, II*
MT	Masoretic Text
MWCD	*Merriam-Webster Collegiate Dictionary.* 11th ed. Springfield, MA: Merriam-Webster, 2003
NA	Neo-Assyrian
Nab	*Building Inscriptions of the Neo-Babylonian Empire.* Stephen Langdon. 4 vols. Paris: Leroux, 1905–12
NAC	New American Commentary
NAR	*North American Review*
Nem.	*Nemeonikai*
NCCS	New Covenant Commentary Series
NICOT	New International Commentary on the Old Testament
NovT	*Novum Testamentum*
NRSV	New Revised Standard Version
NSBT	New Studies in Biblical Theology
OB	Old Babylonian
OBC	The Oxford Bible Commentary
OBO	Orbis Biblicus et Orientalis
OBT	Overtures to Biblical Theology
OCM	Oxford Classical Monographs
OG	Old Greek (Septuagint, LXX)
OHP	*The Oxford Handbook of the Pentateuch.* Edited by Joel S. Baden and Jeffrey Stackert. Oxford Handbooks. Oxford: Oxford University Press, 2021
OSCC	Oklahoma Series in Classical Culture

OT	Old Testament
OTE	*Old Testament Essays*
OTL	Old Testament Library
OTP	*Old Testament Pseudepigrapha*. Edited by James H. Charlesworth. 2 vols. New York: Doubleday, 1983, 1985
OTR	Old Testament Readings
OTS	Old Testament Studies
OtSt	*Oudtestamentische Studiën*
OWN	*Oudtestamentlich Werkgezelschap in Nederland*
Pan.	*Panarion (Adversus haereses)*
PBM	Paternoster Biblical Monographs
PH	Primeval History (Gen 1–11)
PresG	*Presbyterian Guardian*
Proof	*Prooftexts: A Journal of Jewish Literary History*
PRSt	*Perspectives in Religious Studies*
PSB	Princeton Seminary Bulletin
Q	Qur'an
R.	Rabbi
Rab.	Rabbah (as in Gen. Rab. or Lam. Rab.)
RBL	*Review of Biblical Literature*
RBS	Resources for Biblical Study
ResQ	*Restoration Quarterly*
RHR	*Revue de l'histoire des religions*
Š	Causative form of the Semitic verb
SAA	State Archives of Assyria
SAALT	State Archives of Assyria Literary Texts
SAK	*Studien zur Altägyptischen Kultur*
SANT	Studien zum Alten und Neuen Testaments
SB	Standard Babylonian
SBLDS	Society of Biblical Literature Dissertation Series
SBLSBS	Society of Biblical Literature Sources for Biblical Study
SBTS	Sources for Biblical and Theological Study
SGT	*The Tafsīr* [تفسير]. R. Saadiah Gaon (d. 942 CE)
SH	Studia Hellenistica

SHCANE	Studies in the History and Culture of the Ancient Near East
SiLTHS	Siphrut: Literature and Theology of the Hebrew Scriptures
SJLA	Studies in Judaism in Late Antiquity
SJOT	*Scandanavian Journal of the Old Testament*
SO	Sources Orientales
SocR	*Sociology of Religion*
StBP	Studia Post-biblica
StudBib	Studia Biblica
Summa	*Summa theologica*
Suppl.	*Supplices*
SWBA	Social World of Biblical Antiquity
SymS	Symposium Series
t.	Tosefta
TBN	Themes in Biblical Narrative
TBST	The Bible Speaks Today
TDOT	*Theological Dictionary of the Old Testament.* Edited by G. Johannes Botterweck and Helmer Ringgren. Translated by John T. Willis et al. 15 vols. Grand Rapids: Eerdmans, 1974–2006
TEP	Tale of the Eloquent Peasant
Tg. Neof.	Targum Neofiti
Tg. Onq.	Targum Onqelos
Tg. Ps.-J.	Targum Pseudo-Jonathan
Th	*Theology*
ThSt	Theologische Studiën
TOTC	Tyndale Old Testament Commentaries
UBCS	Understanding the Bible Commentary Series
UNP	*Ugaritic Narrative Poetry.* Edited by Simon B. Parker. WAW 9. Atlanta: Society of Biblical Literature, 1997
UTB	Uni-Taschenbücher
VT	*Vetus Testamentum*
VTE	Vassal-Treaties of Esarhaddon
VTSup	Supplements to Vetus Testamentum
WAW	Writings from the Ancient World
WBC	Word Biblical Commentary

Wehr	Wehr, Hans. *A Dictionary of Modern Written Arabic*. Edited by J. Milton Cowan. 3rd ed. Ithaca: Spoken Languages Services, 1976. Repr., 4th enlarged and amended ed., Wiesbaden: Harrassowtiz, 1979
WUNT	Wissenschaftliche Untersuchungen zum Neuen Testament
WW	*Word and World*
y.	Jerusalem Talmud
ZA	*Zeitschrift für Assyriologie*
ZABR	*Zeitschrift für altorientalische und biblische Rechtsgeschichte*
ZAW	*Zeitschrift für die alttestamentliche Wissenschaft*
ZDMG	*Zeitschrift der deutschen morgenländischen Gesellschaft*
ZTK	*Zeitschrift für Theologie und Kirche*

Introductory Remarks

THE PURPOSE OF THIS book is to examine several theological polarities animating the ANE text revered as scripture[1] by all three monotheistic faiths (Judaism, Christianity, and Islam).[2] Jews call it Torah (תורה) because of its primary directive to "teach" (ירה) the "law,"[3] recognizing it not only as the

---

1. "Scripture" here refers to a specific text or set of texts held by a given community to be (or contain) the word of God. For Paul the apostle, "scripture" (γραφὴ) is "God-breathed" (θεόπνευστος) (2 Tim 3:16). For W. Smith it is merely "human" and "historical" (*Scripture*, 21). For Childs, however, "biblical literature is not correctly understood or interpreted" unless "its role as religious literature is correctly assessed" (*Old Testament*, 16).

2. Hughes wonders whether the "unity" among Jews, Christians and Muslims is too "vague and nebulous" to be taken seriously, but admits that all three groups revere the first five books of the Bible as "Scripture" (*Abrahamic*, 2). The ET titles are transliterations of OG: Γένεσις (*Genesis*, origin, source); Ἔξοδος (*Exodus*, going out); Λευίτικον (*Leviticus*, Levite/priestly matters); Ἀριθμοι (*Numbers*, Vg *Numeri*); and Δευτερονόμιον (*Deuteronomy*, summary of the law). Their Hebrew titles derive from the first word in each scroll: *Genesis* is בראשית (*Bereshit*, in the beginning); *Exodus* is שמות (*Shemot*, names) *Leviticus* is ויקרא (*Vayiqra*, then he called); *Numbers* is במדבר (*Bemidbar*, in the wilderness); and *Deuteronomy* is הדברים (*Hadebarim*, the words).

3. Lit., teach the teaching. Heb תורה (Torah) is a nominal form of the verb ירה (to instruct, teach) (Isa 28:9; 1 Kgs 8:36), a term usually translated νόμος in OG (law) (Exod 12:49; Lev 11:46; Num 5:29; Deut 1:5). Syr ܢܡܘܣܐ is a transliteration of νόμα, not תורה. The earliest Tanak reference to written Torah occurs in Hos 8:12, אכתב לו רבי תורתי כמו זר נחשבו (Though I write for him the principle requirements of my Torah, they are considered by him to be strange). Cf. MacIntosh, *Hosea*, 325; Van der Toorn, "Before," 386–88.

bedrock of Tanak,[4] but as the religio-cultural foundation of all Judaism.[5] Muslims hold it to be sacred to all "People of the Book" (ياهل الكنب),[6] situating it upon a religio-cultural trajectory dominated by Qur'an (القران)[7] and the hadiths (احاديث).[8] Christians sometimes refer to it as the "Old Testament of the Old Testament,"[9] and while some would contest it, the Judeo-Christian tradition prompted by this text is the religio-cultural backbone of Western civilization.[10]

Greek readers are the first to call it Πεντάτευχος (Pentateuch), a compound term comprised of two simpler ones: πέντε (five) + τεῦχος (container).[11] The first is a plain mathematical term, while the second denotes "containers" for tools,[12] weapons,[13] clothing,[14] ballots,[15] beehives,[16]

---

4. Tanak is an acronym for *Torah-Nevi'im-Ketuvim*, the three major sections of the Hebrew Bible (Torah, Prophets, and Writings). Seeking to understand why the Samaritans accept only Torah as Scripture, Knoppers asks, "How do the Samaritans and the Jews come to share the same basic set of holy scriptures . . . ? Does one simply borrow the written Torah from the other, or is the Pentateuch itself, in the end, the result of a prolonged collaboration between the two communities?" He concludes that "the latter option seems much more likely than the former, given historical conditions and the analysis of manuscript evidence from the DSS" (*Jews*, 178).

5. J. Collins contends that "the Torah of Moses is an attempt to mold Judean identity in a particular way. . . . There are still Judeans well into the Second Temple period who do not define themselves by reference to the Torah (e.g., as seen in the earlier wisdom literature) and some . . . who may not even have been aware of its existence. Eventually, however, the composite Torah . . . comes to be the dominant expression of Judean identity" (*Invention*, 183).

6. Q 5:15 (lit., the Writing). Carimokam recognizes that "People of the Book" is Qur'an's "most frequent title for Jews and Christians" (*Muhammad*, 7-8).

7. Lit., the Reading; cf. the cognate term מקרא (the Reading) (Neh 8:8).

8. Lit., the Traditions (Berg, *Development*, 1-5; Ma'oz, *Civilizations*). Levenson doubts whether Muslims truly accept الكتاب (the Writing) as "scripture" (*Inheriting*, 175).

9. Moberly, *Testament*, 176-202. The Nazarene prophet cites from all five Torah scrolls: e.g., Gen 1:27 (cited in Matt 19:4); Exod 16:15 (cited in John 6:31); Lev 19:18 (cited in Matt 22:39); Num 30:2 (cited in Matt 5:33); and Deut 6:5 (cited in Matt 22:37).

10. Heller, "Judeo-Christian," 133; Zucker, *Torah*, 1-2; Nathan and Topolski, "Myth"; Pavlac, "Chosen"; Maritain, *Christianisme*, 29; Westbrook, "Punishments," 5:555-56; G. Walsh, *Religion*, 103-66. Periodically it becomes fashionable in some circles to deny the impact or even the existence of a "Judeo-Christian tradition" (e.g., Cohen, *Myth*), but even a historian as critical as Thompson admits that the "Western Asiatic metaphor of 'law' as Torah may well reside close to the roots of Western jurisprudence" ("Discipline," 350).

11. Cf. Shectman, "Themes," 67.

12. Homer, *Il.* 14.381.

13. Euripides, *Andr.* 617.

14. Xenophon, *Anab.* 7.5.14.

15. Aeschylus, *Eum.* 742.

16. Aristotle, *Hist. an.* 625a.26.

libations,[17] bathwater,[18] papyrus scrolls,[19] and the like. Its first known appearance occurs in a private letter penned by Ptolemaeus, a disciple of the Gnostic ideologue Valentinus (d. 179 CE), in an off-the-cuff reference to "the law embedded within the Πεντάτευχος of Moses."[20] The lawyer-theologian Tertullian (d. 220 CE) utilizes a Latin transliteration of the term (*Pentateuchos*) in a tractate denouncing the work of Marcion of Sinope,[21] and after this it appears to take on a life of its own among readers eager to call it something besides "Torah."

The following "short theological introduction" is hardly the first attempt to examine this "great text,"[22] nor is it likely to be the last. After all, billions of souls have long held it to be the inspired word of God.[23] Interpreting it from so vast a distance is challenging, of course, but some attempts are better than others. To explain, many academic programs in religious studies require students to take an introductory course on the Pentateuch, even in schools where the discipline of biblical studies is marginal to the curriculum.[24] Yet many of the textbooks chosen to facilitate this course often fail to connect with the minds and hearts of twenty-first-century students. Occasionally this happens because of a simplistic "old is bad, new is good" mentality

---

17. Aeschylus, *Cho.* 99.

18. Aeschylus, *Ag.* 1128.

19. Let. Aris. 179. In other words τεῦχος possesses a much broader semantic range than, say, βίβλιον (scroll).

20. νόμος ὁ ἐμπεριεχόμενος τῇ Μωσέως πεντατεύχῳ (Ptolemaeus, *Letter to Flora*, cited in Epiphanius, *Pan.* 33.4.1; cf. G. Smith, *Valentinian*, 20). Neh 8:1 speaks of ספר תורה משה (the book of the law of Moses), and John 7:23 reads ὁ νόμος Μωϋσέως (the law of Moses).

21. Tertullian, *Marc.* 1.10. What especially bothers Tertullian is Marcion's determination to excise the Pentateuch from the canon of sacred books (cf. Lieu, *Marcion*, 50–85).

22. Reiner ("Literatur") and Foster ("Literature") critically define what makes up a "great text" (Moore, *WealthWatch*, 22–25).

23. Cf. Levenson, *Inheriting*, 173–76; Marshall, *Inspiration*, 31–47.

24. Contemporary schools facing declining enrollments are under tremendous pressure to "streamline our programs" and "balance the budget." Correlative to this is the desire among some administrators to "increase market share" by eliminating anything in the curriculum perceived to be too intellectually challenging for students to handle (e.g., the biblical languages). Market-driven decisions like these tend to preoccupy administrators much more than, say, how to reform the elitist tenure system. In fact, many tenured faculty care more about their sabbaticals than with equipping students with the exegetical tools needed to interpret Scripture competently (Washburn, *University*, ix–xxi). This problem is not new. Benjamin Warfield criticizes similar "corner cutting" at Princeton in 1912 (Woolley, "Princeton," 28).

students sometimes bring to the classroom,[25] but the greater problem by far is the protracted influence of eighteenth- to nineteenth-century Continental scholarship on contemporary textbook writers,[26] many of whom still slice and dice the Pentateuch into bits and pieces, then speculate endlessly about the "histories" lying behind each piece.[27] Occasionally such atomistic conjecture is tempered by a proviso or two on how these bits and pieces make their way into the hands of (post)exilic editors,[28] but such disclaimers do little to help students appreciate the Pentateuch's literary integrity, not to mention its

---

25. Cf. T. Miller et al., *Expectations*, 10–23; Brickell and Paul, *Curriculum*, 30–31; Sibler, *Students*, 89–92; R. H. Miller, *Campus*, 467–70.

26. Contemporary interpretation of the Pentateuch suffers two extremes. On one end of the spectrum, readers dissect it into thousands of atomized parts, dismissing the literary framework in which they appear and marginalizing the ANE "great literature" against which they take fundamental shape. Some view this "great text" as little more than political propaganda created by homeless exiles desperate to redefine themselves through selective memory. Others view it as religious propaganda designed to promote a narrow religiopolitical ideology (i.e., monotheistic Yahwism). On the other end of the spectrum populist readers imagine the Pentateuch to be a "holy book" written by "holy authors" inside a "holy bubble." Dismissing it as a revelatory message resonating within "clay jars" and "human hearts," populists overemphasize its *transcendence* to the virtual exclusion of its *immanence*. Sustaining all this takes great energy, of course, yet populists tend to believe it to be the best (if not the only) way to protect their most cherished religious beliefs from "defilement."

27. Classic examples of this atomistic approach include Eissfeldt, *Introduction*, 155–241; Sellin and Fohrer, *Introduction*, 103–95; and Kaiser, *Introduction*, 33–133. More recently Kratz speculates that "the priestly writing reduces the hexateuch, which had become an enneateuch, to a tetrateuch. The literary joining together with the non-priestly origin and patriarch stories in Genesis and the exodus stories in Exodus-Numbers isolates Deuteronomy, which itself becomes the substance of the laws in Joshua-Kings. The corresponding additions in Deut 31–34 further isolate the Pentateuch, which is already dominated by the priestly writing, expanded by the priestly spirit" (*Komposition*, 224). Carr, however, categorically rejects such speculation, cautioning students that "all too often, biblical studies have attempted to trace in detail every step in the growth of a biblical text to its present form. Some have found 'evidence' of eight to fifteen (or more) layers of sources and redactional expansions in a single chapter or set of verses. Yet I suggest that these more complicated reconstructions of textual prehistory have not stood and will not stand the test of time" (*Hebrew Bible*, 4).

28. Some overreact to the point of presuming that the discordant sections of, say, the flood narrative (Gen 6–9) or the Balaam cycle (Num 22–24) show no evidence of literary-historical development (e.g., Fokkelman, "Genesis"; Gross, *Bileam*). O'Neill questions both extremes ("Criticism"), while Edelman presumes that the Pentateuch "addresses concerns in the sociopolitical setting of the Persian period . . . when the books are likely to have come together to form a written core" ("Preface"). Grabbe observes that "there are good reasons for seeing the fourth century BCE as the period when the Pentateuch was compiled and promulgated, though it may have taken time to be accepted as authoritative" ("Last," 20).

religio-spiritual authority.[29] The simple fact is that most twenty-first-century students find nineteenth-century interpretations of the Pentateuch puzzling and confusing, if not altogether bewildering.[30]

Yet not all introductions are pedagogically inept. Terry Fretheim's *The Pentateuch*,[31] for example, engages several questions *behind, in*, and *in front of* the Pentateuch,[32] converging on the last of these to fashion a theology shaped by the concerns of twenty-first-century readers in a methodological approach often called "reader-response criticism."[33] Reading *behind* the text he evaluates the ins and outs of various historical approaches.[34] Reading *within* it he ponders its literary/structural possibilities.[35] Yet such approach-

29. Polzin views much contemporary scholarship as a "dehusking procedure" ("Job," 182), while Carr finds in it too much "hypothetical reconstruction" (*Hebrew Bible*, 36). The presumption here is not that this type of scholarship is innately invalid, but that apart from hard evidence interpreted within clear methodological parameters such methodologies easily fade into feathery speculation (cf. Perrin, *Redaction*, 1–13; Vermeylen, *Job*; Moore, Review of *Jehu*).

30. Pleading the pedagogical case, Bailey observes that "the difficulty" teachers face is "finding an articulate, up-to-date, readable work that presents a succinct history of research, while focusing on the most cogent arguments and issues. Often problems arise when an author attempts to present the contemporary state of research to the uninitiated (beginning graduate students who are just starting their scholarly studies)" (*Torah*, 269). But beginning students are not alone in their frustration. Seasoned scholars are frustrated as well (Sommer, "Pseudo-Historicism"). Realizing this *état de choses*, Baden and Stackert introduce "pentateuchal studies as a lively and multifaceted area of biblical studies," recognizing that "the differences represented in the field show no sign of abating"("Introduction," 15). Römer is more blunt: "The lack of any consensus is probably the first thought that comes to mind when one tries to describe the current state of historical and critical pentateuchal research" ("Sojourn," 419).

31. Introductions to the Pentateuch usually appear at the beginning of standard introductions to the Hebrew Bible/Old Testament (e.g., Childs, *Introduction*, 109–225; LaSor, *Survey*, 3–14; J. Collins, *Hebrew Bible*, 25–190; M. Hamilton, *Word*, 107–236; and Dillard and Longman, *Introduction*, 37–106).

32. Fretheim, *Pentateuch*, 23–24.

33. E. Davies, *Biblical Criticism*, 11–35; R. Fowler, *Reader*, 7–58. Longman defines "reader-response criticism" as a subjectivist reading strategy where "meaning resides in the reader, not in the text" (*Literary*, 38). Similarly, Perdue defines "postmodernism" as "an extensive array of evocative modulations" formulating an epistemology which "places the source of understanding within the interaction of the mind of the interpreter" (*Reconstructing*, 240). McKnight, however, is careful to note that not all reader-response critics ignore the text's historical development (*Post-Modern*, 174), and Silva observes how competent instructors "resist the temptation to eliminate the (historical) tensions" in ancient texts like the Bible (*Misread*, 38).

34. Law recognizes that legitimate historical criticism "leads to original, stimulating, and nuanced insights into the different writings which make up the Bible and sheds light on the processes by which they come into existence" (*Historical-Critical*, viii).

35. Clines and Exum observe that the "magisterial four-document theory of the

es he finds problematic whenever they dismiss the questions preoccupying contemporary readers standing *in front of* the text.[36] *Response:* The pages below acknowledge the validity of legitimate reader-response criticism,[37] but in no way do they affirm the postmodern ideology of *presentism*; i.e., the belief that the thinking of contemporary readers is inherently superior to that of all others, including the biblical writers themselves.[38] "Reader-response," in other words, can easily masquerade as a glossy moniker for what used to be called "eisegesis."[39]

Heavily impacted by the postmodern thinking of Bernard Lonergan and Hans-Georg Gadamer,[40] Seán McEvenue's *Interpreting the Pentateuch* sets out to identify the theological objectives of the Pentateuch's so-called "documentary sources"; i.e., the Yahwist, Elohist, Deuteronomic, and Priestly "documents" first hypothesized in nineteenth-century Europe to explain the Pentateuch's literary-historical development.[41] Agreeing with John van

---

sources of the Pentateuch given classic formulation by Julius Wellhausen (*Prolegomena*, 3-4), and the still regnant hypothesis of a Deuteronomistic edition of Joshua-2 Kings proposed by Martin Noth (*Studien*) are showcases of the methods and results of traditional literary criticism.... The 'new' literary criticism," however, "is not a historical discipline, but a strictly literary one" in which the text is treated as "an object, a product, not a window upon historical reality" ("Criticism," 11). Alter observes that "the new literary criticism of the Bible tends to uncover unities where previous biblical scholars, following the hidden imperative 'the more atomistic, the more scientific,' find discontinuities, contradictions, duplications, and fissures" ("Introduction," 25; cf. Heard, "Genesis," 110).

36. Momigliano laments the fact that historians today are not expected to be "accurate, cautious, and factual," but "inventive, imaginative, and creative," often at the expense of historical accuracy ("Method," 5).

37. Cf. Zevit, *Garden*, 48-53.

38. Cf. Hunt, "Problem"; Korson, "Problem." Hardmeier warns of two dangers associated with reader-response criticism: (a) "leaving the meaning of texts entirely to the reader's creativity without corroborating them with reliable criteria for their examination; and (b) uncritically submitting them to the prevailing trends and needs of reader-response in specific interpretive communities" ("Achilles," 121). Martin challenges readers to "break out of the captivity of Scripture to modernity" and "reclaim the premodern heritage" (*Pedagogy*, 98).

39. *Eisegesis* (εἰσάγω, "to go in") is the opposite of *exegesis* (ἐξάγω, "to come out"). Mailloux recognizes that Bleich's (*Subjective*) approach to the reading of ancient texts presumes "the absolute priority of individual selves as creators of texts" (*Conventions*, 31), while E. Davies cautions that reader-response criticism should not simply replace literary-historical criticism. In fact, if the latter *is* "on the decline," he argues, "it is not because of the force of the intellectual argument against it," but because "it no longer seems appealing or exciting to a new generation of biblical scholars" (*Biblical Criticism*, 3).

40. Cf. Lonergan, *Insight*; Gadamer, *Truth* (cf. Moore, Review of *Theology*).

41. McEvenue, *Pentateuch*, 63-151; Astruc prefers the term *mémoires* (*Conjectures*,

Seters that "no interpretation of the Pentateuch can dispense with the task of understanding its compositional history,"[42] McEvenue tries to salvage as much of DocH as possible,[43] but not so much to trace the "histories" of the JEDP "sources" as to help readers "define and distinguish between the activities of interpreting, communicating, and theologizing" prompted by the "interpersonal aspect of reading."[44]

Aware of DocH and its many clones,[45] Michael Guinan's *The Pentateuch* nonetheless sidesteps them in a well-meaning attempt to usher readers more-or-less directly into the Pentateuch's "spiritual message."[46] Thus Genesis is about "the fortunes and misfortunes of imagehood" because "the living God of Israel can be imaged only by living beings who do what God does."[47] Exodus is about "how God delivers the Israelites from Egyptian op-

2). DocH in its Wellhausenian form alleges that four separate documents (abbreviated JEDP) independently circulate prior to the Pentateuch's final formation (cf. discussions in Childs, *Introduction*, 112–35; and LaSor, *Survey*, 10–11). Some readers, like Cross, imagine P (Priestly) not as a stand-alone "document," but as an editorial framework for J (Yahwist) E (Elohist) and D (Deuteronomistic) (*CMHE* 301). Others, like Weinfeld, argue that D is in many ways a secularized revision of the cultic mentality enshrined in P (*School*, 44, 180; "Deuteronomy," 2:175–77). Still others, like Schmidt (*Pentateuch*), Friedman (*Bible*), and Baden (*Composition*), contend that DocH is the only way to explain the Pentateuch's developmental history. Working separately from H. Schmid (*Jahwist*), Rendtorff challenges the Western academic obsession with written "documents," proposing in its place a "fragmentary hypothesis" wherein "larger units" (like the "Promises to the Patriarchs" and the "Revelation of the Law on Sinai") gradually meld together over time (*Problem*, 29–79). Presaging Rendtorff, Gunkel argues that Gen 1 "is not the composition of a 'writer' [*Schriftsteller*], but merely the 'transcript' [*Niedersteller*] of a tradition harking back to primordial antiquity" (*Schöpfung*, 14).

42. Van Seters, *Pentateuch*, 183. Recognizing the developmental differences between the law codes in Exodus, Leviticus, and Deuteronomy, Cazelles suggests that "if one can contest these four documents (JEDP) as 'sources' of the actual Pentateuch, (then) one must still recognize that its distinctly juridical strata refer to societies possessed of different social structures" ("Statut," 4; cf. Wright, *Inventing*, 29–120).

43. Nicholson summarizes the history of the DocH discussion (*Pentateuch*, 222–68).

44. McEvenue, *Pentateuch*, 43. Cf. Van Inwagen, "Listen"; and Provan, "Knowing."

45. Cf. discussions in Van Seters, *Pentateuch*; Alexander, *Paradise*; Bradford Anderson, *Pentateuch*; Bailey, *Pentateuch*; Gottwald, *Hebrew*, 89–130; Sailhamer, *Narrative*, 81–480; Stackert, *Deuteronomy*; Mendenhall, *Law*; Ska, *Introduction*; Shectman, *Women*; Gooder, *Pentateuch*; Watts, *Pentateuch*; Houston, *Pentateuch*; K. Schmid, *Scribes*; Laffey, *Pentateuch*; and Wenham, *Exploring* (this list is not exhaustive).

46. Guinan, *Pentateuch*, 14–20. This book appears in a Roman Catholic series called the Message of Biblical Spirituality. Chalier, a Jewish philosopher, approaches the Pentateuch in a similarly "spiritual" way (*Torah*).

47. Guinan, *Pentateuch*, 21, 24. Peterson contends that "interpreting the *imago dei*" in terms of "human identity is exegetically and theologically preferable to substantialist (Aquinas, *Summa*, 1a.93.7.ad.1), functionalist (Middleton, *Image*, 36–41), and

pression" in the hope that they will follow their Emancipator into Sinai and points north.[48] Leviticus is revealed in toto on Mt. Sinai in order to address the persistent problem of defilement because while holiness stems from an "attachment to God," it cannot coexist alongside anything "unholy, unclean, impure, or sinful."[49] Numbers depicts the forty-year wilderness wandering period as a long and painful training class on how to put the Sinai covenant into practice, especially when dealing with external/internal conflict.[50] Deuteronomy expounds the theological correlation between covenant blessing and covenant faithfulness without woodenly presuming the former to be dependent upon the latter.[51] *Response:* Guinan patiently discusses a number of important pentateuchal motifs and themes, but regrettably this book suggests no metric for assessing their relative significance.[52]

Instead of focusing on specific texts,[53] motifs,[54] and themes,[55] Victor Hamilton's *Handbook on the Pentateuch* provides, in the words of one reviewer, a veritable "mini-commentary on the entire Torah."[56] Historical concerns *behind* the text (like the historicity of the patriarchs or the date of the exodus) are left unaddressed because the main objective here is to identify the Pentateuch's *contents*, not just its *contexts*. Like many others, Hamilton finds DocH untenable, but out of respect for his readers he lays out its basic pros and cons before encouraging them to decide for themselves.[57] Thus Genesis may or may not be the product of (post)exilic editors stitching together an

---

relational (Barth, *Dogmatik*, 3.1.3–4) interpretations" (*Identity*, 173; cf. Chalier, *Image*, 12–15).

48. Guinan, *Pentateuch*, 40.

49. Guinan, *Pentateuch*, 75–76. Cf. Douglas, *Purity*; Douglas, *Leviticus*; Eichrodt, *Theology*, 2:373–74; Levine, *Presence*; Moore, "Divine," 166–67.

50. Cf. Noth, *History*, 58–59; Coats, *Rebellion*; G. Davies, "Wilderness Wandering"; Kunin, *Incest*, 11–18; Moore, "Numbers."

51. Cf. McConville, *Deuteronomy*, 10–20; Fee, *Disease*; Bowler, *Blessed*; Vogt, *Torah*, 227–30; Moore, *WealthWatch*, 100–167.

52. Cf. Bailey, *Pentateuch*.

53. Fretheim, *Pentateuch*.

54. Hendel defines "motifs" as "essential semantic units of biblical narrative," and that "to elucidate them adequately requires knowledge of language, literary and religious traditions, and cultural context, as well as an eye for intertextuality and the nuances of literary style" (Review, 127).

55. Guinan, *Pentateuch*; Alexander, *Pentateuch*.

56. Hummel, Review, 32.

57. Contrast the frontal assault on DocH by Kikawada and Quinn (*Abraham*) vs. Mowinckel's sober critique (*Erwägungen*, 1–9), not to mention Engnell's rejection of hypotheses which refuse to take seriously the authenticity of oral tradition (*Testamentet*, 168–85).

already circulating collection of written "documents,"[58] but it is myopic not to see in it a "unified composition neatly arranged by an author (or narrator or editor)"[59] guided by the highest standards of "literary artistry."[60]

Thomas Dozeman's *The Pentateuch: Introducing the Torah* is a hefty seven-hundred-page volume subdivided into four sections: Section 1 "clarifies the plot, setting, and central characters in the overarching story of Genesis-Deuteronomy" and "explores the relationship of Torah to the Prophetic literature and the Writings." Section 2 "introduces the history of research on the formation of the Pentateuch . . . from the traditional understanding of Moses as the author to the identification of anonymous authors by 18th- and 19th-century historical critics."[61] Section 3 introduces each pentateuchal book in terms of its outlines, central themes, literary designs, and comparisons to other ANE texts. Section 4 explores the aftermath of the Pentateuch; i.e., the "different ways in which readers bring meaning to Torah."[62] Of all the introductory textbooks in print today, Dozeman's is certainly one of the most comprehensive.[63]

Joseph Blenkinsopp's *The Pentateuch: An Introduction to the First Five Books of the Bible* defends the historical-critical approach from what he believes to be a surging synchronic wave hyper-impacting the minds

---

58. Gerstenberger thinks that "the beginnings of a new constitution of the defeated are already present during the era of Babylonian domination," but that "the granting of free religious practice by the Persians is still needed for a comprehensive regeneration of Yhwh's people," esp. with regard to the creation of the Pentateuch (*Israel*, 30). Grabbe argues that the Elephantine community in Egypt "knows nothing of the Pentateuch" because its trove of Aramaic texts make no mention of Moses or Aaron or even the word תורה (torah) ("Last," 20).

59. V. Hamilton, *Pentateuch*, 18 (cf. Whybray, *Making*, 221–23). Van Seters logically argues that if "Genesis is the gradual accumulation of traditions," then "the form of the whole demands as much explanation as that of its parts" (*Prologue*, 1). Berlin contends that "it is well known that the Bible borrows themes and motifs from elsewhere in the ancient Near East; Kikawada and Quinn posit the same type of borrowing for structural forms. The credit that Rendsburg reserves throughout most of his book for a redactor, Kikawada and Quinn give more readily to an author" (Review, 252).

60. V. Hamilton, *Pentateuch*, 134. Alter insists that he has "no quarrel with the courage of conjecture of those engaged in what Sir Edmund Leach shrewdly calls 'unscrambling the omelette' [Leach and Aycock, *Structuralist*, 3], but the essential point for the validity of the literary perspective is that we have in the Bible, with far fewer exceptions than the historical critics will allow, a very well made omelette indeed" ("Introduction," 25).

61. Cf. Gröger, *Wegbereiter*.

62. Dozeman, *Pentateuch*, xxv–xxvi. Part 4 tries to explain the dynamics of the blurry transition from reception-history to reader-response critique.

63. Dozeman wisely recommends to beginning students that they read parts 1 and 3 before parts 2 and 4 (*Pentateuch*, xxvi).

of many biblical scholars.⁶⁴ Like McEvenue, he tries to salvage as much of DocH as possible,⁶⁵ but at the same time he ponders the possibility that the Pentateuch may well be an official document commissioned by Persian authorities to define the status of Jerusalem subsequent to the arrival of Ezra and Nehemiah; i.e., that it might be a legally authorized "constitution" in which the interests of the returning Jewish community happily converge with those of their Persian overlords.⁶⁶

Showcasing the Pentateuch as "great literature," Thomas Mann's *The Book of the Torah: The Narrative Integrity of the Pentateuch* contends that this "great text" should be read "both in terms of its final form" *and* in terms of its "internal complexities."⁶⁷ To illustrate his point he brings a handcrafted wooden box to class and invites a student to describe it. Receiving the reply "It's a wooden box shaped like a heart," he opens the lid to reveal its contents. Soliciting a second description, he hears, "It's a wooden heart containing an intricate three-dimensional puzzle comprised of scores of carefully interlocked pieces of wood."⁶⁸ Then he asks, "Which is more beautiful, the exterior or the interior?" The point, of course, is that like all "great texts"⁶⁹

---

64. Blenkinsopp, *Pentateuch*, vii–x. Cf. Moore, Review of *Abiding*.

65. Blenkinsopp, *Pentateuch*, 229–43. Tigay points out that "the hallmark of the critical approach to the history of ancient literature (biblical and classical, as well as Mesopotamian) ... is its necessary reliance on critical analysis of late, usually final, versions of compositions. By analysis of the received texts, critics attempt to find embedded within them signs (contradictions, thematic and stylistic variants) or earlier stages of the traditions or the literary sources which combine to produce those texts, then to hypothetically reconstruct those earlier stages, and finally, to infer the processes by which the texts reach their final form. Since actual copies of these earlier stages are almost never available for consultation, the results, though impressive, remain hypothetical. For this reason biblical and classical scholars remain acutely aware of the need to gain some empirical perspective on the hypothetical critical methods which have come to dominate their fields. ... By showing what happens in a field where the history of a composition can be documented" (like *GE*), it can be suggested *quid pro quo* "what may also happen ... in fields where the history cannot be documented (like the Pentateuch)" (*Evolution*, 2).

66. Cf. Frei, "Zentralgewalt"; Crüsemann, *Tora*; Blenkinsopp, "Constitution"; Ska, *Introduction*, 217–29; and Moore, *WealthWarn*, 122–42. Blenkinsopp notes that Persian imperial policy "insists on local self-definition inscribed primarily in a codified and standardized corpus of traditional law. ... In Babylon, the neo-Babylonian laws would remain in force," and "as for Egypt, the Demotic Chronicle (papyrus 215 of the Bibliothèque Nationale in Paris) informs us that, as an aspect of the reorganization of the empire, Darius I sets up a commission of warriors, priests, and scribes to codify the traditional Egyptian laws, the final draft of which is written up in Aramaic and demotic Egyptian" (*Pentateuch*, 239–40).

67. Mann, *Torah*, 1.

68. Mann, *Torah*, 1.

69. Mugerauer argues that the primary function of "great literature" is to challenge

the Pentateuch cannot be defined *only* by its external appearance, nor can it be defined *only* by its internal complexities.[70]

Of all the textbooks in print today Norman Whybray's *Introduction to the Pentateuch* looks more like the present volume than most others, at least in terms of basic structure.[71] Both textbooks set out to be concise, not comprehensive. Both examine historical *and* literary questions. Both investigate textual *and* intertextual questions. Both engage the Pentateuch diachronically *and* synchronically.[72] Both highlight the importance of theological analysis. Both question the "evidence" for DocH, Whybray proposing that the Pentateuch may in fact be the product of a single author drawing upon multiple oral and written sources, blissfully unaware of twenty-first-century notions about literary symmetry, orthographical consistency, and stylistic finesse.[73]

At any rate, the following pages examine the Pentateuch from three angles: (a) as an *epic* text intertextually comparable to other ANE epics;[74] (b) as a *literary* text comparable to anything written by Homer or Virgil or Sîn-lēqi-unnini;[75] and (c) as a *theological* text designed to draw readers deeper into the mind of God. To this end the great Torah scholar Baruch Levine suggests that the best way "to get to core issues is to study conflict" because "arguably it is the most reliable index of what is most important in life."[76] Taking this axiom to heart, the pages below will focus on what seem to this writer to be the Pentateuch's most obvious theological polarities: *chaos vs. creation* (Genesis), *slavery vs. freedom* (Exodus), *defilement*

---

entrenched value systems that have become corrupt ("Literature").

70. Another way to put this is that the Pentateuch can and should be interpreted both synchronically and diachronically.

71. Whybray, *Introduction*. Moberly rather unfairly accuses Whybray of (a) having "little to offer by way of positive alternative" to DocH, and (b) "attempting no exegesis and interpretation of his own" (*Testament*, 176).

72. Whybray, *Introduction*, 135.

73. Whybray, *Making*, 221–23.

74. Nordheim recognizes that "disputation with ANE notions at different times in Israel's history highlights the exemplary character of specific texts" (*Selbstbehauptung*, 185–86).

75. According to Lambert an Assyrian curriculum list names Sîn-lēqi-unnini as the *āšipu*-priest responsible for preserving the Gilgamesh "series" (*iškaru*) ("Catalogue"). Alter warns that "some who have embraced literary perspectives have chosen to ignore text-critical analysis and the rigors of philology, even though in the polemic zeal of *The Art of Biblical Narrative*, I made clear that these perspectives were indispensable tools for dealing with ancient texts" (*Art*, x).

76. Levine, "Foreword," viii. Cf. his commentaries on Leviticus and Numbers (listed in the bibliography).

vs. holiness (Leviticus), *wilderness vs. homeland* (Numbers), and *conflict vs. covenant* (Deuteronomy).[77]

---

77. Clines attempts to trace a common theme (sg.) throughout the Pentateuch. This single theme, he claims, is the partial fulfilment of the promise made to the patriarchs, a promise possessed of three distinct elements: *progeny, divine-human relationship,* and *land*. Differing aspects of this promise occur in different books. In Gen 12–50 the promise of *progeny* predominates. In Exodus and Leviticus the emphasis is on the *relationship between Israel and Yhwh*. In Numbers and Deuteronomy the focus is on *the land soon to be possessed*. PH he sees ending with God's wrath falling on the nations, after which the patriarchal narratives effectively function as the "mitigation" element of the Babel story by reaffirming the deity's intentions for Israel and humanity as a whole (*Theme*).

1

Genesis: Chaos or Creation?

THE GENESIS SCROLL IS comprised of four main sections: the Primeval History (Gen 1–11), the Abraham cycle (Gen 12–24), the Jacob cycle (Gen 25–36), and the Joseph novella (Gen 37–50).[1] Not only does it set the tone for the rest of the Pentateuch (and indeed, for Tanak as a whole), but its intertextual resonance with other ANE epics helps greatly in developing a clearer understanding of this "first book of Moses."[2]

PRIMEVAL HISTORY

Much like an overture to a great symphony, the Primeval History (Gen 1–11) introduces both the Genesis scroll and the Pentateuch at large. Whether or not its first line ("In the beginning God created") is an

---

1. The connective tissue between these sections is largely the work of priestly scribes or, as Van der Toorn puts it, "The Hebrew Bible is both a product of and a monument to the scribal culture of ancient Israel" (*Scribal*, 143).

2. D. Christensen and Narucki contend that "the theological hermeneutic sees the horizontal procession of history from a vertical relation. If God is ultimately the norming norm who reveals himself within the history of Israel, and if history is shaped by real persons, then we are now in a position to begin to affirm the person of Moses as a normative influence within the history of the people of Israel. So in this sense of a creative norming event happening through a particular person for a particular people we can claim Moses' authorship of the Pentateuch" ("Pentateuch," 465).

indication of *creatio ex nihilo*,³ Genesis consists of four *sagas*⁴ expounding the chaos-creation polarity (a) in the first human generation (Adam and Eve) (Gen 1–3); (b) in the second human generation (Cain and Abel) (Gen 4–5); (c) in the world at large (the flood) (Gen 6–9); and (d) among the nations (the tower of Babel) (Gen 10–11).⁵

---

3. "Creation out of nothing." Kaufmann imagines *creatio ex nihilo* as "the basic idea of Israelite religion" (*Religion*, 60), but Levenson disagrees, arguing that contrary to modern Western conceptions of "creation" as *origination*, the creation language of the Bible concerns itself with *mastery, lordship*, and *kingship* (*Creation*, xxix). Aware of this debate, Heard agrees that whereas *creatio ex nihilo* "fits Western philosophical notions," the "creation of a chaotic earth would jar an ANE reader, who would understand creation as the taming and ordering of chaos (Isa 45:18)" ("Genesis," 108). *Question*: "If *creatio ex nihilo* is prototypically "Western," how then is the following axiom to be interpreted—οὐκ ἐξ ὄντων ἐποίησεν αὐτὰ ὁ θεός, "God did not make things out of existing things" (2 Macc 7:28)? Cf. Rubio, "Time," 3–4; Moore, "Maccabees," 1065–71.

4. Gunkel discusses the literary-historical (dis)similarities between saga, history, legend, and myth (*Genesis*, vi–xii). Kratz, on the other hand, refers to PH as "Israel's myth" (*Komposition*, 226).

5. Scurlock insightfully summarizes previous study on the chaos-creation polarity ("Introduction," ix–xiv). Tsumuraya observes a literary pattern in Genesis that (in her opinion) cannot be coincidental: (a) Gen 1–3 consists of two accounts, 1:1—2:4a and 2:4b—3:24, which together form one paired creation account; (b) the first account includes ten repetitions of the phrase ויאמר אלהים (and God said), while the second is a תולדות (generations) account comprised of two parts, the first half (2:4b–25) retracing the themes of Gen 1 from beginning to end in ascending order, the second half (3:1–24) retracing the course of creation from end to beginning in descending order; (c) the first nine ויאמר אלהים (and God said) in Gen 1 lead up to the commitment formula designating human beings as creatures made in the *imago Dei* (1:29); (d) this corresponds to the structure of Gen 2, where the first nine mentions of יהוה אלהים (Yhwh Elohim) climax with the commitment formula designating the first couple as covenant partners (2:23); (e) the ten ויאמר אלהים (and God said) formulae in Gen 1 correspond to the ten ויאמר אלהים (and God said) formulae from Noah (6:13) to Israel (46:2) to the ten תולדות אלה (these are the generations) from Adam (5:1) to Jacob (37:2); and (f) the ten ויאמר אלהים (and God said) formulae in creation also anticipate the Ten Commandments at Sinai (Exod 20:1–17), which profoundly reshape the identity of Israel, and indeed the entire creation ("Genesis," 316–17).

Chaos vs. Creation in the First Generation (Gen 1–3)

Creation epics tend to express a given culture's deepest values.[6] In this sense PH is no different from any other creation epic.[7] Several feature plots, characters, and motifs similar to those found in PH, yet one stands closer than all the others—the Babylonian epic of Atrahasis.[8] Unlike the Babylonian creation epic Enūma eliš,[9] Atrahasis not only preserves two episodes parallel to those in PH, but *in exactly the same order:* (a) the creation of humanity followed by (b) the re-creation of humanity after the great flood.[10]

With regard to the first of these episodes, Enūma ilū,[11] like Enūma eliš,[12] presumes (a) a primeval conflict between "greater gods" and "lesser gods"; (b) a decision to appease the "greater gods" by sacrificing the rebel ringleader of the "lesser gods"; (c) a belief that the blood of this rebel ringleader can bring magically inseminated clay to life;[13] and (d) a belief that the

---

6. Komoroczy insists that the divine society portrayed in ancient myths "is nothing else than the human world" ("Work," 37), while Fishbane argues that "monotheism and myth are neither mutually exclusive nor incompatible" (*Myth*, 16; cf. Lambert, *Myths*, v–viii; Moore, *WealthWatch*, 27–28). T. Lewis distinguishes between the terms "mythopoeic" (μῦθος + ποιέω [myth making]) and "mythopoetic" (μῦθος + ποιητικός [mythic imagery]) (*Origin*, 37).

7. Gilan surveys the Anatolian ("Anatolia"), Töyräänvuori the Egyptian ("Egyptian"), Sonik the Greek and Latin ("Chaos"), and Campbell the Hurrian epics ("Theogonies").

8. Cf. Lambert and Millard, *Atra-Ḫasīs*; Frymer-Kensky, "Atrahasis." Echoing Day (*Conflict*, 4), R. D. Miller insists that the creation motifs in the Psalter most likely "derive" not from Mesopotamian, but Canaanite mythology ("*Chaoskampf*," 207).

9. Scurlock thinks that "Genesis 1 is written with Ee in mind," but that this "by no means requires placing God in the role of Marduk defeating primordial Chaos" ("Chaos," 268); instead it simply "provides an opportunity to discern the nature of God as Creator as this is understood by the authors of the Genesis narrative" ("Searching," 49). Ollenburger, on the other hand, argues that God's creative words function as a "weapon" which, though different from the violence involved in Marduk's killing of Tiamat (Ee 4.102–4), is still violent (*Creator*, 81). Cf. Sparks, "Mimesis," 629–32.

10. Cf. Lambert, *Myths*, 3–144, 330–405, 366–75, 387–95; Frymer-Kensky, "Atrahasis," 148; Moran spotlights the symmetrical intentionality of Atr's bicameral structure ("Considerations," 245–46). Guinan argues that "creation has nothing to do with modern science or modern scientific explanations," but is instead "a religious statement, a statement of faith" (*Pentateuch*, 23).

11. Akk "When the gods" (Atr 1.1), the first line of Atrahasis.

12. Akk "When on high" (Ee 1.1), the first line of the Babylonian Creation Epic.

13. Qur'an also holds that God "initiates" (بدأ) the creation of "people" (الانسن) from "clay" (طين) (Q 32:7; 37:11), but that the "creation" (الخلق) of the heavens and earth is "greater" (اكبر) than the creation of "people" (الناس) (40:57).

clay creatures thereby produced can liberate the "lesser gods" from "hard labor."[14]

At first glance this sequence of scenarios looks nothing like the material in PH, but underneath the polytheistic veneer lie some remarkable parallels.[15] Like all myths, Atrahasis reflects the major socioeconomic concerns of the culture from which it originates, what Norman Gottwald rather simplistically calls "the exploiters vs. the exploited."[16] Creation in Atrahasis begins with the "greater gods" constructing "clay creatures,"[17] who, in Tikva Frymer-Kensky's words, "do the work of the (lesser) gods" by "relieving them" of "hard labor."[18] The clay creatures in Genesis,[19] however, serve a function which is *representational*, not *substitutional*.[20] Never are they enlisted to resolve conflicts between rival powers, nor are they ever called upon to pinch-hit for one group against another. The rationale for their creation, as Ryan Peterson makes clear, is simply "to establish an earthly image of God in the world."[21] That is, the clay creatures in PH are formatted to serve the agenda of a Creator determined to populate his creation with creatures capable of emulating the *imago Dei* "on earth as it is in heaven" (Matt 6:10). This creation theology pops up repeatedly in Tanak, especially in the great poetic assemblages of Job and the Psalms.[22] For example,

---

14. Atr 1:1–243. Cf. the similar plotline in Ee 6.31–34: "They bound and held him [i.e, Qingu, Tiamat's 'counselor'] before Enki / They imposed the punishment on him and shed his blood / From his blood he made humankind [*a-me-lu-tu*] / He imposed the hard labor [*dul-lu*] of the gods" (cf. Talon, *Creation*, 63).

15. Like Ee and Atr, the Sumerian myth of Enki and Ninmaḫ also presumes an aboriginal conflict where "the great gods supervise the lesser gods as they do the work" (DIĜIR ŠAR$_2$-ŠAR$_2$ KIĜ$_2$-ĜA$_2$ AL-SUG$_2$-GE-EŠ DIĜIR TUR-TUR DU$_2$-LUM IM-IL$_2$-IL$_2$-E-NE) (EN 1.9).

16. Gottwald, "Social," 4 (cf. Marx and Engels, *Manifesto*; Moore, *WealthWatch*, 73–81).

17. Atr 1.212. Akk *awīlūtu*, like Gk ἄνθρωποι, means "humankind" (*CAD* A.2.57–62).

18. Frymer-Kensky, "Atrahasis," 149.

19. *Adam* (אדם [man]) is created from the *adamah* (אדמה [ground]) (Gen 2:7), and woman (אשה) is created from man (איש) (Gen 2:23).

20. N.b. that Inanna cannot leave the netherworld until a *substitute* is found to replace her: UD-DA ^{D}INANA KUR-TA BA-ED$_3$-DE$_3$ SAĜ DILI SAĜ-ĜA$_2$-NA ḪA-BA-AB-ŠUM$_2$-MU (If Inanna is to ascend from the netherworld, let her provide a substitute for herself) (ID 288–89).

21. Peterson, *Identity*, 1.

22. The whirlwind speeches in Job 38–41 are widely recognized to be a premier example of Yahwistic creation theology (Perdue, *Wisdom*, 168–79; Schifferdecker, *Whirlwind*; Pelham, *Job*).

לא לנו יהוה לא לנו	Not to us, O Yhwh, not to us,
כי לשמך תן כבוד	but to *your* name bestow honor....[23]
למה יאמרו הגוים איה נא אלהיהם	Why should the nations say, "Where is their God?"—
ואלהינו בשמים כל אשר חפץ עשה	when our God is in heaven doing whatever he wants?[24]

Yet like the clay creatures in Atrahasis, the clay creatures in PH remain, in the words of Jon Levenson, "fragile" and "vulnerable" to chaos long after its initial suppression.[25] Atrahasis conveys this by depicting Enlil, the deity responsible for providing the original clay,[26] as a fearful character willing do whatever is necessary to muffle their "clamor" (*rigmu*).[27] The PH directives to be fruitful and multiply,[28] on the other hand—as well as those stipulating "subjugation" and "dominion" (Gen 1:28)[29]—are issued not to *muffle*, but to *involve* Eden's clay creatures in the Creator's "labor" (Gen 2:2).[30]

Promoting the values of *their* culture, the scribal authors of Atrahasis specify that the best way to deal with chaos is to offer up a blood sacrifice powerful enough to neutralize it, in this case the "blood" of a "lesser god."[31] Postmodern readers wink at this "solution," of course, because after all, how

---

23. Clifford translates, "Not for us, Yhwh, not for us, but for the sake of your name bring glory" ("Psalm 115:1," 294).

24. Ps 115:1–3. R. Watson examines in detail the Psalter's attraction to creation theology (*Chaos*).

25. Levenson, *Creation*, xxix. Blenkinsopp finds this fragility to be present "whether creation is limited to an event—the coming into existence of the world and humanity—or extended to include the created order, the phenomenal world in relation to God as its origin and the source of its intelligibility" (*Creation*, 176). Reading PH in the context of the Pentateuch as a whole, Muilenburg ventures that "the creation account in Genesis 1 is not only prologue to the history which follows it, but is also a development of the election-historical life, of the redemptive history which has the Exodus at its center" ("Time," 242). Sonik aptly observes that the definition of "cosmos" in *MWCD* 282 "incorrectly suggests ... an absence of chaotic or disruptive elements" ("Chaos," 2n5).

26. Atr 2.1.3–8. Enlil is one of the three great deities of the Sumero-Akkadian pantheon, the other two being Anu and Enki (Wang, *Enlil*; Schneider, *Introduction*, 58–59).

27. Atr 2.1.7 (*CAD* R. 328–34). Cf. Exod 1:13–22.

28. That MT רבה (to become great) is often translated "multiply" in Gen 1:28 is largely because of the vv.: OG πληθύνω (to multiply); Syr ܪܒܐ (to increase); Vg *multiplicare* (to multiply).

29. כבשו ורדו.

30. מלאכתו (his labor); OG τὰ ἔργα αὐτοῦ (his labors); Syr ܥܒܕܘܗܝ (his labors); Vg *opus suum* (his labor).

31. The deity they sacrifice, ᴰWe-ila (Atr 1.223), is renowned for his innate $ţe_4$-e-ma (intelligence).

can an incorporeal entity "shed blood"?[32] In Genesis, at any rate, the deity does not sacrifice his clay creatures; he simply expels them from the protection of the garden (Gen 3:3),[33] a decision leading Chris Heard to remark that "God does not need to fight Chaos to create the world. God simply commands, and Chaos obeys. By introducing God as a king who commands primordial Chaos, Genesis departs sharply from its Mesopotamian counterpart."[34]

The clay creatures' assignment in Atrahasis is to relieve the "lesser gods" of "hard labor," but for Eden's clay creatures, "hard labor" results from abandonment of the *imago Dei* (Gen 3:16–19). Each tradition speaks of "hard labor," but the definitional values assigned to each are different. One is the product of an urban, authoritarian, slaveholding economy determined to maintain the status quo,[35] while the other refers to a nomadic/agrarian culture inclined to believe that the only way to fend off chaos is by emulation of the Creator.[36] Both epics feature the "labor" motif, but whereas the Babylonians treat it as something objectionable, the Hebrews worship a deity who not only "delights"[37] in his "labor" (Gen 2:2),[38] he projects this delight onto his clay creatures by repeatedly inviting them to participate in the management of his creation.[39]

---

32. Abusch observes that "the killing of a god seems to be depicted already on seals dating to the Old Akkadian period, but enters the literary tradition of the OB period possibly as a consequence of the settlement of the tribal Amorites in Mesopotamia" ("Sacrifice," 46).

33. OG reads MT Gen 2:8 גן בעדן (garden in Eden) as παράδεισος (paradise). N.b. that even though the deaths of the first couple are postponed, they are not altogether revoked (Gen 3:19). Feinman lists five of the more common interpretations of the Garden of Eden ("Eden," 173–75).

34. Heard, "Genesis," 110. Con. Gunkel (*Schöpfung*, 78–80), Westermann denies any organic connection between the Hebrew and Babylonian traditions, arguing that "Gen 1:2 belongs to a history of creation narratives in which the motif of the primeval deep, with or without darkness, very often represents the situation before creation, but that the link between creation and the struggle of the gods is not part of its pre-history" (*Genesis 1–11*, 106).

35. That is, without abolishing slavery (Moore, *WealthWatch*, 88–89).

36. Guinan, *Pentateuch*, 21, 24.

37. In Job 40:29, Leviathan is a creature in whom the Creator takes "delight" (MT שחק in the D form). Cf. Jer 15:17; Prov 26:19; Syr ܪܩܕ (to dance); OG παίζω (to play).

38. ויכל אלהים ביום השביעי מלאכתו (On the seventh day God completed his labor).

39. Carr views the "labor" motif in Genesis as "fundamentally ambivalent" (*Formation of Genesis*, 17).

Chaos vs. Creation in the Second Generation (Gen 4–5)

Not only does chaos impair the vertical relationship between the Creator and his creatures, but it also impacts the horizontal relationships between the creatures themselves (Gen 2–3).[40] PH depicts the first woman as the first creature to abandon the *imago Dei*, but to associate chronological sequence with severity is a mistake. Both creatures dismiss the *imago Dei*, and coercion plays no role in either dismissal.[41] The man makes a freewill decision to abandon the *imago Dei*, and so does the woman.[42] Where things become theologically significant is when each creature tries to defend themselves by "playing the victim card."[43]

ויקרא יהוה אלהים אל האדם	Then Yhwh Elohim called to the man
ויאמר לו איכה	and said to him, "Where are you?"
ויאמר את קלך שמעתי בגן	And he answered, "I heard your voice in the garden,
ואירא כי עירם אנכי ואחבא	but I was afraid because I was naked; so I hid."
ויאמר מי הגיד לך כי עירם אתה	Then he said, "Who told you that you were naked?[44]

---

40. Wenham argues that the depiction of Adam and Eve represents an attempt to "apply the principles of the first marriage to every marriage" (*Genesis*, 70). Kikawada sees in Gen 2:7 a second phase of creation in which the main concern is the reproduction of humanity after the first initial act of creation ("Double"), but Espak finds this hypothesis "not well grounded" because in his opinion Gen 2:7 "represents only a detailed repetition of the first creative act of God by the author(s)" (*Enki*, 172).

41. Picirilli, *Free Will*, 19–23.

42. While it's important to recognize that female human beings are rarely mentioned as main characters in Atr or Ee or any other ANE creation epic, Espak suggests that the creation of Eve in PH echoes Enki's creation of the first female in EN 88 (reading CAG₄-BA as "womb," following Kilmer, "Baby") (*Enki*, 171–74), but this hardly "parallels" the much more developed character of Eve in PH.

43. Writing from the perspective of a Western journalist seeking justice for Liberians unjustly treated by corrupt officials in Sierra Leone, Jefferson recounts the terrors of real victims of real evil ("Victimhood"). But this situation is light-years away from that involving two clay creatures who, in spite of their perfect environment, still try to disavow the allegations brought against them by their Creator.

44. The wild beast Enkidu does not become "human" until he displays "reason and great wisdom" (*ṭ [é-ma r]a-pa-áš ḫa-si-sa*) (GE 1.202) and puts on "clothes" (*lu-bu-šú*) (2.34–35).

המן העץ אשר צויתיך	Have you eaten from the tree
לבלתי אכל ממנו אכלת	from which I commanded you not to eat?"
ויאמר האדם האשה אשר נתתה עמדי	And the man answered, "The woman you gave to me
היא נתנה לי מן העץ ואכל	offered to me from the tree and I ate."
ויאמר יהוה אלהים לאשה	Then Yhwh Elohim said to the woman,
מה זאת עשית	"What is this you have done?"
ותאמר האשה	And the woman answered,
הנחש השיאני ואכל	"The serpent tricked me ... so I ate."
	(Gen 3:9–13)⁴⁵

Confronted by the Creator first, the man "passes the buck" onto the woman just as quickly as she "passes the buck" onto the serpent.⁴⁶ The theological issue here is not who sins first, nor even who most obstinately refuses to take responsibility for their sin.⁴⁷ The issue is that such behavior is inevitable among clay creatures abandoning the *imago Dei*.

At any rate, these choices generate lethal repercussions.⁴⁸ Much like Ishtar's seduction of Gilgamesh,⁴⁹ the Cain and Abel saga⁵⁰ features a powerful deity engaging iconic characters who in turn symbolize iconic vocations: *farmer* vs. *shepherd*.⁵¹ The Sumerian story of Dumuzi and Enkimdu depicts a

---

45. MT נשא (to beguile); OG ἀπατάω (to cheat); Syr ܢܟܠ (deceive, seduce); Vg *decipere* (deceive); Tg חויא אשייני בחוכמתיה ואטעיני ברישעותיה (the serpent beguiled me with his wisdom and deceived me with his wickedness).

46. Cf. McCoy, "Parable."

47. Much is said about the "rights" of Eve vs. the "rights" of Adam. Augustine (*Genesi* 12.11.35), e.g., argues that Adam and Eve sin equally according to pride, but unequally according to sex (i.e., Eve's guilt is greater because of her sex).

48. Some teach that *sin* passes down from generation to generation, but the prophet Ezekiel teaches that "the soul that sins, it shall die ... nor shall a child suffer for the sin of the parent" (Ezek 18:20). The apostle Paul teaches that what passes down from generation to generation is *death*, not *sin* (Rom 5:12).

49. GE 6.6–21 (Moore, *WealthWatch*, 51–67).

50. Cain (קין [acquisition]) is a עבד הארץ (servant of the land); Abel (הבל [weakness]) is a רעה הצון (herder of sheep) (Gen 4:2). Qur'an calls these characters قابيل (Qabil, from قبل [to guarantee]) and هابيل (Habil, from هبل [to take advantage]) (Q 5:27, 32). Like the "wise man" vs. "wild man" conflicts in other ANE texts, this conflict reflects a traditional socioeconomic rift (cf. Mobley, "Wild"; Moore, *WealthWatch*, 29–73).

51. Heard explores the intratextual dynamics of these polarities (*Dynamics*), and Von Rad discusses their history of transformation (*Theology*, 1:105–28). E. Leach argues that this episode reflects a binary paradigm much like that recurring in the first two creation narratives (*Genesis*), but Carroll disagrees ("Leach").

similar polarity,[52] only here the shepherd (Dumuzi) is the aggressor, not the farmer (Enkimdu). As in PH, the deity's favor falls upon the shepherd, but not because the farmer is somehow undeserving. It falls upon the shepherd because he is the one who successfully woos the goddess Inanna.[53] Similarly, Adam's sons try to "woo" Yhwh[54] with their respective gifts, Cain's from the field and Abel's from the herd.[55] The text is silent as to why Yhwh's favor falls only upon Abel, but in light of Dumuzi and Enkimdu the reason may simply have to do with the fact that blood is much more precious than grain.[56] Whatever the case, the Sumerian story ends with fraternal reconciliation while the Hebrew story ends with fratricide and banishment.[57] *Conclusion:* Chaos may begin with a decision to abandon the *imago Dei*, but it takes only one generation for such a choice to bear unthinkably violent fruit.[58]

Chaos vs. Creation in the Natural World (Gen 6–9)

The second part of Atrahasis focuses on the great flood,[59] a tradition acknowledged not only by the Babylonians and Hebrews, but by some sixty other cultures.[60] The Babylonians and Hebrews utilize similar motifs in their

---

52. ETCSL c.4.08.33.

53. Cf. Wolkstein and Kramer, *Inanna*, 29–50; Alster, "Tammuz," 831–32; Moore, *WealthWarn*, 4–16.

54. Technically Yhwh is not formally introduced until the burning bush encounter (Exod 3:15). The fact that this name occurs so early in Genesis does not mean that the scribes want to challenge this history, only that the Torah's final draft presumes Yhwh to be active from the beginning.

55. That this conflict is not occasional is indicated by the story of the Rechabites in Jer 35:6–10, a sect refusing to sow seed, plant vineyards, and live in settled houses.

56. N.b. that blood is precious because נפש הבשר בדם הוא (the life of the flesh is in the blood) (Lev 17:11). Byron discusses several interpretations of this saga, listing the opinions of various thinkers, some even suggesting that Cain is condemned because he is not Adam's son, but is more likely the spawn of a בן האלהים (divine being) like those mentioned in Gen 6:2 (*Cain*, 11–38).

57. Like the Sumerian tale of Dumuzi and Enkimdu, the Egyptian Tale of Two Brothers also ends in reconciliation (BM-10183; *ANET* 23–25; cf. Hollis, *Brothers*; Wettengel, *Erzahlung*). Schlimm emphasizes that although this earliest sibling episode in Genesis ends in fratricide, the final one ends with fraternal forgiveness (Gen 45:4–5) (*Genesis*, 4).

58. Later interpreters are very hard on Cain, one labeling him an "unrighteous" man (ἄδικος) (Wis 10:3) whose behavior is at least partially responsible for "bringing on the flood" (κατακλύζω) (10:4); cf. discussion in Byron, *Cain*, 207.

59. Qur'an alludes to the flood as الكرب العظيم (the great distress) (Q 37:76).

60. Cf. Peake, *Flood*, 124–25, cited in J. Lewis, *Flood*, 1. With regard to how (post) moderns read the flood saga, Longman and Walton recognize that "the biblical author

respective epics, but again, the meanings assigned are different. Whereas the first part of Atrahasis addresses the labor concerns of Babylonian managers (Igigi myth), the second part (flood myth) portrays the clay creature workforce becoming so big it begins to "bellow in the land like a bull,"[61] creating a "tumult" (*ḫubūru*)[62] making Enlil so "fearful" (*adāru*)[63] he sends drought, famine, pestilence, and disease to try and stop it.[64] When these "solutions" all fail, he secures a mandate from his colleagues to flush them away with floodwater drawn down from the heavens[65] and up from the ABZU.[66]

Neither epic portrays the flood simply and only as divine punishment, but as a necessary prelude to *re-creation*. That is, *creation* followed by *un-creation* can—and often does—lead to *re-creation*.[67] Whereas the flood in Atrahasis pacifies Enlil,[68] the flood in PH occurs as a carefully measured response to a moral crisis in which "every inclination" of humanity's "daily thinking leans only toward evil" (Gen 6:5).[69] The situation is dire, to be

---

is not authoritatively describing an event (in a way that would prove its historical authenticity to the satisfaction of a sceptic), but is authoritatively interpreting what God is doing through the event using his own perspectives and conventions" (*Flood*, 177).

61. Akk *[m]a-tum ki-ma li-i ša-a-bu* (Atr 2.1.3; cf. Moore, *WealthWatch*, 81–82).
62. Atr 2.1.3-8 (cf. *CAD* Ḫ.220–21).
63. Atr 1.355 (cf. *CAD* A.1.105–7).
64. Pharaoh recommends a similar strategy to control the Hebrews (Exod 1:9–10).
65. Adad roared in the clouds (*iš-ta-ag-na* ᴰ*Adad i-na er-pé-ti*) (Atr 3.2.49).
66. Atr 3.1.29. Sum ABZU (Akk *apsû*) refers to the underground fresh water managed and maintained by the god Enki (ECTSL 1.1.4.4). The same notion appears in Gen 7:11 when נבקעו כל מעינת תהום רבה (all the great fountains of the deep burst forth). In Atr 3.22–52 Enki warns Atrahasis (the Babylonian "Noah") of the coming catastrophe and commands him to "build a boat," put animals and his family in it, bolt the door, and seal it with pitch. Than after the floodwaters subside, Nintu the birth goddess (ᴰ*Nin-tu sassūru*) facilitates the beginning of a new created order, including "women who give birth" and "women who do not" (Atr 3.6.43–47.8). Qur'an's description of the flood specifies that groundwater erupts as if bursting from a *tannur*-"oven" (تنور) (Q 11:40), i.e., a bulging section of land resembling the convex "oven" commonly used to bake bread.
67. This "restart" motif is a main fixture of the Pentateuch (Blenkinsopp, *Creation*). Ross alleges that Gen 1:2 refers to a *pre-creation* evil chaos, and that 1:3 actually begins the account of the *re-creation* (*Creation*, 106–7). Noting the deity's suggestion that after destroying Israel he can easily "start over" again with Moses (Exod 32:10), Sanders remarks that were this actually to happen, "Moses would have a role similar to Noah's" (*Theology*, 61). Qur'an similarly teaches that God "intentionally" (بالحق [lit., in truth]) "creates the heavens and the earth, but if he so desires it he can remove you and produce a new creation" (بخالق جديد) (Q 14:19).
68. Atr 1.353.
69. וכל יצר מחשבת לבו רק רע כל היום. Qur'an teaches that the "soul" (النفس; cf. נפש in Gen 2:7) "is ever inclined toward evil" (Q 12:53).

sure, but things *really* fall apart when several "sons of God" cross over from the unseen world into the seen world to impregnate several "daughters of men" (Gen 6:1–4).[70] Granted, there is more than one way to interpret this text,[71] but two facts remain certain: (a) the Genesis "tumult"[72] *intertextually* parallels the Atrahasis "tumult"[73] and (b) the punishment levied in the flood saga *intratextually* mirrors the punishment levied in PH's other three sagas: (a) the expulsion of the first couple from Eden, (b) the banishment of their murderous son, and (c) the confusion of the languages at the tower of Babel.[74]

Chaos vs. Creation among the Nations (Gen 10–11)

The final PH saga brings the chaos-creation polarity full circle. Whereas the "sons of God" invade the seen world before the flood (Gen 6:2),[75] the "sons of Adam" set out to invade the unseen world via a "tower whose summit reaches to the heavens" (Gen 11:4).[76] Instead of emulating Adam's

---

70. The Nephilim (MT נפלים [fallen ones]; OG γίγαντες [giants]; Syr ܓܢܒܪܐ [mighty ones]; Tg שמחזאי ועוזיאל [Shamḥazai and Uzziel]) generated by these unions find parallels in the "demigods" of Greek tradition (C. Collins, "Noah, Deucalion"). The poet Pindar, for example, tells the story of Zeus impregnating the human princess Alcmene in order to produce a ἥρως θεός (hero god) named Heracles (*Nem.* 3.22), and Poseidon impregnates the human princess Aethra to produce the demigod Theseus (the famous slayer of the Cretan Minotaur) (Apollodorus, *Library*, 2:3.15.7).

71. One Second Temple interpreter describes this behavior as a violation of "the law of heaven" (1 En. 106:13). Doedens lists the major interpretations of בני האלהים (the sons of God) as (a) angels; (b) mighty ones; (c) Sethites; and (d) divine beings, selecting the last of these options as the most "tenable" (*Sons*, 178–250). Kugel imagines Gen 6:1–4 as an "insertion" designed to complete the genealogies in 5:28–32, and that it is therefore not originally intended to be read as a rationale for the flood ("Descent," 216–19).

72. Gen 6:11, חמס (cf. Jer 20:8; 1QH 14.5); OG ἀδικία (injustice); Vg *iniquitate* (iniquity); Syr ܥܘܠܐ (evil); Tg. Neof. חמסין וגזלנין (violence and robbers); Arab حمس (*ḥms*) means "to be hard, firm, strong, strict or rigorous in religion, in fight, in courage, and in affairs" (Lane 643), the adjectival form meaning "unflinching, staunch, zealous, fiery" (Wehr 205).

73. Atr 2.1.4 (*ḫubūru*) (CAD Ḫ.220–21).

74. Cf. Chaloupka, "Daughters," 366n4.

75. בני האלהים. So prominent is this incident, some Second Temple texts refer to it. In the Genesis Apocryphon from Qumran Cave 1, e.g., Lamech (Noah's father) (Gen 5:28), has a conversation with his wife in which he questions the identity of the father responsible for her pregnancy, and she assures him that "this seed comes from you, not from... any of the sons of heaven" (בני שמין, [1QapGen 2.15–16]).

76. בני האדם. Further, whereas 6:1–4 functions as a literary trigger for the flood saga, 11:1–9 functions as a literary trigger for the Abraham cycle.

assignment to name the world's creatures (Gen 2:19–23), these "sons of Adam" seek to "make a name for *themselves*" (Gen 11:4). In other words, the chaos responsible for derailing the first couple, murdering their son, and generating the flood now spreads its tentacles over "the whole earth" (כל הארץ) (Gen 11:1). Whereas the flood fails to drown chaos (as if such were possible),[77] the tower of Babel saga highlights the danger of violating what one reader calls the "law of heaven" (1 En. 106:13).

Similar motifs operate within a Sumerian epic called Enmerkar and the Lord of Aratta,[78] a story in which both King Enmerkar of Uruk and his rival, an unnamed monarch from Aratta,[79] seek to please the goddess Inanna by building her "a house brought down from heaven."[80] Inanna, however, makes it clear that she wants her "house" to be built in Uruk, not Aratta, a preference Enki[81] tries to explain to the "many-tongued" laborers from Šubur, Ḥamazi, Sumer, Akkad, and Martu.[82] In a speech to these laborers he shares his vision that someday they will all be able to "speak the same language"[83] and that "humanity's speech will indeed become one."[84] Given this obvious, albeit antonymous parallel to the fourth saga in PH, the latter looks to be hammering away not only at humanity's inclination to renounce the *imago Dei*, but especially its determination to replace it with the *imago sui*. Is it merely coincidental that this Sumerian story promotes the dream of a single language while this Hebrew saga so openly challenges it?[85]

---

77. Qur'an claims that despite all the horrors of "the flood" (الطوفان), Noah's generation still persists in "wrongdoing" (ظالمون) (Q 29:14).

78. ECTSL 1.8.2.3. Enmerkar appears in the same king-list as Gilgamesh, a later king of Uruk (ECTSL 2.1.1.102).

79. Arrata is likely situated in what is now called Afghanistan.

80. ECTSL 1.8.2.3.43 (E_2 AN-TA [ED_3-DA KI]-GUB-BA-ZA). Building "houses/temples" for deities is one of the quickest ways to secure their favor. In Canaanite myth the god Ba'al pushes to have El build him a "house" on his schedule and to his liking (CAT 1.4.4.62–65.1), while his temporary replacement (Athtar) complains that no one will ever build a "house" for him (CAT 1.2.3.19–20). Cf. Moore, *WealthWarn*, 43–46.

81. Enki is the deity who most often intercedes with Enlil on behalf of his clay creatures (cf. Atr 3.1.1–37; Espak, *Enki*, 171–74).

82. Sum EME ḪAMUN (many-tongued) (ECTSL 1.8.2.3.142).

83. Sum EME 1-AM$_3$ HE$_2$-EN-NA-DA-AB-DUG$_4$ (ECTSL 1.8.2.3.146).

84. Sum EME NAM-LU$_2$-ULU$_3$ 1 I$_3$-ME-[A] (ECTSL 1.8.2.3.155). Tg. Ps.-J. Gen 11:1 reads, "All the earth was of one language [לישן], one speech [ממלל], and one counsel [עיטא]. In the holy tongue [לישן קודשא] they spoke, the one by which the world was created [אתבריא] in the beginning." Talmud presumes this "holy tongue" to be Hebrew (b. Šabb. 115a).

85. Batto argues that the Genesis narrator "is certainly cognizant of the polemical character of this story and likely retains it as reinforcement of his anti-Babylonian campaign" ("Combat," 236).

Reading this saga from a slightly different angle, John Walton suggests (a) that the tower of Babel is most likely designed, like all ziggurats,[86] to lure the gods down from heaven in order to put them at the disposal of this or that priesthood; and (b) that such behavior is not unexpected from "a religious system defined not by faith or doctrine," but by a cultural imperative to "feed and care for the gods."[87] Such systems, Walton observes, tend to create "a codependence ... between gods and humans which is entirely transactional."[88] The people take care of the gods, and the gods ... bring them prosperity."[89] The mindset thus created not only (a) presumes that deities are controllable by clay creatures, but (b) explains why a Yahwistic text would so bluntly challenge it, even to the point of compressing this challenge into a single imperative verb:

הבה נלבנה לבנים	*Come*, let us make hardened bricks. (Gen 11:3)[90]
הבה נבנה לנו עיר ... מגדל ... ושם	*Come*, let us build for ourselves a city ... a tower ... and a name. (Gen 11:4)
הבה נרדה ונבלה שם שפתם	*Come*, let us go down and confuse their language. (Gen 11:7)

Whereas the first two imperatives demonstrate the *imago sui* mentality of the "sons of Adam," the third shows that the deity *is* willing to descend to earth, though not to submit to this or that human priesthood.

---

86. At Uruk (present-day Warka) stand the ruins of one of the largest ziggurats ever discovered (from Akk *zaqārum* [to build high, project] [*CAD* Z.55–56]).

87. Cf. Walker and Dick, *Induction*, 4–31.

88. Cf. Moore and Klunzinger, "Codependency."

89. Walton, "Babel," 76. This, in essence, is the core ideology of the predominantly American "health-and-wealth gospel." But again, just as Adam and Eve are *expelled* (not killed), the Shinar workers are *dispersed* (not destroyed).

90. This common verb (יהב) appears in the Tell Fekheriye inscription (line 10), the Sefire inscription (*KAI* 222B.38), at Tell Deir ʿAllā (*DA* 1.9), and other texts (cf. *DNWSI* 442–48). MT הבה is the ipv form of יהב, a polysemantic verb meaning "to come" (Gen 38:16; Exod 1:10) and/or "to give" (Gen 29:21; 30:1; 47:15; Judg 1:15; 1 Sam 14:41; Prov 30:15). N.b. that Enmerkar comes from "brick-built Kulaba" (ŠEG$_{12}$ KUL-ABA$_4^{KI}$-KE$_4$) (ECTSL 1.8.2.3.15, 32, 235), an early epithet of Uruk.

Summary

For several reasons PH is one of the most thoroughly scrutinized sections of the Bible,[91] not least because, as Lurquin and Stone observe, "origin myths are wonderful, meaningful stories that reflect both universal human concerns and distinctive cultural conceptions."[92] Eliciting the attention of millions for millennia, PH can be appreciated from several perspectives—literary, sociological, ideological, intertextual—to name just a few of the more popular. From a *theological* perspective, however, PH focuses upon several key aspects of the chaos-creation polarity, aspects which continue to resonate throughout the remainder of Genesis:

1. Chaos and creation are dynamic forces, not static entities.

2. Creation suppresses chaos, but does not eliminate it.

3. Chaos is suppressed by no other power than that which emanates from the *imago Dei*.

4. The damage caused by chaos is not irreparable. Creation can be *un*-created ... but it can also be *re*-created.[93]

ABRAHAM CYCLE

Whereas the Shinar workers set out to make a great "name" for *themselves*, Yhwh calls Abraham out of Mesopotamia[94] to make a great "name" of *him* (Gen 11:4; 12:2).[95] Clearly there is nothing wrong with having a "great name." The question, of course, is "To what end?" Is it to glorify the *imago Dei* or the *imago sui*? Genesis highlights this contrast via a deft literary maneuver in which the term שם (name) at the end of PH (Gen 11:4) crops up again at the beginning of the Abraham cycle (12:2)[96] as a catchword linking

---

91. Cf., e.g., Westermann, *Genesis 1–11*; Hendel, *Genesis 1–11*; Carr, *Genesis 1–11*; Day, *Genesis 1–11*; Mathews, *Genesis 1—11:26*; Davidson, *Genesis 1–11*; Jiang, *Genesis 1–11*; Good, *Genesis 1–11*; Bandstra, *Genesis 1–11*. This list is not exhaustive.

92. Lurquin and Stone, *Myths*, 20.

93. Qur'an stresses the same point in Q 17:99: "Do they not see that Alla, the One who creates the heavens and the earth, can re-create them?" (يخلق مثلهم [lit., create their like]).

94. Ur of the Chaldees (Gen 11:31). Cf. Margueron, "Ur."

95. "Abram" does not technically become "Abraham" until 17:5, but for the sake of consistency the present study uses only the more familiar name.

96. Parunak describes this phenomenon as a transitional technique based on the repetition of a "keyword" ("Transitional," 529–30). Tomlinson calls it a "hooked

these two major sections.⁹⁷ Moreover, in contrast to the rather impromptu activity succeeding the flood,⁹⁸ the Abraham cycle begins with a carefully considered, long-term plan to re-create that which chaos un-creates in PH.⁹⁹ Why this long-term plan focuses upon a single individual or why this particular individual is chosen over all others are interesting questions, but from a theological perspective unimportant.¹⁰⁰ What *is* important is that the Creator wants his long-term plan through Abraham to "bless all the families of the earth" (Gen 12:3).¹⁰¹ Yet even as it unfolds via a series of promises to his "re-creation agents" (Gen 12:4; 13:16; 14:19; 15:5, 18; 17:4–9; 22:17–18), chaos repeatedly interrupts.¹⁰²

---

keyword" ("Cohesion," 98). J. Walsh refers to it simply as a "thread" (*Style*, 188), while Marcus calls it a "catchword" ("Masora," 218). These descriptions all go back to Lucian of Samosata (d. 180 CE), an early literary critic who defines the technique as follows: "All parts must be independently completed, but when the first is completed, the second is brought into essential connection with it. Attached like one end of a chain to another ... the first does not merely sit next to the second, but stands in fellowship [κοινωνεῖν] with it, their extremities [ἄκρα] intermingling [ἀνακεκρᾶσθαι]" (cited from H. Fowler and Fowler, *Lucian*, 2:133).

97. Nogalski notes several examples of catchwords linking individual books in the Book of the Twelve (Hosea-Malachi) (*Precursors*, 21–57).

98. Noah's sacrifice elicits from God the promise that he will never again curse the land (Gen 8:21), but never is Noah promised that through him "all the families on the earth will be blessed" (12:3).

99. Speiser thinks that Gen 12:1–3 "signals the beginning of the integral history of a particular group as opposed to background episodes in the prehistory of the race as a whole. The story commences with one individual, and extends gradually to his family, then to a people, and later still to a nation. Yet it is not to be the tale of individuals or a family or a people as such. Rather, it is to be the story of a society in quest of an ideal" (*Genesis*, 87).

100. Levenson observes that "the claim that Abraham is a source of reconciliation among the three traditions increasingly called 'Abrahamic' is as simplistic as it is now widespread. Historically, Abraham functions much more as a point of differentiation among the three religious communities than as a node of commonality" (*Inheriting*, 8–9).

101. MT ונברכו, OG ἐνευλογηθήσονται, and Vg *benedicentur* are all future passive forms ("they will be blessed"), but Syr ܘܢܬܒܪܟܘܢ is a future reflexive form ("they will bless themselves").

102. Westermann assigns great theological significance to the "ancestral promises" (*Promises*), and Flury-Scholch counts the passage in Gen 12:1–4 "among the most important" in Tanak "because of its theological depth" (*Segen*, 1).

Abraham Lies about His Wife

The first interruption occurs when Abraham succumbs to a temptation similar to that ensnaring the first couple. He lies. He lies to Pharaoh about the status of his wife (Gen 12), then he lies about her again to the Canaanite chieftain Abimelech (Gen 20).[103] In spite of his great wealth, Abraham finds himself forced by the infamous Palestinian famine cycle to take his family down to Egypt to find food (Deut 11:10–12).[104] Preparing Sarah for the journey, he warns that the Egyptians may assassinate him to abduct her.[105] Most rabbinic interpreters focus on Abraham's survival in this episode, highlighting his acquisitional victories and downplaying his improprieties.[106] Few read it from a perspective shaped by the chaos-creation polarity,[107] thereby ignoring two important questions: (a) Why does Abraham *presume* Sarah's abduction? and (b) How does this description of Egyptian behavior resonate with other descriptions? Questions like these would be easier to engage, however, were not so many of the story's earliest interpreters so blatantly racist. One rabbinic commentator, for example, denigrates Egypt as a land filled with "black and ugly" people,[108] while another goes out of his way to smear the pharaonic court as a cesspool of immorality.[109] Still another goes so far as to suggest that even after Pharaoh learns of Sarah's marital status he tries to seduce her anyway, though this flatly contradicts his words in Genesis: "What is this you have done to me? Why did you not tell me that she was your wife? Why did you say, 'She is my sister,' so that I took her as my wife?" (Gen 12:18–19).[110]

---

103. Isaac later lies about his wife Rebekah (Gen 26:7–11). *Pace* Throntveit ("Things," 24), what Abraham does here is much more than mere "indiscretion." Whether or not these episodes are historical duplications, the repetition of this motif is significant.

104. Cf. Rabinowitz, "Famine"; Moore, *Faith*, 139–53.

105. Firestone, "Difficulties."

106. As Firestone sees it, "Abraham seems to be caught in a moral double bind: quite simply, the patriarch appears either as a liar or as involved in a relationship of incest" ("Prophethood," 336). Fretheim examines these options carefully (*Abraham*, 46–65), but Kunin argues that the wife/sister texts in Genesis are there to help Israel resolve its ambivalence over the choice of endogamy vs. exogamy in the aftermath of foreign invasion (*Incest*, 65–93).

107. Moore, *WealthWatch*, 117–21.

108. Gen. Rab. 40:4.

109. *Sifra* 7:11; Josephus, *A.J.* 1:162. Shapiro presumes (without a shred of evidence) that "it was common practice for Egyptians to abduct the wives of strangers for sexual purposes" ("Moses," 494).

110. Con. Gen. Rab. 41:2.

Genesis spotlights these questions by mirroring the wife/sister incident in ch. 12 with the wife/sister incidents in chs. 20 and 26, leading some readers to wonder whether each incident originates from its own "source."[111] Others imagine all three incidents coming from the same "source,"[112] while still others view the episodes in chs. 20 and 26 as free-flowing refractions of a partially preserved folktale lying underneath ch. 12, sometimes to the point of hypothesizing the episodes in chs. 20 and 26 as "solutions" to the "problems" in ch. 12.[113] No hard evidence exists, however, to prove the existence of such "sources," nor do chs. 20 and 26 consciously set out to fix any "problems" "caused" by them.[114] Following a suggestion from Umberto Cassuto,[115] Moshe Weinfeld argues that the Egyptian decision to exchange "gifts" for Sarah reflects the ethos of a legal statute mandating that any man who "journeys" with another man's wife must compensate him by (a) taking an oath and (b) giving him a "gift."[116] Presumably the purpose of this oath is to validate the oath taker's ignorance of her marital status, whereas the "gift" is designed to compensate the offended husband for the social "contempt" he suffers.[117] At any rate, some insist that Pharaoh never touches Sarah,[118] even to the point of conflating the stories in chs. 12 and 20 to "protect her purity."[119]

From a historical perspective even the most cursory analysis shows this episode to be a rather accurate reflection of a blatantly sexist world in which women are treated as a "primordial means of social exchange."[120] In this world Egyptians take their neighbors' daughters in marriage without

111. In chs. 20 and 26, e.g., Abraham receives no financial compensation "on her behalf" בעבורה, (12:16). See Dillmann (*Genesis*, 226, 278-79, 322-23); König (*Genesis*, 56-57, 67); Skinner (*Genesis*, 242-43, 315, 363); Speiser (*Genesis*, 91); Von Rad (*Genesis*, 193, 235).

112. Koch, *Formgeschichte*, 121-48.

113. Van Seters, *Abraham*, 167-91; Westermann, *Genesis 12-36*, 187-88, 389-90, 516-17. Presuming a connection between "woman's body" and "social body," Frick argues that "the sexually endangered matriarch represents the vulnerability of the Israelite community amidst more powerful nations" ("Political," 203).

114. Firestone suggests that "the latter rendition of the story appears to have served, at least in part, as exegesis on the Genesis 12 rendition" ("Prophethood," 335). Cf. Alexander, "Wife/Sister."

115. Abrahams and Roth, "Cassuto."

116. Weinfeld, "Sarah" (cf. *ANET* 181, §A22).

117. In cases like these it's wise to question, with Wells ("Law"), which laws reflect actual practice and which do not.

118. Cf., e.g., Philo, *Abr.* 98; Josephus, *B.J.* 5.381.

119. Wise suggests that the Genesis Apocryphon from Qumran Cave 1 reads Gen 12 through the "eyes" of Gen 20 (*Scrolls*, 99-102).

120. Avruch, "Reciprocity," 163.

reciprocating their own,[121] a one-sidedness likely reflecting the probability that Egyptians regard *their* women as inherently superior,[122] but also that women in general are more likely to be assigned to the category of "tribute" than "gifts" as part of a socioeconomic policy designed to create the illusion that women are "exchangeable property."[123] Betsy Bryan suggests the further possibility that inheritance customs are so fragile, political marriage in Egypt may have evolved into little more than a minimalist paraphrase of "foreign invasion."[124]

Some rabbinic interpreters find Abraham's behavior troubling because, as Elihu stresses to Job, "righteous heroes" are not generally thought of as "wrongdoers."[125] Gershon Hepner, however, suggests that the "verbal resonance" between two biblical texts—Gen 12:13 and Jer 38:20–23—is strong enough to suggest that Gen 12 has primarily to do with the notion that Judean women must constantly be protected from "captivity and rape."[126] A similar notion is suggested in an Aramaic retelling of this episode in the Genesis Apocryphon,[127] a text in which:

1. Abraham dreams about loggers preparing to cut down two trees, a cedar and a palm,[128] but as they approach the cedar, the palm tree begs them to spare it. *Interpretation:* Pharaoh's emissaries will surely kill Abraham (the cedar), unless Sarah (the palm) persuades them otherwise. Thus, to "fulfill Abraham's dream" Sarah *has* to support her husband's "white lie."[129]

---

121. Kunin cites several examples (*Incest*, 164).

122. Aeschylus illustrates this attitude in a story about an Egyptian king's fifty daughters who refuse to be manipulated by his court into political marriages designed to "seal" international treaties (*Suppl.* 1–18). Spier argues that their resistance has less to do with a fear of "loveless marriage" than "marriage in general" ("Motive," 315).

123. Liverani, *Relations*, 6.

124. Bryan, "Egyptian," 82.

125. Elihu asks Job, "Would you condemn someone who is righteous and mighty?" (Job 34:17b; cf. Moore, *Retribution*, 65–66). Rickett recognizes that "one of the chief concerns" of early interpreters "is to shift the focus away from any potential difficulties surrounding Abraham" (*Separating*, 89).

126. Hepner, "Abraham," 143. N.b. that one of Boaz's first acts with Ruth is to protect her from being "touched" (נגע [Ruth 2:9]; Vg *molestus*).

127. Text and translation in *DSSSE* 1:28–49.

128. 1QapGen 19.14–27. In Gen 20:3–7 God speaks to Abimelech in a dream.

129. Creating alternative scenarios via dreams is not uncommon in the ancient literary world. Whereas Oppenheim distinguishes between "message dreams" and "symbolic dreams" in Mesopotamia (*Dreams*, 187–91), Mouton finds the Anatolians distinguishing more between "message dreams" and "bad dreams" (*Rêves*, 29–62).

2. The deity's attack against Pharaoh is not explained in Genesis, but his response in the Genesis Apocryphon, rather than being vengeful, is simply to answer the prayer request of his "re-creation agent." *Interpretation:* God is not to blame for the suffering of "innocent" Egyptians, especially those who abduct the wives of foreign visitors.[130]

3. Like Philo, the Genesis Apocryphon emphasizes that Sarah never has intercourse with anyone other than her husband, a detail not explicitly mentioned in Genesis.[131] *Interpretation:* One can be absolutely sure that Sarah's son Isaac is Abraham's biological son.[132]

4. In Gen 12:16 Pharaoh "pays" for Sarah with goods and gifts *before* she enters the palace, but in 1QapGen 20.31–33 Egyptian gifts arrive *after* she returns to her husband.[133] *Interpretation:* Like the fleecing of the Egyptians after centuries of captivity (Exod 12:35–36), the fleecing of the Egyptians after Sarah's captivity is not inappropriate.

"Rewritten Scripture" like the Genesis Apocryphon posts revealing glimpses into the minds of the writers responsible for its production, but it needs to be read against two irrefutable facts: (a) it never enjoys equal status and authority with canonical Scripture;[134] and (b) it is but one of many attempts to interpret the canonical text to a later audience.[135] The theological point, at any rate, is that no matter how many interpreters try to "rescue" Abraham's reputation, the fact remains that he "passes the buck" just like the clay creatures before him. Cain's contemptuous question, "Am I my brother's keeper?," might well be cited by Abraham as "Am I my wife's keeper?" Both episodes demonstrate the power of chaos to ensnare even God's "re-creation agents," even the one for whom he promises to make a "great name."[136]

---

130. Le Grys shows how reticent many readers are today to recognize the deity's implacable justice, concluding that "a truly biblical vision of God is always multitextured, highly contoured—and distinctly uncomfortable" ("Difficult," 118).

131. Philo, *Abr.* 98; 1QapGen 20.17. Gen 20:6, however, also highlights her purity.

132. Lot's status as Abraham's "heir" is effectively cancelled when he commits incest (Gen 19:30–38; Lev 18:6).

133. Gen 20:14–16 shows Abraham also receiving gifts *after* Sarah's return.

134. Cf. Vermès, *Scripture*, 67–126; Segal, "Between"; Tov, "Rewritten"; and Bernstein, "Rewritten." Elledge lays out five criteria for evaluating the "authority" of rewritten biblical texts like 1QapGen and Jubilees ("Re-Writing," 93–95).

135. Segal, e.g., thinks that the book of "Jubilees presents a sequence that is secondary to that reflected in the Genesis Apocryphon" ("Literary," 75).

136. Goldingay concludes that "the story does not aim to provide readers with a good or bad example of faithfulness. It's about God's faithfulness to his purpose, even when his people are unfaithful" (*Genesis*, 215).

Abraham's and Lot's Companies Clash over Resources

It's tempting to presume that the reason for the conflict between Abraham's and Lot's companies is simply that "money is the root of all evil," or that "absolute power corrupts absolutely." But simplistic platitudes like these do little to identify the densities embedded within this complex uncle-nephew relationship (Gen 13:1–11).[137] Within the immediate context it's important to be aware that Abraham has not yet sired a biological heir,[138] a detail which might seem unimportant to Westerners, but one which ancient Near Easterners cannot ignore.[139] What this means is that absent a biological heir Abraham has to maintain a healthy relationship with his nephew Lot, even if it means he has to improvise on occasion.[140]

So when a conflict develops between their companies, much is at stake here besides land and resources.[141] Granted, access to potable water is a persistent problem in this part of the world, often leading to what Tobias von Lossow calls "water weaponization."[142] Indeed, access to potable water shapes the contours of Middle Eastern politics up to the present day. In 1967 CE, for example, Israel forces Syria to hand over control of the Banias, a freshwater spring originating from a cave in the Golan Heights.[143]

---

137. Granted, this is implied by the emphasis on Lot resolving their conflict by choosing land that is משקה (lit., drinkable; NRSV reads "well-watered"), but n.b. that the "water rights" motif occurs more noticeably in 26:15–22.

138. On the socioeconomic phenomenon of primogeniture, cf. Moore, *WealthWatch*, 129–35.

139. "In the overall Genesis narrative, whether or not Sarah and Abraham have a child matters. Will there be a next generation? Will Yhwh's promises prevail? It all depends on the birth of a child. This is one of several biblical stories of miraculous or unexpected births, through which Yhwh bestows blessing upon God's people, renewing the divine promise and moving the saga of Israel's redemptive role in the world along to a new stage" (Gaiser, "Sarah," 273).

140. Ignoring the intertextual context (e.g., the conflict between Kirta and Yaṣṣib in *CAT* 1.16.6.41–53; cf. Moore, *WealthWatch*, 124–29), Rickett imagines the episode's essential point to be the separation of Lot from Abraham (*Separating*, 12–28), but this downplays the Abraham cycle's obvious desire to highlight Abraham's character, especially his patriarchal desire for a legitimate biological heir. Inheritance is no minor notion in the Pentateuch, nor in the cognate literature. At Ugarit, e.g., the Kirta epic bears testimony to its importance in no uncertain terms (*CAT* 1.14–16; cf. Hendel, *Epic*; Helyer, "Separation"; Moore, *WealthWatch*, 117–37; Moore, *WealthWarn*, 197–98).

141. Granted, Gen 13 is less than forthcoming about the details of the dispute between Abraham's and Lot's herdsmen, but in light of the explicit conflict over water rights in the Jacob cycle (Gen 26:19–22), it's difficult to avoid a similar conclusion here.

142. Lossow, "Water." Cf. also King, "Watershed."

143. Cf. Sofer, *Rivers*, 123. The Banias is one of the major freshwater springs feeding the Jordan River.

Moreover, Palestinian farmers justifiably resent the fact that Israeli farmers drain approximately 80 percent of the Mountain Aquifer for their crops, even though approximately 85 percent of it comes from rain fallen upon Palestinian land.[144]

From a theological perspective, however, this episode has fundamentally to do with how decisively Abraham suppresses the forces of chaos before it can seriously damage the family through which "all the families of the earth are to be blessed." Refusing to argue or negotiate with his nephew, Abraham instead invites Lot to take first choice of the land and its resources. Not to cast aspersions on his character,[145] it's nevertheless naive to conclude that he simply wants to be a "nice uncle."[146] More likely this offer is just as much calculated to avoid endangering a relationship with his de facto heir.[147]

Lot Taken Hostage in a Regional Conflict

Again their relationship is tested when Lot is taken hostage in a skirmish between regional warlords.[148] Whoever these warlords are and whatever can be known about their territorial claims are important historical questions,[149] but again, basically irrelevant here. Instead, what is of greatest theological interest is how the Creator uses his "re-creation agent" in this chaotic situation to restore order to his creation. Here it is important to notice what Abraham does after securing Lot's return: (a) he builds bridges with the Canaanites by tithing the spoils of battle to Melchizedek, king of Salem and priest of El Elyôn (Gen 14:22);[150] and (b) he refuses to share spoil with the Sodomite king because of an earlier oath pledged to this same "El Elyôn, Yhwh, the *Creator* of heaven and earth" (Gen 14:22b).[151]

---

144. Cf. Shuval, "Water," 3.

145. Philo suggests that Abraham treats Lot graciously because he "seeks a life free from strife and so far as lay with him of tranquility, thereby showing himself to be the most admirable of men" (*Abr.* 37.214–16).

146. Why does Lot reject Abraham's leadership? Probably not because he believes his uncle to be "corrupt," but rather because he feels a desire to free himself from the socioeconomic restrictions ingrained into all tribal cultures, hoping instead to network himself more lucratively into the "breadbasket of the Jordan" (ככר ירדן) (Gen 13:10).

147. Josephus bluntly writes that "Abraham, having no legitimate son, adopts Lot" (*A.J.* 1.154). N.b. how different this behavior is from that extended by Jacob to his sons.

148. The first test is internal; the second is external.

149. Attempts to engage these questions span an intellectual spectrum from Speiser (*Genesis*, 105–9) to Gertoux (*Chederlaomer*, 3–30) to S. Collins and Scott (*Sodom*).

150. MT אל עליון (God Most High). Cf. Lack, "'Elyôn."

151. N.b. that (a) Yhwh is identified with El Elyôn, and (b) this identification is

Abraham's Childlessness

Several factors contribute to Abraham's childlessness,[152] but of greatest interest here is how the Creator helps him resolve it. *First*, as evidenced by the previous two episodes, Lot is an important figure in Abraham's life as his de facto heir.[153] Yet Lot's decision to move to Sodom significantly endangers this relationship.[154] Not only does it eventuate in the death of his wife, but in the wake of Sodom's destruction, his daughters dupe him into committing the sin of incest (Lev 18:6).[155] *Second*, Abraham sires Ishmael with Sarah's Egyptian maid, Hagar. Examining this episode from a literary feminist perspective, Phyllis Trible justly categorizes it as a "text of terror,"[156] applying it to the needs of a contemporary world grown numb to the terrors of psychosexual, socioeconomic, and emotional abuse. But this is not the only way to read this text.[157] The Abraham cycle can just as easily be read from Sarah's or Lot's or Isaac's point of view, revealing Abraham to be enacting less-than-stellar roles like wily husband, ambivalent uncle, and fretful father.[158] *Third*, he fathers a child with Sarah in his old age. The boy's name,

---

extended further to קנה שמים וארץ (Creator of heaven and earth). Gese's attempt to interpret this as a "triad" (Yhwh/El Elyôn/Creator) is too rigid ("Altsyriens," 114), much like Parpola's attempt to posit a "trinity" in NA prophecy (*Prophecies*, xxvi–xxviii). N.b. that 1QapGen 22.16, 21 reads מרה שמיא וארצא, "Lord [not 'Creator'] of heaven and earth."

152. Moss and Baden elaborate how childlessness affects five famous women in Tanak—Sarah, Rebekah, Rachel, Samson's mother, and Hannah (*Infertility*, 21–69).

153. Louis H. Feldman observes that "the Greek or Roman reader" examining this text "would expect a hero, if childless, to adopt a son in order to ensure the maintenance of his name and estate" (in Josephus, *Antiquities*, 1.55)

154. Grenz argues convincingly that the Sodomites' sin in Gen 19 is not just the denial of hospitality to Lot's guests, but their "abominable" (תועבה) (Ezek 16:50) homosexual behavior (*Welcoming*, 35–40; cf. Moore, Review of *Welcoming*).

155. *CH* prescribes different punishments according to the type of incest: with a daughter—banishment (154); with a daughter-in-law—death (155); between mother and son after the father's death—death for both (157). Not to be forgotten is Lot's earlier attempt to offer his daughters to the men of Sodom (Gen 19:8).

156. Trible, *Terror*, 9–36 (Gen 16:1–16; 21:9–17). The other texts she discusses are Judg 11:30–40 (Jephthah's daughter), 2 Sam 13:1–22 (Absalom's sister Tamar), and Judg 19:1–30 (the Levite's concubine).

157. Graybill commits to "carving out a space for reading *after terror*: that is, not letting the suffering or darkness of the texts consume all the interpretive space around them" (*Terror*, 2; emphasis original).

158. Some of these roles are enacted by another childless patriarch—Kirta, king of Khubur (*CAT* 14–16; cf. Moore, *Reconciliation*, 35–48). Gossai sees Abraham as someone afflicted by a "personal barrenness" (*Barrenness*, 19).

Isaac (יצחק), comes from the verb צחק (to laugh)[159] because Sarah laughs at the promise of a child in her old age (Gen 18:12).[160]

Abraham's Revealing Test

The climactic episode of the Abraham cycle justifiably garners a great deal of attention.[161] Jewish readers call it the *Aqeda*[162] because the "binding" of Isaac is to many a disquieting portent of later "bindings," like the "binding" of Jews in the Spanish inquisition,[163] the "binding" of Jews in the Russian pogroms,[164] and the "binding" of Jews in the Nazi prison camps.[165] Christians and Muslims, however, tend to focus on Abraham. Adopting Vg *temptatio* as the clearest translation of נסה (to test, tempt), many Christians read this chapter as the story of Abraham's "temptation,"[166] but Qur'an more accurately refers to it as Ibrahim's البلكوا المبين (revealing test).[167]

Examining this Hebrew episode alongside Homer's *Odyssey* and other "great texts," Erich Auerbach attends to all three characters—Elohim, Abraham, and Isaac. In his groundbreaking study *Mimesis*[168] he argues (a) that unlike Zeus, Elohim is a deity "not fixed in form or content,"[169] but wor-

---

159. The hospitality meal at which this occurs finds a parallel in *CAT* 1.15.4.1–16; 1.17.5.14–33, and laughter (Ug *ṣḥq*) regarding the birth of a child finds a parallel in *CAT* 1.17.2.10–11.

160. GNT is careful not to imply that Sarah is "faithless" because "by faith even Sarah, who was past childbearing age, was enabled to bear children because she considered him faithful who had made the promise" (Heb 11:11).

161. Gen 22:1, נסה (to test—this same verb describes Solomon's "testing" by the queen of Sheba in 1 Kgs 10:1); cf. OG (πειράζω); Syr (ܢܣܐ); Vg (*temptavit*); Tg. Onq. נסי; Tg. Ps.-J. omits.

162. Gen 22:9, עקד, "to bind."

163. J. Anderson, *Spanish Inquisition*, 87–103.

164. Veidlinger, *Pogroms*.

165. Milton, "Expulsion" (cf. Dershowitz, *Tunnels*, 1–4).

166. Cf. Moore, "Abraham's."

167. Q 37:106 identifies the son to be sacrificed as Ishmael, not Isaac, though Isaac eventually receives a title of his own, نبيا من الصالحين (prophet among the righteous) (Q 37:112).

168. Nixon calls *Mimesis* "an unignorable landmark in post-WWII literary and cultural studies, and in the growing emphasis within these fields on how literature helps us understand ourselves *historically*—as persons ineluctably drawn towards the representation of ourselves within our particular space and time" (*Auerbach*, 1). Wellek contends that what Auerbach accomplishes in *Mimesis* is nothing less than "a short history of the human condition" as seen through literary "glimpses into reality from many centuries and societies" ("Realism," 299).

169. Moses is extended a visual aid in the "burning bush," but not Abraham.

shiped by the Hebrews "in competition with the far more manifest gods of the surrounding Near Eastern world";[170] and (b) that Abraham is an individual understandably perplexed by the deity's command to sacrifice his "only son" (Gen 22:2),[171] thereby making his journey to Mt. Moriah "a silent progress through the indeterminate and the contingent, a holding of the breath";[172] and (c) that Isaac is not so much a "person" as a "personage" whose primary function is to demonstrate "how terrible Abraham's temptation is," not to mention that "God is fully aware of it."[173]

Driven by a desire to protect Abraham's reputation, Omri Boehm adopts Maimonides' suggestion that the actions in vv. 10-12—the passage where Abraham picks up the knife to kill his son—must be absent from the original text.[174] Whatever the (de)merits of this suggestion,[175] the theological point does not change; viz., that sometimes it's difficult to tell the difference between the forces of chaos and the forces of creation, particularly when the Creator tolerates behavior which at first glance appears to look more like the former. *Conclusion:* Chaos is persistent, yes, but the Creator is more so, the proof being his unflinching readiness to test the covenant loyalty of anyone, even his "re-creation agents."[176]

JACOB CYCLE

Like the Erra poem, the Jacob cycle gingerly straddles the canyon dividing "city dwellers" from "field dwellers" through several vignettes designed to

---

170. Auerbach, *Mimesis*, 39.

171. בנך יחידך (so Syr; OG omits); Vg *unigenitum* (only begotten; cf. John 3:16).

172. Auerbach, *Mimesis*, 40. Porter sees Auerbach characterizing Abraham as a wretched soul fated to "march through empty, blank space for three days to arrive at the sacrificial altar," the space "being that of an abstract moral universe" where "time elapses like a symbolic eternity" ("Auerbach," 129). Boehm sees this "empty blank space" as "progressively hinting, up to the moment that Isaac is bound on the altar, that Abraham's obedience should not be taken for granted" (*Isaac*, 41-42).

173. Auerbach, *Mimesis*, 40. Interestingly enough, Auerbach, a Jewish refugee from the Nazi regime, does not favor the *Aqedah* interpretation.

174. Boehm, *Isaac*, 43 (citing Maimonides, *Guide*, 3.24).

175. Noth, on the other hand, suggests that this episode is based on an old "human sacrifice" ritual in which a ram is homeopathically substituted at the pivotal moment (*History*, 114-15).

176. "Now I know that you fear God, because you have not withheld from me your son, your only son" (Gen. 22:12). Cf. the similar testing of Jacob and Joseph, and also Deut 8:16.

contrast the "wild man" from the "field"[177] and the "civilized man"[178] who lives "in tents" (Gen 25:27). Like Enkidu, a "mantle of hair" covers the "wild man's" body (Gen 25:25),[179] and like Gilgamesh, the "civilized" man's heroism has a dark side.[180] Meir Malul thus concludes that this section of *Genesis* manipulates the sibling rivalry metaphor in order to spotlight a "conflict between two ways of life, one of a member of what has become . . . the civilized society, and the other of a member of the sphere of lawlessness."[181]

Divine sibling rivalry stories tend to fall into one of three categories: (a) sibling deities of fertility vs. death;[182] (b) sibling deities of founders vs. foreigners;[183] and (c) twins—heroes vs. villains.[184] In Egypt the sibling rivalry motif is featured in the entertaining Tale of Two Brothers,[185] a story loosely analogous to the Cain and Abel saga. The story of Jacob and Esau, however, is much more densely layered. Even those who read Genesis only as literature find it to be one of the most honestly human stories ever told.[186] But those who read it as the word of God find that it does more than merely entertain, as the opening prophecy to Rebekah makes clear:

---

177. שדה; Erra 1.55-56. Like Enkidu, Esau is a "man familiar with wild game" (איש ידע ציד).

178. תם (integrity/complete).

179. אדרת סער. Cf. GE 1:105, *šuʾur šartu* (hairy with hair).

180. Mobley, *Empty*, 19-74.

181. Malul, "Heel," 206.

182. Tutt observes that "as death is a reality to human existence, every culture features a death deity and nearly all myths have a fertility or life-giving sibling to counteract death personified. Therefore, as these deities represent two sides of the same coin, they are often depicted as siblings, if not twins" ("Sibling," 6).

183. Tutt recognizes that a "prevalent theme of sibling myths involves the jealousy between a powerful leader and his/her underappreciated sibling. While these stories describe sibling rivalries, they also represent a core element of human civilization, the dichotomy of order and chaos" ("Sibling," 38).

184. Tutt argues that "on the one hand, twins can be the most powerful of heroes, coming from humble beginnings, gaining strength and skills through their lives together, and saving humanity through great feats of heroism. On the other hand, twins can represent a deeper divide between the dualistic ideologies represented in other sibling myths, most drastically the divide between good and evil. Twin deities therefore represent the most extreme examples of the sibling deity myths" ("Sibling," 62.)

185. *ANET* 23-25; cf. Hollis, *Brothers*.

186. Cf. Fokkelman, "Genesis," 45-47.

שני גוים בבטנך	Two nations are in your womb,
שני לאמים ממעיך יפרדו	two peoples fighting within your belly.
לאם מלאם יאמץ	One nation will be stronger than the other,
ורב יעבד צעיר	for the older will serve the younger.
	(Gen 25:23)[187]

Several things may be said about this prophetic preamble, but what is most literarily distinctive is the fact that it organically links a family *story* to a larger *history* in what Hugh White calls a "symbolic narrative."[188] That is, the micro-conflict between Jacob and Esau parallels the macro-conflict between Israel and Edom, and failure to recognize this parallel makes it difficult to appreciate the Jacob cycle in its literary-theological depth.

What White means is that *history* in symbolic narratives can and does bleed over into *story* and vice versa.[189] Here the two blend together so seamlessly it can be difficult to tell where one ends and the other begins, a circumstance made observable by putting to this text a few simple questions: Who is the hero? Who is the villain? Who is responsible for the conflict? Does it resolve? If so, how? On the surface these queries look simple, yet symbolic narratives are complicated texts intentionally designed to challenge readers to *un*tangle that which has been so deliberately *en*tangled.[190]

Esau, for example, seems far too gullible to be a "villain," at least not in the usual sense of the word.[191] Yet what is he, if not the "bad guy"?[192] Impetuous and impatient, he marries Hittite wives against the wishes of his parents (Gen 25:36; 28:9). He surrenders his birthright to his brother for a bowl of stew, yet still expects his father's blessing (Gen 27:4).[193] When this

---

187. Calling Rebekah a "decisive matriarch," Jeansonne thinks that her character is basically designed to "ensure that God's designated choice, Jacob, the second-born, receives Isaac's blessing" (*Women*, 53).

188. White, *Narration*, 58.

189. Similarly, priestly ritual sometimes makes it difficult to distinguish human from divine participants (cf. Kowalzig, *Singing*, 13–23).

190. White observes that "it is precisely in this polyvalent friction between individuals, classes, and circumstances that this narrative exhibits another feature" because "each character remains unfinished, open to the future and the other characters, and it is precisely in this ambiguous communicative interaction between these distant social worlds that the story achieves its aesthetic (and religious) power" (*Narration*, 185).

191. Cf. V. Propp, *Morphology*, 21–23; and Alter, *Art*, 94–96.

192. Esau is the "wild man" to Jacob's "civilized man" (cf. Mobley, "Wild," 226–28; Moore, *WealthWatch*, 129–35).

193. N.b. the parallel on Nuzu Tablet G 51: "The adoption tablet of Nashwi son of Arshenni. He adopted Wullu son of Puhishenni. As long as Nashwi lives, Wullu shall give (him) food and clothing. When Nashwi dies, Wullu shall be the heir. Should

fails (due in part to the admittedly devious activity of Jacob and Rebekah) he finds himself engulfed in a chaos much like that which paralyzes the prediluvians in PH (Gen 27:41–46).[194] In short, Esau comes across as an immature, impulsive, rather arrogant young man at the beginning of the Jacob cycle.[195]

Jacob, on the other hand, seems far too devious to be a "hero." Instead he looks very much like what his name implies, a "trickster."[196] The first time he appears in the story he is gouging his brother out of his birthright (Gen 25:31).[197] After this he participates in a deceitful scheme to steal his brother's blessing by tricking their blind father into believing that he is Esau (Gen 27:18–29).[198] Later, fleeing Esau's wrath, he has a dream in which he hears the same promise made earlier to his grandfather Abraham:

זרעך כעפר הארץ	Your descendants will be like the dust of the earth....
נברכו בך כל משפחות	All the families on earth will be blessed through you
האדמה ובזרעך	and your descendants. (Gen 28:14)

Awakening from this dream, he cries out,

Nashwi beget a son, (the latter) shall divide equally with Wullu but (only) Nashwi's son shall take Nashwi's gods. But if there be no son of Nashwi's, then Wullu shall take Nashwi's gods. And (Nashwi) has given his daughter Nuhuya as wife to Wullu. And if Wullu takes another wife, he forfeits Nashwi's land and buildings. Whoever breaks the contract shall pay one mina of silver (and) one mina of gold" (from Gordon, "Nuzu," 5). The duty of a father to bless his children finds a parallel in CAT 1.16.6.55–59, and the filial duty of preparing game for one's father finds a parallel in CAT 1.17.5.33–39.

194. Cf. above on Gen 6–9.
195. This is the side of Esau described in Heb 12:16–17.
196. Heb יעקב (Jacob) means "heel grabber" (Gen 25:26) or, to use more contemporary language, "wheeler-dealer" or "con man." The use of disguises finds a parallel in CAT 1.19.4.33.63.
197. Trying to be objective, Weiss wrestles with whether Jacob acts ethically in the "birthright trading incident" or unethically in order to "seize a propitious opportunity to exploit Esau's predicament" ("Ethics," 142).
198. Steinmetz, Kinship, 30–85. Snyman finds plenty of blame to go around, asking, "Who perverts justice, and for whom should the readers reserve their disgust? Is it Rebekah and Jacob for deceiving Isaac, and robbing Esau of his blessing? Is it Jacob for exploiting Esau's nonchalance regarding his birthright? Is it Esau for neglecting the birthright tradition, or is it Isaac for neglecting his role as patriarch?" Steinmann (Genesis, 445) points out the parallel between Isaac's blindness here and Jacob's blindness later (48:10), particularly how each case affects a patriarch's ability to recognize his (grand)children ("Disgust," 446).

מה נורא המקום הזה	How fearful is this place!
אין זה כי אם בית אלהים	This is none other than the house of God!
זה שער השמים	This is the very gate of heaven! (Gen 28:17)[199]

Yet in spite of this "fearful" experience he still tries to dictate to the Creator the terms of their relationship:

אי יהיה אלהים עמדי ושמרני	If God will be with me, and will guard me[200]
בדרך הזה אשר אנכי הולך	on this path I am taking,
ונתן לי לחם לאכל ובגד לבלש	and will give me bread to eat and clothing to wear
ושבתי בשלום אל בית אבי	so that I can return to my father's house in peace,
והיה יהוה לי לאלהם	then Yhwh shall be my God. (Gen 28:20–21)[201]

Quite an interesting set of preconditions for a liar and a cheat, no? Granted, this speech *may* be interpreted as a budding indicator of an embryonic "faith,"[202] but in light of the chaos-creation polarity it's more likely that its intention is to disclose the power of chaos to destroy Jacob. Certainly it is one of the few places in the Bible where a clay creature dares to dictate covenant terms to its Creator.[203]

---

199. ANE peoples almost universally imagine a "gate" between the seen and unseen worlds, usually one that can be locked and bolted (cf, e.g., *DA* 1.6, *tpry skry šmyn b'bky* (lock up and bolt the heavens with your cloud). That Jacob sees angels freely ascending and descending between these two worlds is thus intended to be taken as extraordinary.

200. MT שמר (to guard, protect) is the same term used by Cain when he asks whether he is obligated to be Abel's "keeper" (4:9).

201. Analyzing Jacob and Joseph as prototypical "younger brothers," Niditch observes that their stories exemplify "the *Bildungsroman*, the tale of maturation," their characters being "underdogs, youngest sons who inherit, exiles who outwit their masters, marginal people who end their tales with financial and social success" (*Prelude*, 70).

202. De Pury asks, "What can be more natural than for Jacob to make a vow and pledge himself to worship the deity?" (*Promesse*, 438), but Humphreys emphasizes that in spite of everything Jacob has done the "remarkable" thing is that "God is willing to stick with this family he elected, and especially those within it who are particularly chosen" (*Character*, 172).

203. This is not the only time in Tanak where a clay creature makes a vow to the Creator (cf. Num 21:2; Judg 11:30–31; 1 Sam 1:11; 2 Sam 18:8), but it is by far the most peremptory. See Moshe Weinfeld, "ברית," *TDOT* 2:253–79; and Dumbrell, *Faith*, 34–39.

Still, Jacob seems to be the protagonist of the story—if not the "good guy," then at least the guy who eventually *tries* to be good.[204] It is Uncle Laban's job to mold this soft clay into something more concrete. So, from the day they first meet, Rebekah's brother drafts Jacob into a graduate course on "deceivership." He administers repeated, hefty doses to Jacob of his own medicine. He lies to him about his daughter, switching Leah for Rachel on the night of their wedding.[205] For fourteen years he treats him more like an indentured servant than a beloved son-in-law. The irony, of course, is that during this time Jacob, the thief who steals his brother's blessing, has his own *wife* stolen; that Jacob, the man who deceives his blind father, is *himself* deceived.[206] After fourteen years of this he naturally begins to wonder whether life back home, even life with Esau, might somehow be better than life with Laban. Confrontation, with all its risks, begins to look preferable to exploitation. So he decides to go home and "face the music." Finagling a relatively honest, non-manipulative agreement with Laban, he successfully extracts his family from his uncle's control and heads home. The question he faces now is "Can a deal with Esau be possible? Can I be reconciled to my brother after so many years of bad blood?" (Gen 31:44–50).[207]

The episode where the two brothers meet, the "showdown" for which the narrator has so carefully prepared us, occurs within one of the most textured sections of Genesis. Attention to this texture is necessary if we are to understand and appreciate creation's ability to rout chaos at a critical moment in history. Reprising the symbolic approach used earlier in the preamble, the narrator now interweaves Jacob's horizontal encounter with Esau into his vertical encounter with God, laying everything out in five parallel stages. In the *vertical* encounter Jacob (1) meets a troupe of divine "messengers" (Gen 28:12);[208] then (2) responds with an exclamation of awe (Gen 28:17);[209] then (3) names the place of the encounter "two camps" (Gen 32:2);[210] then (4) "wrestles" with a superhuman being (Gen 32:22–

---

204. Kaminsky suggests that Genesis preserves this story to highlight "the problems which arise when someone is mysteriously singled out as God's special elect" ("Reclaiming," 135).

205. The motif of leaving home to find a wife finds a parallel in *CAT* 1.14.2.30–33.44.

206. N.b. the difference between the realistic portrait of Jacob in Genesis and the more glowing portrayals in Hos 12:1–6; Matt 8:11; and Rom 9:10–12.

207. This is basically the same question Joseph later faces with his Hebrew brothers as Zaphenath-Paneah (41:45).

208. The word for "angel" and the word for "messenger" are the same Hebrew word, מלאך.

209. See above.

210. MT מחנים (*maḥanaim*) means "two camps."

32);²¹¹ then (5) changes his name from יעקב (Jacob—trickster) to ישראל (Israel—struggler with God) (Gen 32:28). In the *horizontal* encounter Jacob (1) encounters four hundred "messengers" from Esau (Gen 33:1);²¹² then (2) divides his entourage into "two camps" (Gen 33:1–2);²¹³ then (3) bows seven times in respect for Esau (Gen 33:3); then (4) engages in an awkward "wrestling match" over who will be the first to forgive the other;²¹⁴ then (5) publicly declares his new name. Whereas the vertical encounter climaxes with "Jacob" becoming "Israel," the horizontal encounter climaxes with the building of an altar named "El Elohê Israel," which means "God, the God of the one who wrestles with God" (Gen 33:20).²¹⁵ With this altar Jacob publicly affirms his new identity. "Israel" is no longer "Jacob," no longer a deceiver of his father, no longer a cheater of his brother, no longer a slave of his uncle, no longer a clay creature bargaining with the Creator for a "better deal."²¹⁶ This *un*-created trickster now becomes a *re*-creation agent.

JOSEPH NOVELLA

The Joseph novella²¹⁷ considerably amplifies the parameters of the chaos-creation polarity identified in the previous two cycles, only here the conflict is between twelve brothers, not two, all vying for their father's approval. The conflict here is not just about deciding which *son* to favor (Abel vs. Cain; Isaac vs. Ishmael; Jacob vs. Esau), but which *family* to favor (Joseph's Hebrew family vs. Zaphenath-paneah's Egyptian family) (Gen 41:45).²¹⁸ Here the chaos-creation polarity plays out on a much grander stage, and like most "great literature" it can be read from a number of perspectives. One can read it from Jacob's perspective, the *re*-created "trickster" who, after hearing of his favorite son's "death," collapses into a mournful stupor from which he

211. Technically, Jacob's wrestling partner is a "man" (איש); cf. the "man" conferring earlier with Abraham (18:10, 13).

212. Heb מלאך here and in 28:12 can mean "messenger" and/or "angel."

213. Leah and her children in the front; Rachel and her children in the back.

214. Esau offers Jacob an expensive gift of livestock, and Jacob politely refuses it. Esau then "urges" him to accept it until Jacob gives in (Gen 33:8–11).

215. אל אלהי ישראל.

216. Gossai recognizes that "the alternative to wrestling with God is more devastating and costly than wrestling with God" (*Barrenness*, 56).

217. According to Gunkel ("Josephsgeschichte") and Von Rad ("Josephsgeschichte," 120), novellas contain more (and more complex) characters and more (and more convoluted) plotlines than those structuring sagas, myths, and/or epics.

218. Heb צפנת פענח is an attempt to transliterate Eg *Ḏ d-p-nṯ r-jw.f-ʿnḫ* (the god speaks and he [the bearer of the name] lives).

never fully recovers. One can read it from the perspective of Joseph's brothers, who, after seeing how much Jacob favors Joseph, become so enraged at him they decide to sell him into slavery.[219] One can read it from the perspective of the Egyptian Pharaoh, the powerful monarch who experiences nightmarish dreams only to find himself forced to rely on a *reṯenu* convict to interpret them.[220] Or one can read it from Joseph's perspective, a young man mistreated by his brothers, his Egyptian master's wife,[221] and a foreign prison system from which it looks like he cannot escape. Beset by a father who dotes on him, a pack of older brothers who hate him, and a foreign culture which isolates him, Joseph is a survivor who, like all survivors, has to learn how to weather the problems and ordeals which drive cowards to despair.

Joseph and His Father

Leah's sons receive far less attention from their father than do Rachel's sons, Joseph and Benjamin. Simply by being Rachel's firstborn, Joseph receives preferential treatment hidden behind a cryptic tapestry of generational prejudices.[222] Evidently Jacob is aware of his sons' "envy" (Gen 37:11),[223] but paternal preference can be so strong, a law has to be passed to protect the rights of the *un*-preferred:[224]

---

219. Originally they mean to kill him, but Reuben intervenes (Gen 37:20–21). Later, of course, Joseph tells his long-estranged brothers that it was not them, but God who brought him into Egypt (Gen 45:5).

220. Eg *reṯenu* refers to "Asiatics/Palestinians" (*CDME* 154; Murnane, "Egypt," 2:700).

221. Qur'an imagines Potiphar's wife defending herself by inviting several women to a banquet and displaying Joseph's "beauty" to them, after which they cut themselves and exclaim, "This one cannot be human [بشر (lit., flesh)], but a noble angel" (ملك كريم) (Q 12:31).

222. Passing over the older for the younger is not unusual in ancient "brother stories." Niditch, in fact, charts the following sequence: (a) unusual birth, (b) conflict over status, (c) journey/adventures, (d) success in new environment, and (e) resolution of rivalry (*Prelude*, 70).

223. MT ויקנאו בו אחיו ואביו שמר את הדבר (His brothers envied him, but his father kept the matter [to himself]); OG πατὴρ αὐτοῦ διετήρησεν τὸ ῥῆμα (his father kept a close watch on the matter); Syr ܐܒܘܗܝ ܗܘܐ ܢܛܪ ܦܬܓܡܐ (and his father watched over the matter); Vg *vero rem tacitus considerabat* (he considered the matter silently).

224. Milstein believes that Israel never has law collections like those in other ANE cultures, and that when Hebrew scribes want to legislate something, they repurpose scribal legal exercises, reframing and revising them to their specific needs (*Case*, 53–89; cf. Farber, Review).

כִּי תִהְיֶיןָ לְאִישׁ שְׁתֵּי נָשִׁים	If a man has two wives,
הָאַחַת אֲהוּבָה וְהָאַחַת שְׂנוּאָה	and he loves one but hates the other,
וְיָלְדוּ לוֹ בָנִים הָאֲהוּבָה וְהַשְּׂנוּאָה	and both the loved one and the hated one bear him sons,
וְהָיָה הַבֵּן הַבְּכוֹר לַשְּׂנִיאָה	but the firstborn son issues from the hated wife,
אֲשֶׁר יִהְיֶה לוֹ וְהָיָה בְּיוֹם הַנְחִילוֹ אֶת בָּנָיו	on the day he wills his property to his sons
לֹא יוּכַל לְבַכֵּר	he shall not hand over the privileges of the firstborn
אֶת בֶּן הָאֲהוּבָה	to the son of the beloved wife
עַל פְּנֵי בֶן הַשְּׂנוּאָה הַבְּכֹר	instead of the firstborn son of the hated wife. (Deut 21:15–16)[225]

In other words, Jacob is supposed to transfer his birthright to Reuben as his legitimate firstborn,[226] but considering the way Laban tricks him into marrying an unpreferred wife, it's understandable why he would (subconsciously?) repeat the same toxic cycle with *his* sons.[227] Observing this dynamic at play, John Goldingay summarily remarks that "the Jacob family illustrates the dynamics of many a family, with someone loved too much, someone loving too much, and some not feeling loved enough."[228]

Joseph and his Brothers

At any rate, Joseph tries to make a go of it with his dysfunctional family.[229] As the story opens we see him "searching" for his brothers, and not just geographically (Gen 37:17).[230] Having openly shared his dreams with them—

---

225. For a partial parallel cf. CH 170: "If the first wife of a gentleman [*awīlum*] has borne his sons and also his slave-girl has borne him sons . . . and the man dies . . . the heir, the son of the first wife, shall have the choice of which share to take."

226. Sternberg's emphasis on serialization as a means by which to project cumulative force (*Poetics*, 109–13) certainly applies to what Syrén calls the "forsaken firstborn" motif (*Forsaken*, 140).

227. This appears to betray the fact that "Israel" still has some of the old "Jacob" (trickster) in him, but not to be overlooked is the fact that Reuben sleeps with Rachel's handmaid Bilhah (Gen 35:22). Engel talks about how difficult it is to identify, much less stop the *legacy* of abuse (*Abuse*, 9–57).

228. Goldingay, *Genesis*, 570.

229. Lennox, *Joseph*, 1.

230. MT וַיֵּלֶךְ יוֹסֵף אַחַר אֶחָיו (Joseph walked after his brothers).

dreams they find bizarre and offensive—he obeys his father's injunction to go out and check on them as they tend his flocks. Precisely why Jacob sends Joseph on such an errand is not clear, but whatever his rationale one has to wonder (a) whether he is at all sensitive to the depth of Leah's sons' anger, and (b) if so, why he would expose Rachel's firstborn to it, especially after having earlier experienced such a painfully similar situation in *his* family.[231] During his "search," at any rate, Joseph seems to have no idea what is happening, though this naïveté may be to some extent generated by the narrator's desire to heighten the contrast between the young innocent Joseph and the older seasoned politician Zaphenath-paneah. Whatever the case may be, at this point he is little more to his brothers than an irritating reminder of opportunities never extended and privileges never granted.

This fraternal resentment comes to a head when Joseph delivers an "evil report" to Jacob about his brothers (Gen 37:2).[232] To speculate about the precise contents of this report is tempting, but futile. The text simply does not say, though a similar phrase is used to describe the "evil report" of the ten men recruited by Moses to scout out the land of Canaan (Num 14:37).[233] Whatever the specifics, all that can be certainly said is that this report significantly fuels the rage of Reuben and his brothers, a result the text relays via some rather clever wordplay. The name "Joseph" means "the one added on," a fitting name for a little brother "added on" to an already sizeable family (Gen 30:24).[234] When he shares his dreams with his family the text twice repeats this word to describe his brothers "*adding* more hatred upon him" (Gen 37:5, 8).[235] Brick by brick, in other words, they keep "adding on" more and more hatred onto their brother until a brick wall materializes which no one can cross—not Joseph, not Jacob, not Benjamin, not even Yhwh. Life behind this wall becomes a twisted cul-de-sac in which the unthinkable becomes thinkable and the unspeakable speakable. In short, Joseph's

---

231. Qur'an explains this by having Jacob say to Joseph, "O my dear son! Do not relate your vision to your brothers, or they will devise a plot against you" (Q 12:5). Goldingay comments that "it is both surprising and not surprising that Jacob has not learned from the role that favoritism plays in his parents' relationship with him and his brother" (*Genesis*, 570).

232. Jacobs argues that "the primacy of the conflict that is to characterize the story is introduced by the account of Joseph giving an 'evil report' (דבה רעה) about his brothers to their father" ("Dynamics," 313).

233. The other two, Joshua and Caleb, do not agree with their colleagues' "evil report" (דבת ... רעה).

234. MT יוסף is the G act. ptc. of the verb יסף (to add on).

235. ויוספו עוד שנא אתו

"search" for his brothers runs terribly awry. Instead of "finding" them, what he discovers instead are kidnapping thugs ready to dispose of him.²³⁶

Joseph in Egypt

Many of the motifs in the Joseph novella echo those animating an Egyptian story called the Tale of Sinuhe,²³⁷ a text Richard Parkinson calls "a masterpiece of Egyptian literature" and Miriam Lichtheim calls "the most accomplished piece of Middle Kingdom prose."²³⁸ There are several parallels between these two stories, but the most prominent can be captured by a single word: *home*. Just as the court official Sinuhe begins life in Egypt, then flees to Canaan, then returns to Egypt, so Joseph begins life in Canaan, is sold into Egypt, then eventually returns home to Canaan.²³⁹ Each of these stories pivots around what Parkinson tellingly describes as a persistent "incursion of chaos."²⁴⁰ In the Tale of Sinuhe, the protagonist is driven from his home at a dark moment of political panic.²⁴¹ In the Joseph novella, chaos attacks Abraham's descendants at a dark moment when Joseph's brothers sell him into Egyptian slavery as the servant of a government official named Potiphar (Gen 39:1).²⁴²

---

236. Not to be forgotten is the fact that their first response is to kill Joseph, a tragedy avoided only by Reuben's intercession (Gen 37:21-22).

237. The Tale of Sinuhe is the story of a government official in the court of Pharaoh Amenemhat I (d. 1962 BCE) who, at the Pharaoh's death, flees the country to escape the draconian repercussions so often accompanying major political transitions.

238. Parkinson, "Sinuhe," 26; *AEL* 1:222. Parkinson calls Sinuhe a "funerary autobiography" designed to "encourage reflection on the nature of Egyptian life" ("Sinuhe," 21), but Spalinger finds it to be a "totally artificial presentation" ("Orientations," 324). English translations appear in *ANET* 18-22, *AEL* 1:222-35, and *COS* 1:77-82.

239. In Gen 50:13 Joseph and his brothers bury Jacob's body next to Abraham in the cave of Machpelah purchased by Abraham for Sarah's burial. In v. 14 Joseph returns to Egypt, but eventually his bones are carried back to Canaan and buried in Shechem (Josh 24:32; Judg 9:6-7). Staubli calls Joseph the "Israelite Sinuhe" ("Impacts," 64).

240. Parkinson, "Sinuhe," 25.

241. Hollis argues that since the Egyptians view themselves as living at the center of the cosmos, their literature often portrays other countries as places of punishment and exile (a motif dominating not only Sinuhe, but also the Story of Two Brothers and the Prince and His Fates). Each of these stories involves (a) the belief that "Asia" (Syria–Palestine) is a place of exile, death, and transformation; and (b) a hero forced to undergo trial in a foreign land before triumphantly returning home ("Otherworld").

242. פוטיפר is a rough transliteration of Eg *pdy pr'* (the one given by Ra). The Hebrew story of Joseph's seduction by Potiphar's wife and the Egyptian Tale of Two Brothers stand in a literary genre where "a young man is propositioned by an older woman and, when he resists the seduction, is denounced to another man who then

Lest the obvious be overlooked, however, Egypt is a long way from "home," not geographically, but culturally and religiously. Egypt is a polytheistic society in which Yahwism is the religion of a *reṭenu* deity. Indeed, monotheism itself is shunned,[243] as Pharaoh Thutmose IV later discovers.[244] On the surface Joseph seems to handle everything in stride. He goes from prison rags to royal riches overnight when Pharaoh springs him from prison and appoints him to high position. The Yahwistic text unsurprisingly attributes this rise to Yhwh, not Pharaoh, but for some readers this leaves too many loose ends, some suggesting that Yhwh *miraculously* shields him from chaos. Such is the opinion of the Jewish historian Artapanus, who imagines him as a shrewd politician who invents a new standard of weights, becomes the "very first" ruler to divide Egypt equitably between the rich and the poor,[245] and engineers his own "kidnapping" because he knows how much Egypt is going to need his gifts.[246]

The biblical story, however, never engages in such speculation. Predictably, it never *overtly* describes Joseph's life in Egypt,[247] but *covertly* it mentions three details which taken together prove to be quite revealing. *First*, he marries the daughter of an Egyptian priest in the service of the sungod Ra (Gen 41:45).[248] Her name is Aseneth and their "romance" becomes

---

inflicts severe punishment upon the innocent victim. After an exile of some sort, the young man returns; his innocence is recognized, and he advances to a higher state, sometimes even becoming king" (Kelly, Review). Not all of these elements are observable in the Hebrew story, but Qur'an claims that the reason why Joseph resists Potiphar's wife is because he "sees a sign" (برهن [lit., proof]) sent to help him "keep away evil and indecency" (Q 12:24).

243. Sensitive to the dangers of Egyptianization, Qur'an has Joseph say, "I follow the faith of my fathers: Abraham, Isaac, and Jacob. It is not for us to associate anything with Alla. . . . Whatever you worship instead of him are just names which you and your forefathers have made up. . . . Alla commands that you worship no one but him" (Q 12:38–40).

244. Pharaoh Thutmose IV (d. 1390 BCE) famously changes his name to Akhenaten (servant of the sun disc) because he wants Egypt to put their faith in only one deity. Yhwh worship comes much later to an island in the southern Nile, but not until the fifth century BCE (cf. Van der Toorn, *Becoming*, 1–9).

245. Equitable land reform is a major theme in TEP, and Redford reads DILA as a timely response to the "calamitous condition of human society" ("Literature," 2234).

246. Artapanus' history is preserved by the early church historian Eusebius in his work *Preparation for the Gospel* (cited in Holladay, *Historians*, 205–9).

247. That is, Tanak tends to avoid what Stanley Hopper calls "inscaping" ("Sonnets," 63).

248. MT כֹּהֵן אֹן (priest of On); OG ἱερέως Ἡλίου πόλεως (priest of Heliopolis); Vg *sacerdotis Heliopoleos* (priest of Sun City).

the stuff of later Jewish legend.[249] The text does not describe what life is like as the son-in-law of an Egyptian priest, but biblical passages elsewhere tend to cast such situations in a negative light.[250] *Second*, he gives symbolic Hebrew names to his sons, Ephraim and Manasseh (Gen 41:50–52).[251] Joseph chooses these names to thank God for rescuing him from distress, yet each exudes irony. Years later when his brothers come asking for food, it immediately becomes clear that he has not "forgotten" what they did to him and that he still struggles with the "fruit" of their cold-bloodedness. *Third*, in addition to his ability to interpret dreams (*oneiromancy*) (Gen 41:25–32), Joseph practices other forms of divination in a "silver cup," most likely with oil (*lecanomancy*) and/or water (*hydromancy*) (Gen 44:2, 4).[252] This is not the place to introduce a detailed discussion of ANE divination or why Israel eventually comes to abhor it (Deut 13:1–5).[253] The point here is that something inevitably happens to Joseph when he changes his name to Zaphenath-paneah. Politically, socially, and religiously he becomes isolated from his Hebrew roots, and soon finds himself forced to stand in a place where chaos threatens to *un*-create that which the Creator has worked so hard to (*re*)-create.

The text mentions these details to set readers up for the eventual meeting between Joseph and his brothers.[254] In this meeting Joseph has to make a decision. Should he reconcile with his Hebrew family? Or should he make himself at "home" in Egypt? *Question:* Why risk so much to reconnect with a family who sells him into slavery then lies to his father about it? *Answer:* Because to do otherwise threatens to undo everything done so far to fulfill Yhwh's promise to "bless all the families of the earth."

---

249. The pseudepigraphal Jewish legend of Joseph and Aseneth wrestles with the problem of Joseph's marriage to a polytheistic woman, the author stressing that Joseph marries Aseneth only after she destroys her idols and converts to Yahwism (cf. Burchard, "Joseph"; Bloch, *Drehbühnen*, 1–28). TgRuth explains Ruth's marriage to Boaz in the same way (cf. Moore, *What Is This Babbler*, 193–95).

250. Cf., e.g., Ahab's marriage to the daughter of Ethba'al, king of the Sidonians (i.e., Jezebel) (1 Kgs 16:31), Samson's marriage to a Philistine woman (Judg 14:3), and Esau's marriage to Hittite women who make Rebekah say קצתי בחיי (I loathe my life) (Gen 27:46); cf. 2 Cor 6:14.

251. Ephraim (אפרים) comes from a verb which means "to be fruitful" (פרה), and Manasseh (מנשה) comes from a verb which means "to forget" (נשה).

252. Cf. נחש ינחש (practice divination) (44:5, 15). Cf. Ulanowski, *Divination*, 171; Jeffers, *Magic*, 160–66.

253. Cf. Moore, *Balaam*, 42–43.

254. Similar preparational depth goes into the story of Jacob's encounter with Esau, only not in such detail.

Summary

The preceding pages are an attempt to chart how deeply the chaos-creation polarity reverberates within the Abraham, Jacob, and Joseph cycles, albeit to varying degrees. This is not the only theological polarity in Genesis, of course, but few others exercise as much influence on the formation of its theology. As suggested above in the summary for PH, this polarity has four aspects.

Chaos and creation are dynamic forces, not static entities.

The Abraham cycle depicts chaos as a dynamic force persistently threatening Abraham's life, a situation obviated by the way he treats his wife, his nephew, and his sons Ishmael and Isaac. The Jacob cycle continues this trajectory by showing how the *un*-creation caused by chaos in the Jacob-Esau rivalry eventually gravitates to *re*-creation. The Joseph novella reprises this polarity on a much grander scale as chaos threatens to disable Joseph's interactions with the sons of Leah, Potiphar's wife, the Egyptian prison system, the trappings of high office, and his own understanding of "home."

Creation suppresses chaos, but never eliminates it.

Examining this polarity from the "other side of the aisle," the Creator repeatedly suppresses chaos via his "re-creation agents," Abraham, Israel, and Joseph. Yet it never goes away, not completely. It's always there, ready to gum things up at a moment's notice. *Examples:* Lot survives the horrors of Sodom, then commits incest with his daughters. Sarah survives captivity in Pharaoh's palace, then laughs at Yhwh's promise to grant her a child. Jacob survives Esau and Laban, then allows Rachel's firstborn to fall into the hands of Leah's children. Reuben saves Joseph's life, then sleeps with Rachel's handmaid Bilhah. Judah spares Jacob the anguish of losing Benjamin, then commits adultery with his daughter-in-law Tamar. Chaos is not only dynamic and persistent; it is relentless.

Chaos is suppressed by no other power than that emanating from the imago Dei.

Over and over again in Genesis an afflicted clay creature tries to save itself, only to learn that emulation of the *imago Dei* is the only way to do so—from the first couple to their murderous son Cain to Noah's family to the Shinar workers to Abraham to Jacob to Joseph's brothers. Chaos cannot be dispelled apart from the Creator's involvement, and that help is inaccessible to clay creatures unwilling to emulate the *imago Dei*.

The damage caused by chaos is not irreparable. Creation can be un-created, but it can also be re-created.

Banishment is not the last word. The flood is not the last word, nor is any attempt to build a ziggurat skyscraper to the heavens. Barrenness is not the last word. Famine is not the last word. Prison is not the last word. Pharaoh is not the last word. Slavery is not the last word. Creation can be *un*-created, yes, but it can also be *re*-created. In fact, the Creator has a long-term plan to do so.

2

Exodus: Slavery or Freedom?

ISRAEL'S SOJOURN INTO EGYPT turns out to be much more than a mere "sojourn." In fact, it turns out to be one of the most difficult periods in Israelite history, an era plagued by centuries of "hard labor" borne under the bootheel of the "world's first superpower."[1] This "hard labor" continues until Yhwh emancipates "the children of Israel" (Exod 1:9),[2] leads them to his holy mountain, and reveals to them his law. Brevard Childs points outs that the second book of the Pentateuch "begins by recapitulating information ... already given in Genesis,"[3] but for Nahum Sarna this "second fifth" book[4] is less a continuation of the first than "the seminal book of the Hebrew Scriptures" because Exodus describes "the pivotal events of Israel's history and the fundamental institutions of its culture and religion."[5] The revelation of the law on Mt. Sinai is one of the most important of these events, to be sure,[6] but what triggers all the *action* in this narrative is the slavery-freedom polarity, a theme most clearly revealed when Israel "performs," in William

---

1. W. Christensen, *Egypt*, 5; Hoffmeier, *Israel*, 248–49.

2. בני ישראל (lit., sons of Israel), usually translated "children of Israel" or "Israelites" (this is the first appearance of this appellation). For Coats, Exodus "builds around one dominant motif: the Egyptians oppress the Israelites with hard labor" (*Exodus*, 5). N.b. that "hard labor" is a major motif in Ee, Atr, and PH.

3. Childs, *Exodus*, 1.

4. חומש שני (b. Sotah 36b).

5. Sarna, "Exodus," 2:690. For Watts "it is in the book of Exodus as it now stands that the pilgrimage motif and the reciprocity of law/instruction and narrative are most fully displayed" (Review, 129).

6. M. Smith, *Exodus*, 264–84.

Propp's description, a "blood ritual on the night of Passover," thereby changing their "social status from slavery to freedom."[7]

Different readers see different literary patterns in Exodus.[8] For Frank Moore Cross, the Song of Victory (Exod 15:1–21)[9] clearly parallels the Canaanite Ba'al cycle at three major points:[10] (a) the victory of the Divine Warrior (יהוה איש מלחמה [Yhwh is a man of war]) over the "sea" (*yam*) (15:3–4; cf. *CAT* 1.1–2); (b) the consecration of Israel at the מקדש (sanctuary) situated on the הר נחלה (mountain of possession) (15:17; cf. *CAT* 1.3–4); and (c) the acknowledgment of Yhwh's eternal kingship (יהוה ימלך לעלם ועד) (Yhwh will reign forever and ever) (15:18; cf. *CAT* 1.5–6).[11] At present there is an ongoing debate not so much about the historicity of the exodus as the degree to which the ANE combat myth frames the tradition in its final form.[12]

Doug Stuart voices the mainstream opinion that the book clearly divides into "two main parts, a first part telling the story of God's rescue of the people of Israel from Egypt and his leading them to Mount Sinai (chapters 1–19), and a second part describing his covenant with them (chapters 20–40)."[13] Mark Smith agrees in principle with this bicameral structure, but suggests that the dividing line is in the wrong place, pointing out that whereas chs. 1–14 narrate *Moses'* movement from Egypt to Midian, involving two calls (3:1—4:16 and 6:1–8) and two confrontations (2:12 and

---

7. W. Propp, *Exodus*, 35. Snell argues that "the desire for personal freedom is ... a universal value in all human societies" (*Flight*, 154), and that it is particularly "central to how the West behaves in the modern world and the assumptions we Westerners bring to it" (*Flight*, 9). Noticing the absence of the slavery-freedom polarity in other passages about Egypt (esp. Ezek 20), Kugler echoes K. Schmid ("Genesis and Exodus") in imagining the slavery-freedom polarity to be only one of several ways to portray Israel's Egyptian stay ("Egypt"). Moses, however, describes Israel's Egyptian sojourn as an "iron smelter" (כור הבזרל) (Deut 4:20).

8. Jenson admits that "it has always been difficult to sum up Exodus by just one theme" (Review, 150).

9. The first half of the song celebrates Yhwh's role in Israel's emancipation (15:1–12) while the second half alludes to challenges yet to come on the road ahead (15:13–21; M. Smith, *Exodus*, 190). For Cross, the song "is not merely one of the oldest compositions preserved by biblical sources," but "the primary source for the central event in Israel's history, the Exodus-Conquest" (*CMHE* 123).

10. J. Collins also recognizes that "the theophanies of Yhwh in the Bible (e.g., on Mt. Sinai) are described in language that is very similar to descriptions of Ba'al in the Ugaritic texts" ("Israel," 182).

11. *CMHE* 112–44; *UNP* 81–180.W. Propp observes that these parallels apply only if Yhwh (not Moses) is the hero/protagonist (*Exodus*, 34).

12. Batto, e.g., argues that the Exodus scroll is a full-blown "adaptation of the Combat Myth" ("Dimensions," 188).

13. Stuart, *Exodus*, 19.

7:1—11:10), chs. 16–40 narrate *Israel's* movement from Egypt to Midian, involving two covenants (24:3 and 34:10) and two sets of tablets (32:19 and 34:1). Presuming a priestly connection between literary structure and cultic calendar,[14] he further suggests that (a) the exodus event coincides with Pesach (Exod 12:1–49),[15] (b) the revelation of the law with Shavuoth,[16] and (c) the forty-year wilderness wandering with Succoth.[17]

What has yet to be fully acknowledged, however, is the crucial role played by the "hard labor" motif.[18] As noted above, the crisis precipitating all the action in Atrahasis is the "hard labor" of the "lesser gods"—in fact, were this not the case, the creation of the *awīlūtu* (clay creatures) would not be necessary.[19] Genesis duly recognizes this "hard labor" motif, but not until Exodus does it develop most fully (Exod 1:11, 14; 2:11; 6:6, 9; 13:3, 14; 20:2). Like the "greater gods" in Atrahasis, Yhwh looks down on the "hard labor" of his clay creatures and responds. He utilizes Moses and Aaron to incarnate this response, to be sure, but as several Tanak passages make clear, *Yhwh* is the Great Emancipator, not Moses (Deut 5:6; 6:12; 7:8; 8:14; 13:5, 10; Josh 24:17; Judg 6:8; Jer 34:13; Mic 6:4).[20] The next question, then, is twofold: (a) What contribution does the "hard labor" motif make to the shape of Exodus?[21] (b) How does this shaping underwrite its contribution to pentateuchal theology?

PRELUDE: THE SLAVERY-FREEDOM POLARITY IN GENESIS

The slavery-freedom trajectory in Genesis begins with little more than a trickle. Both Sarah and Lot experience slavery to some degree, as does Jacob

---

14. M. Smith suggests that "pilgrimage supplies the priestly redaction of Exodus with a ready model in order to understand the journey to, and call and commission at, the divine mountain" (*Exodus*, 46), but the intertextual parallels with the Ba'al cycle best explain the sacrality of the holy mountain scene in Exodus.

15. Pesaḥ (פסח) is the Festival of Passover.

16. Shavuoth (שבעות) is the Festival of Weeks (Exod 23:16; Deut 16:10).

17. Succoth (סכות) is the Festival of Booths (Deut 16:13). Alexander finds this literary-calendrical hypothesis less than convincing (*Pilgrimage*, 493; cf. *CMHE* 84).

18. Dozeman draws little attention to the "hard labor" motif, but instead argues that the book's "two central themes (are) the character of divine power and the nature of divine presence in this world" ("Exodus," 140).

19. Atr 1.212 (see above).

20. Ford is blunt: "The story of the Exodus is primarily a story about Yhwh" (*God*, 1).

21. N.b. that the "wandering Aramean" confession in Deut 26:6 also mentions עבדה קשה (hard labor).

in his fourteen years of servitude to Laban. But it is in the Joseph novella where it begins to gain serious traction. Joseph's brothers sell him into slavery for twenty pieces of silver. His Midianite/Ishmaelite owners then sell him to an Egyptian government official who promptly throws him into prison on a trumped-up charge.[22] Eventually Pharaoh springs him from his prison cell to appoint him prime minister of Egypt's agro-economy, enlisting him in the stockpiling of grain for seven years, then selling it to hungry consumers when famine strikes—first for silver, then for livestock, then for land, then for themselves as slaves of the state (Gen 47:13–21).[23]

HEBREW "HARD LABOR"

So by the first chapter of Exodus the "hard labor" motif is well established. Two more parallels from Atrahasis, however, shed more light on this pentateuchal text: (a) the rapid multiplication of clay creatures forced into "hard labor"[24] and (b) the failure of their overseers to regulate it.[25] The clay creatures in Atrahasis relieve the "lesser gods" from "hard labor," but Enlil panics when he discovers that he cannot regulate their growth.[26] Exodus replicates this sequence. After Joseph's death a new Pharaoh comes to power who not only enslaves Joseph's descendents,[27] he attempts, like Enlil, to regulate their

---

22. Qur'an contends that Potiphar's wife's friends dub him her "slave-boy" (فتىٰ, Q 12:30).

23. Mendelsohn categorizes several types of slavery: (a) POWs, (b) sale of minors, (c) self-sale, and (d) defaulting debtors ("Slavery," 74–80; cf. Moore, *WealthWatch*, 83–89). Chirichigno points out that debt slavery "is caused by various interrelated socioeconomic factors, including taxation, the monopoly of resources and services among the state and private elite (i.e., rent-capitalism), high interest loans, and the economic and political collapse of higher kinship groups" (*Debt-Slavery*, 142). Whatever type of debt slavery is experienced by the Hebrews in Goshen, it seems imprudent to suggest that they are not seriously affected by it.

24. Atr 1.1–6.

25. Atr 2.1.3–8.

26. Atr 2.1.7. Urbainczyk observes that "slaves rebel in various ways in the ancient world. Sometimes, when they have the opportunity, they run away. Sometimes they take up arms and fight their masters. Spartacus is a name familiar to many, but he is only one of tens of thousands of slaves from antiquity who form armies to fight for their freedom" (*Revolts*, 1).

27. Doubtless this is at least partially driven by Pharaoh's decision (a) to conscript Hebrews for his building projects or (b) put to work those Hebrews unable to pay off their debts in any other way. Like Enlil, Pharaoh proactively attempts to quell the dissidence fomenting within his workforce before it can break out into open rebellion. Realizing that the Hebrews are more numerous than other *reṭenu*-populations in his workforce, he makes a fateful decision to rely on the "stick" instead of the "carrot."

growth by "thinning the herd."²⁸ Both Enlil and Pharaoh seek to justify their slaveholding policies with dire warnings about impending disaster should anything happen to alter the status quo.²⁹ Yet it's difficult to find an ANE parallel similar to the Hebrew experience.³⁰ The clay creatures in Atrahasis and Exodus endure slavery, but only the clay creatures in the Pentateuch experience a relatively bloodless *exodus*.³¹

MOSES' FIRST ATTEMPT TO EMANCIPATE ISRAEL

However well-intended, Moses' first attempt at emancipation fails for four reasons: (1) it consists of little more than an emotional reaction bereft of planning,³² (2) it occurs without the support of Israel's deity, (3) it occurs without the support of Israel's elders, and (4) it occurs in secret.³³

---

28. "The Israelites were fruitful and prolific [MT שרץ (lit., to swarm)]; they multiplied and grew exceptionally strong, so that the land was filled with them" (Exod. 1:7). The vignette about the midwives' "inability" to reach their pregnant clients in time is pure comic relief. Shiphrah and Puah are to Exodus what Rosenkrantz and Guildenstern are to Hamlet.

29. The slave revolt led by the Thracian gladiator Spartacus comes immediately to mind (cf. Strauss, *Spartacus*), but slaveholders throughout history tend to hide behind such "dire warnings" (cf. Baptist, *Slavery*, xv–xxix; Beckert and Rockman, "Capitalism").

30. Manumission can be common when, say, a new ruler comes to power (for examples, see Moore, *WealthWarn*, 81–82), but to release thousands of slaves at one time is not.

31. Gk ἔξοδος (way out).

32. Philo contends that Moses is in complete control of his emotions (*Mos.* 1.40–44). Exod 2:11–14 reads, "One day, after Moses had grown up, he went out to his people and saw their hard labor [סבלות, from סבל (to burden); cf. Akk *zabālu* (to carry bricks/water) (*CAD* Z.2); OG πόνος (hard labor); Syr ܥܡܠܐ (oppression); Vg *adflictionem eorum* (their affliction)]. He saw an Egyptian beating a Hebrew, one of his kinsfolk. Looking this way and that, and seeing no one, he killed the Egyptian and hid him in the sand. When he went out the next day, he saw two Hebrews fighting [Tg. Ps.-J. imagines them to be Dathan and Abiram, two of the ringleaders of the wilderness rebellion in Num 16:1]. Then he said to the assailant, 'Why do you strike your fellow Hebrew?' He answered, 'Who set you up to be a ruler [איש שר] and judge [שפט] over us?'" Syr reads, "Who made you a great man [ܓܒܪܐ ܪܒܐ] and judge [ܕܝܢܐ] over us?" Qur'an changes the interrogative to the declarative: "You only want to be a tyrant [جبارا] in the land [الارض], with no intention of becoming one of the peacemakers [المصلحين] (Q 28:19)]. Who made you a ruler and judge over us? Do you mean to kill me as you killed the Egyptian?"

33. Dozeman recognizes that "although Moses seeks to liberate Hebrews, his first act as an adult is a violent murder performed in secret" (*Exodus*, 87).

MOSES' SECOND ATTEMPT TO EMANCIPATE ISRAEL

His second attempt corrects each of these failings:[34]

- Like the Egyptian courtier Sinuhe,[35] Moses leaves Egypt, eventually winding up as a Midianite shepherd,[36] a *reṯenu* profession "abominable" to Egyptians (Gen 46:34),[37] but one in which the Hebrews are recognizedly proficient (Gen 47:3).[38] This effectively redefines his identity in both the Egyptian and the Hebrew communities.

- Doubtless the single greatest deficiency in his first attempt is his attempt to proceed without the blessing of Yhwh. Far from emotional reaction to the abuse of single individuals,[39] he eventually comes to realize (however grudgingly)[40] that the Great Emancipator wants to free *all* the Hebrews, not just one or two.[41] Whatever his feelings about this commission, it's hard to imagine, as Waldemar Janzen puts it, that he has any time to "prepare" for it. In fact, he appears to be utterly blindsided by that terrifying moment when "God unexpectedly steps into his ordinary shepherd routine and calls him to a new and frightening task."[42]

---

34. Coats points out that whereas most (post)modern models of leadership are built around unrealistic expectations of constant success, the Exodus narrative is more realistic because it allows the protagonist to learn from his (several) mistakes (*Moses*, 115–24).

35. Parkinson, "Sinuhe"; *AEL* 1:222–35 (see above).

36. Eg *reṯenu* refers to "Asiatics/Palestinians" (*CDME* 154; Murnane, "Egypt," 2:700). Cf. above.

37. MT תועבה (abominable); OG βδέλυγμα (abominable); Syr ܡܣܠܝܐ (contemptible); Vg *detestatus* (detestable).

38. Hollis argues that in Pharaoh's eyes Moses (like Sinuhe) is simply another disaffected Egyptian foolishly abandoning his homeland for the "uncivilized" *reṯenu* world ("Otherworld," 334–37).

39. "Whereas Genesis concerns itself with the lives of individuals, the second book of the Torah relates to the fortunes of the people as a whole" (Sarna, "Exodus," 2:690).

40. Responding to Baltzer's attempt to explain the nature of the prophet-deity relationship ("Prophet"), Glazov points out that Baltzer fails to attend adequately to the human side of the equation, doubtless because in his desire to counter the hyper-humanizing trends of the 1960s, he unwittingly camps too close to the divine side, thereby marginalizing "the elements of pain, pathos, wonder and dread underlying many of the prophetic expressions of reluctance to speak and objections to the call" (*Bridling*, 32).

41. Walzer distinguishes *slavery* from *service* as follows: "Slavery is begun and sustained by coercion; service is begun and sustained by covenant" (*Exodus*, 6).

42. Janzen, *Exodus*, 57.

- One of Moses' concerns is that his fellow Hebrews will (again) reject him.[43] Yhwh responds to this concern by empowering Aaron to serve alongside him as a fraternal team,[44] designating Aaron a נביא (prophet) figure to Moses' אלהים (deity) figure (Exod 4:16; 7:1).[45]
- Unlike his first secretive attempt, the second one takes place in a public forum, face-to-face with Pharaoh.

THE FIRST STAGE OF YHWH'S EMANCIPATION OF ISRAEL

The first stage of Yhwh's emancipation is to choose a leader capable of pulling off what looks for all the world to be a "mission impossible." Why Moses is the one called to do this is as cloaked in mystery as why Abraham or Isaiah or Ezekiel is called by Yhwh into service.[46] What is of greater importance, at any rate, is how Yhwh responds to Moses' objections. In the burning bush dialogue, Yhwh (a) identifies himself,[47] (b) tells Moses to "remove your sandals, for you are standing on holy ground" (Exod 3:5);[48] (c) reviews the reality of his people's afflictions,[49] and (d) commands Moses to lead them out of bondage.[50] This generates several objections immediately countered by several assurances.

43. In his first attempt a cynical Hebrew says to him, "Who made you a judge and ruler over us?" (Exod 2:14). Dozeman observes that later interpreters argue over whether Moses is to be viewed as a liberator (e.g., Philo, *Mos.* 1.40–44; Acts 7:23–29) or as a failed leader (e.g., *Midrash on the Passing of Moses*, cited in Leibowitz, *Shemot* 1.44–46 ("Exodus," 145–46).

44. Qur'an claims that Moses asks for Aaron's help (Q 26:13).

45. Römer tries to explain the dynamics of this fraternity: "With Aaron as his mouthpiece, Moses represents Yhwh," just as "Pharaoh is a representative of the Egyptian divinities" ("Moisés," 93). N.b. that "Moses is called the God of Aaron (4:16) *and* the God of Pharaoh (7:1)." Cf. França, "Deus."

46. Recognizing the call of Moses to be a more-or-less typical prophetic "call narrative," Glazov argues (*pace* Habel, "Narratives") that whereas the first set of responses to the deity focuses on the prophet himself, the second set focuses on the specifics of the deity's commission ((*Bridling*, 49; cf. Moore, Review of *Bridling*, 558–60).

47. Yhwh actually identifies himself twice in this encounter—the first being a historical identification (Exod 3:6), the second being a personal one (3:14).

48. Cf. Q 20:12, "I am your lord, so remove your sandals [فخلع نعليك], for you are in the sacred valley."

49. Yhwh observes עני עמי (the affliction of my people) (Exod 3:7; n.b. the alliteration). Here Yhwh identifies the Hebrews as עמי (my people), but later he identifies them to Moses as עמך (your people) (Exod 32:7).

50. Even as the tower of Babel saga is structured around the ipv of יהב (to give,

1. *Moses:* "Why me?"[51] *Yhwh:* "I will be with you ... the proof of which will be your future arrival on this mountain to worship me." (Exod 3:12)[52]

2. *Moses:* "Who are you?" *Yhwh:* "I am who I am." (Exod 3:14).[53]

3. *Moses:* "What if they do not believe me?"[54] *Yhwh:* "Show them signs: (a) your staff can turn into a snake, then turn back into a staff; (b) your hand can become leprous then turn back to normal;[55] (c) the Nile will turn into blood.[56]

4. *Moses:* "What if I cannot be eloquent, but am too slow of speech and heavy of tongue to do the job?" (Exod 4:10).[57] *Yhwh:* "Do not worry; I will teach[58] you what to say with your mouth." (Exod 4:12)[59]

---

come) (Gen 11:3, 4, 7), so the commissions of Abraham and Moses begin with the ipv of the verb הלך (to go, come) (Gen 12:1; Exod 3:10).

51. "Who am I that I should go to Pharaoh and bring the Israelites out of Egypt?" (Exod 3:11).

52. Yhwh pitches this to Moses as a future sign (אות) of his support. Moses uses the same "future-will-tell" argument to distinguish true from false prophecy: "If a prophet speaks in the name of Yhwh but the thing does not take place or prove to be true, it is a word that Yhwh has not spoken" (Deut. 18:22).

53. Cross discusses several ways to interpret אהיה אשר אהיה (I am who I am) (*CMHE* 60–75), but Surls argues convincingly that the name יהוה (Yhwh) is not *formally* unveiled until Exod 34:6 ("Name," 287–90).

54. In Qur'an Moses fears that the *Egyptians* "will reject me" (يكذبون), not the Hebrews (Q 26:12; 28:34).

55. Moses is explicitly told that if the Hebrews will not accept the first two signs, he is to perform a third sign (Exod 4:9).

56. Provision of multiple signs is not uncommon. In Anatolia, e.g., the "augur" (^LÚMUŠEN.DÙ) sometimes serves as a "sign checker" hired to ascertain whether the KIN or KUŠ oracles of the "old woman" (^SALŠU.GI) are true or false (cf. Moore, *Balaam*, 20–30). Perhaps the most obvious example of multiple signs occurs in the Fourth Gospel, the first half of which is the Gospel of Signs (cf. Fortna, *Signs*; Wahlde, *Signs*).

57. MT לא איש דברים בי אדני (lit., in me, my lord, there is no man of words); OG ἰσχνόφωνος καὶ βραδύγλωσσος ἐγώ εἰμι (I am weak-voiced and I stammer); Vg *inpeditioris et tardioris linguae sum* (I am slow of speech and [have] an impediment). McDermott lists Moses as one of twelve "famous stutterers," the other eleven being Aristotle, Demosthenes, Joshua Chamberlain, George VI, Winston Churchill, Byron Pitts, Marilyn Monroe, Peter Brown, John Stossel, James Earl Jones, and John Updike (*Stutterers*).

58. MT הוריתיך אשר תדבר (I will teach [from the root ירה ((to teach)); cf. תורה ((Torah))] you what you shall say); OG reads συμβιβάσω σε ὃ μέλλεις λαλῆσαι (lit., I will bring together for you what you are going to say); cf. Paul's description of the body of Christ as ἐπιχορηγούμενον καὶ συμβιβαζόμενον (nourished and brought together) (Col 2:14).

59. Just hours before the cross the Nazarene prophet promises his disciples that "when they bring you to trial and hand you over, do not worry beforehand about what

5. *Moses:* Can you not send someone else? *Yhwh:* "No! I want you . . . , but I will draft your brother Aaron to help."[60]

THE SECOND STAGE OF YHWH'S EMANCIPATION OF ISRAEL

The second stage of Yhwh's emancipation of Israel involves a series of direct confrontations between Moses and Pharaoh, each targeting a different Egyptian deity.[61]

1. *The Nile turns to blood* (Exod 7:17–25). Egyptian deities associated with the Nile include Ḥapy, the god who annually floods the Nile to prepare for the planting of crops, and Isis, the deity sometimes called "the goddess of the Nile."
2. *The plague of frogs* (8:1–15). Ḥeqet, the goddess of birth and consort of Khnum, is often depicted with the head of a frog.
3. *The plague of gnats* (8:16–20). Seti, god of the desert, is the deity in charge of the "dust of the earth"; i.e., the dust Aaron flings into the air, which turns into gnats.
4. *The plague of flies* (8:21–32). Ḥepri is often portrayed with the head of a scarab beetle or fly.
5. *The plague of pestilence against livestock* (9:1–7). Hathor, the goddess often portrayed with the head of a cow, is in charge of protecting the livelihoods of herdsmen and shepherds.
6. *The plague of boils* (9:8–12). The goddess Seḥmet, daughter of Ra, is in charge of protection against disease and pandemic.
7. *The plague of thunder and hail* (9:13–35). Seti is the god of storms, and Osiris is the deity in charge of crops vulnerable to destruction by hail and thunder.

---

you are to say; but say whatever is given you at that time, for it is not you who speak, but the Holy Spirit" (Mark 13:11).

60. As with Jeremiah, Yhwh is patient with Moses until he runs out of excuses (cf. Moore, *What Is This Babbler*, 81–93). Qur'an claims that it is *Moses* who suggests Aaron's involvement, not God (Q 26:13).

61. Schnittjer (*Torah*, 185, 187) calls the "plagues" (מגפות, Exod 9:14, from נגף, "to strike a blow") "cosmic terrors," but to Yhwh they are simply "my signs" (אתתי) and "my wonders" (מופתי, 7:3).

8. *The plague of locusts* (10:1–20). Osiris is in charge of protecting crops from locust infestation.

9. *The plague of darkness* (10:21–29). Ra is the executive solar deity at the top of the pantheon.

10. *Death of the firstborn* (11:1–10). Min is an old fertility deity (always portrayed with an erect phallus); Ḥeqet is a deity associated with midwifery; Isis is a goddess of fertility; and Pharaoh's son can occasionally be worshiped as a deity.

The plagues *narrative*, on the other hand, boasts three main features:[62]

1. Yhwh increases the pressure on Pharaoh with each new plague, resolutely pushing the Egyptian king to make a decision about whether to free Israel or continue oppressing them with ever-more-increasing "hard labor."[63] Moreover, the literary decision to interweave the Passover narrative into the plagues narrative is as likely to be intentional as the interweaving of Jacob's encounter with Esau into his encounter with God.[64]

2. Yhwh graciously engages Pharaoh at his own "speed,"[65] but does not relent until (a) his firstborn son triumphs over Pharaoh's firstborn son (Exod 4:21–23), (b) the Hebrews witness these events as evidence that Moses and Aaron are indeed his servants,[66] and (c) the Egyptians witness these events as evidence that Yhwh indeed is the one true God.[67]

---

62. Dozeman argues that the plagues narrative is mythopoeically designed because this is the genre most likely to be taken most seriously by ANE readers (*War*, 15–18).

63. Qur'an claims that each "sign" (عايه) shown to Pharaoh is "greater than the one before" (اكبو من اجيها [lit., greater than its sister]) (Q 43:48). On the thorny question of "heart hardening" cf. Q 10:88, "Destroy their riches and harden their hearts [واشدد على قلوبهم] so that they will not believe until they experience the pain of punishment" (cf. Moore, "Obduracy").

64. I.e., as another example of "symbolic narrative" (White, *Narration*, 58, 185). Discovery of the *zukru* spring festival at Tell Meskene (ancient Emar), featuring the prophylactic use of blood on doorways, suggests that the Passover festival may be a Yahwistic adaptation of a well-known rite (cf. Fleming, *Emar*, 48–140; Dozeman, "Exodus," 152).

65. At first glance it looks like Pharaoh is willing to cooperate, but as soon as Yhwh, say, removes all the frogs, Pharaoh changes his mind (e.g., Exod 8:8–15). This back-and-forth ambivalence continues until Yhwh takes Pharaoh's son away from him.

66. Also, Yhwh wants them to realize that he graciously exempts them from the worst effects of the plagues.

67. "I am sending my plagues upon you, your servants, and your people so that you may understand that there is no one like me in all the earth" (אין כמני בכל הארץ) (Exod 9:14). Contemporary Kemetism seeks to revive the religion of ancient Egypt (cf.

3. Pharaoh's response to Yhwh's "signs and wonders" (Exod 7:3)[68] evolves through at least four stages: (a) stubborn pride; (b) paralyzed ambivalence; (c) indignant desperation; (d) wounded anger.[69]

THE THIRD STAGE OF YHWH'S EMANCIPATION OF ISRAEL

The third stage involves two key events: (a) the miraculous crossing of the sea and (b) the revelation of the law on Sinai. As noted above, the portrayal of the first event follows the same literary sequence as that found in the Canaanite text about Ba`al's victory over Yam (Exod 15:4),[70] while the second represents one of the key turning points of history, a groundbreaking event whose significance needs no explanation. It is simply common knowledge that law-abiding societies are preferable to lawless ones, not only because the latter are more likely to enslave the poor,[71] but because only the wealthy and the powerful ever benefit from them.[72] Aware of this truth, King David is quick to recognize the superiority of divine justice over human:

צר לי מאד	(When) I am in great distress
נפלה נא ביד יהוה	let me fall into Yhwh's hands,
כי רבים רחמיו	For his mercies are great.
וביד אדם אל אפלה	But let me not fall into human hands!
	(2 Sam 24:14)

P. Harris, *Egyptologists*; Reidy, *Egypt*).

68. MT אותות ומופתים; Syr ܐܬܘܬܐ ܘܬܕܡܪܬܐ (signs and wonders); OG σημεῖά καὶ τὰ τέρατα; Vg *signa et ostenta*. Only once does Yhwh use the term מגפת (plagues) (Exod 9:14).

69. Qur'an claims that it is Pharaoh's idea that the Hebrews be "driven out" (يستفزهم) (Q 17:103).

70. Heb ים is equivalent to Ug *yam* (sea). Like the biblical stories of Jehu's coronation and Bathsheba's silence, it is not unusual for Hebrew narrators to borrow freely from Canaanite literary sources and Yahwicize them (cf. Moore, "Jehu's"; Moore, "Bathsheba's").

71. E.g., Plato, *Resp*. 4.424–25.

72. Nozick states the issue clearly: "Individuals have rights, and there are things no person or group can do to them (without violating their rights" (*Anarchy*, ix). To this we might add that the Mosaic law code is not the only ANE law code, but it seems no accident that it exercises the greatest influence.

Challenging the mainstream opinion that CC "is the result of a long process of development and accretion, and that its contacts with the Mesopotamian legal tradition are based on oral traditions common in Syria-Canaan early in the second millennium BCE,"[73] David Wright argues that CC is "directly, primarily, and throughout dependent upon CH."[74] Interpreting this to mean that CC is in effect a "plagiarization" of CH, Bruce Wells concedes that "for some readers, the evidence adduced in Wright's book will be sufficient to persuade them of CC's direct dependence on the Laws of Hammurabi," but "for others, including myself, it merely highlights the degree to which Israelite/Judean legal texts are part of the warp and woof of ANE legal culture—as much a part of it as any other written legal collection from that time and place."[75]

Whatever the legal/literary possibilities, the theological presumption here is that slavery most often recurs in societies driven by the law of the jungle ("might makes right") or, to put it conversely, that true freedom is impossible apart from the rule of law.[76] For Mark Smith, "freedom from the Egyptians is made complete only by the Sinai legislation," and "freedom fulfilled is the freedom obtained through law."[77] For Jon Levenson, "Mount Sinai is the intersection of love and law, of gift and demand."[78] For Mark Hamilton, "the law, far from being a set of mindless rules, is a gift that God gives to a rescued people so that they may live free from the tyranny that strangles them in Egypt."[79]

---

73. Malul, Review, 155.

74. Wright, Inventing, 3. Holtz calls Wright's proposal "the most recent manifestation of the 'Brandeis school' of pentateuchal legal studies," citing Levinson (Deuteronomy) and Stackert (Rewriting) as his ideological forerunners (Review, 820).

75. Wells, Review, 559.

76. This is why pagan Canaanite "statutes" (חקות) (Lev 18:3) are unacceptable.

77. M. Smith, Exodus, 268.

78. Levenson, Sinai, 136. The apostle Paul famously wrestles with how to define the law—especially its contours and boundaries—for a Christian audience. On the one hand, he argues, the law is needed to distinguish right from wrong (i.e., identify "sin," Rom 3:20); in fact, without it the boundary between right and wrong is unidentifiable (5:13). Yet divine justice is neither dependent upon the law, nor does it simply nullify it (3:21). As Räisänen puts it, "Paul's teaching does not cancel the law; on the contrary, it ... establishes it" (Paul, 199).

79. M. Hamilton, "Deuteronomy," 204.

THE FOURTH STAGE OF YHWH'S EMANCIPATION OF ISRAEL

In some ways everything just discussed is but a prelude to the most difficult aspect of emancipation: *maintaining* it. It's one thing to be freed from slavery; it's quite another to *stay* free. Realizing the enormity of this challenge,[80] Yhwh creates a specialized community within his "stubborn and stiff-necked" people, a priestly community whose job is to help Israel *stay* free (Exod 32:9; 33:3, 5; 34:9).[81] The priesthood has its problems, to be sure, but its primary *raison d'être* remains incontrovertibly positive—to provide a safe place for broken souls to repair their relationships with God and one another through a carefully administered program centered upon the homeopathic ritualization of sacrificial atonement.[82]

The two focal points of this program are the tabernacle and the priesthood. The tabernacle is the "first draft" of an attempt to create a sacred space on earth functionally able to keep at bay the forces of chaos,[83] whether they be social, political, economic, religious, or spiritual.[84] Its importance cannot be overstated because without it there is no way for "a former group of slaves miraculously freed by Yhwh from Egyptian bondage" to *stay* free.[85] Eventually the tabernacle is furnished with a variety of cultic furniture designed to help animate the various aspects of this freedom (both vertical and horizontal), including the ark of the covenant, the incense altar, the table for the bread of the presence, the lampstand, Aaron's budding rod (Num 17:23–26), the container of manna (Exod 16:33–34), and the scroll of the law.[86] Joseph Blenkinsopp sees a parallel between the seven speeches to Moses delineating

---

80. I.e., that "all sin and fall short of the glory of God" (Rom 3:23).

81. Cf. Moore, "Role."

82. On the anthropological phenomenon of "sacrifice" see Abusch, "Sacrifice"; Moore, *What Is This Babbler*, 16–18; Moore, "Sacrifice." Douglas contends that "when Deuteronomy speaks of sacrifice, sacrifice is all it means. In its more political agenda sacrifice is less important, but Leviticus takes sacrifice in the same spirit as the wisdom literature uses seafaring, trade, or horticulture, and makes it the framework for a philosophy of life. Sacrifice is one of the main figural motifs with which it presents the principles of God's creation, and the divine order of existence" (*Leviticus*, 66).

83. Dozeman views the tabernacle as a "holy place on earth which, when coupled with holy time in the law of the Sabbath (Exod 31:12–17), allows for Israel to commune with God" ("Exodus," 166).

84. The "second draft" is "the house/temple of Yhwh" built in Jerusalem (הבית ליהוה, 1 Kgs 6:1—7:51), and the third draft (for Christians) is the body of Christ ("the church") (1 Cor 3:16–17) populated by the "Israel of God" (Gal 6:16).

85. Klein, "Tabernacle," 265.

86. Friedman, "Tabernacle," 292. In Exod 38:21 the tabernacle is the "tabernacle of the testimony" (משכן העדת).

the tabernacle's building instructions and the opening words of Genesis focusing on the seven days of creation.[87] Ralph Klein agrees, arguing (a) that Moses' "seven speeches... recall the seven days of Creation," thereby implying (b) that "the ultimate goal of Creation is God's full presence with God's people."[88]

Examining several temple construction texts from Mesopotamia and Canaan alongside the tabernacle building instructions in Exodus,[89] Victor Hurowitz concludes that all basically follow the same pattern: (a) a rationale for construction as affirmed by command or consent of the deity; (b) preparations for the project, including the enlistment of workers and the gathering/manufacturing of building materials; (c) description of the building process; (d) dedication of the completed building with ritual celebrations; and (e) submission of prayers and blessings designed to safeguard the building's future utility.[90] Granting that the blueprints in Exodus do not slavishly mirror every aspect of every other shrine (Exod 24:1—31:18), Hurowitz nevertheless finds it "difficult to deny that the Exodus narrative is a fully developed example of them."[91]

The last chapters of Exodus preview the defilement-holiness polarity (more fully expounded in Leviticus) alongside the slavery-freedom polarity in order to spotlight Yhwh's determination to convince his long-enslaved people that the most beneficial counterpoint to "hard labor" is "Sabbath rest" (Exod 31:14–16; 35:2–3).[92] In Deuteronomy the command to observe the Sabbath emphasizes its horizontal aspects:

---

87. Blenkinsopp comes to this conclusion after noting that the conclusion of the priestly creation narrative (Gen 2:1) and the conclusion of the tabernacle instructions (Exod 39:32; 40:33) are practically identical ("Structure"). Cross imagines "that the Israelite system described in the tabernacle legislation of Leviticus probably goes back in its basic outlines to common Semitic practice" ("Tabernacle," 51).

88. Klein, "Tabernacle," 266.

89. Yhwh tells Moses to build it "according to the pattern [MT תבנית, from בנה (to build); OG τύπον (type); Syr ܕܡܘܬܐ (image); cf. דמות (likeness) (Gen 1:26)] which you saw on the mountain" (Exod 25:40).

90. Hurowitz, *Temple*, 311.

91. Hurowitz, *Temple*, 113. Dozeman sees an intertextual parallel in the tabernacle-Sabbath connection of Exod 24:1—31:18 in Nabonidus' description of Šamaš' temple as "the residence of your rest" (*šubat tapšuḫtīka*) (*Nab* 2.6.2—15.16); cf. the Heb cognate שבת [Sabbath]) ("Exodus," 166). Luckenbill identifies the furniture in several well-known Assyro-Babylonian "houses/temples" ("Temples").

92. Cf. CD 3.14; 6.18; 10.14, 17, 21–22; 11.2, 5, 9, 10–15, 17–18; 12.4; Heb 4:9; cf. Ernst Haag, "שׁבת," *TDOT* 4:387–97; and A. Heschel, *Sabbath*.

ויום שביעי שבת ליהוה אלהיך	The seventh day is the Sabbath to Yhwh your God.
לא תעשה כל מלאכה	You shall do no work—
אתה ובנך ובתך	not you, your son, your daughter,
ועבדך ואמתך	or your male and female slaves. . . .[93]

וזכרת כי עבד היית בארץ המצרים	Remember that you were a slave in Egypt. . . .
על כן צוך יהוה אלהיך	Therefore Yhwh your God is commanding you
לעשות את יום השבת	to keep the Sabbath day. (Deut 5:14–15)[94]

In Exodus, however, the focus stays firmly on the vertical:

כי ששת ימים עשה יהוה את השמים ואת הארץ	For six days Yhwh made heaven and earth,
את הים וכל אשר בם	the sea and all that is within them;
וינח ביום השביעי	but he rested on the seventh day.[95]
על כן ברך יהוה את יום השבת	Therefore Yhwh blessed the Sabbath day
ויקדשהו	and made it holy. (Exod 20:11)[96]

SUMMARY

Joel Baden notes that the liberation theologian Gustavo Gutiérrez views the Egyptian slaveholding economy as "a system in which the power of self-determination is withheld" so that "injustice is endemic to its theopolitical system" and that "true freedom not only permits but requires active

---

93. These four lines repeat verbatim in Exod 20:10.
94. Deut 5:14, MT עשה (to do, make), not שמר (to guard, keep), as in 5:12.
95. Gen 2:2 reads, וישבת ביום השביעי (and he rested [שבת, not נוח] on the seventh day).
96. Gen 2:3 reads, ויברך אלהים את יום השביעי ויקדש אתו (and God blessed the seventh day and made it holy).

self-determination."[97] Baden goes on to note that although Gutiérrez's analysis is socially, politically, and religiously predictable, it regrettably "does not seem to engage fully with the nature of the Israelite society that is formed in the wake of the Exodus."[98] The laws in CC, for example, do not condemn slavery per se (particularly debt slavery), only its egregious abuses.[99] So, the most to be concluded here is that slavery-freedom is the primary polarity responsible for triggering all the *action* in Exodus, a pentateuchal scroll opening with enslaved Hebrews suffering "hard labor" in a foreign land, and closing with emancipated Hebrews standing on holy ground before a holy God in his holy tabernacle on his holy Sabbath.

---

97. Baden, *Exodus*, 194–95 (responding to Gutiérrez, *Liberation*, 157).

98. Baden, *Exodus*, 192.

99. "When you buy a male Hebrew slave, he shall serve six years, but in the seventh he shall go out a free person, without debt" (Exod. 21:2).

3

Leviticus: Defilement or Holiness?

THE PRIMARY THEOLOGICAL POLARITY in Leviticus can be readily discerned from a passage near the middle:

והזרתם את בני ישראל מטאמתם	You shall make the Israelites abstain[1] from their defilement.
ולא ימתו בטמאתם	So that they do not die in their defilement
בטמאם את משכני אשר בתוכם	by defiling my tabernacle in their midst. (Lev 15:31)[2]

David Wright suggests that impurity can and should be analyzed on a calibrated spectrum "ranging from least to most severe,"[3] but while this assessment is not inaccurate, it seems obvious that the greatest barrier to fellowship with the Holy One comes down to one word: *defilement*.[4] However

---

1. MT נזר (to make separate, abstain, vow). Cf. OG εὐλαβεῖς ποιήσετε (you shall separate); Vg *docebitis . . . ut caveant* (you shall teach and make them beware); Syr ܘܬܙܗܪܘܢ (you shall make them beware); Tg. Ps.-J. ותפרשון (you shall separate). N.b. that the Nazirite vow (נזר) demands abstinence from particular activities for set periods of time (Num 6:2; Acts 18:18).

2. The verb טמא (to defile) is repeated three times in this passage; cf. OG τῶν ἀκαθαρσιῶν αὐτῶν (their uncleannesses); Syr ܒܛܢܦܘܬܗܘܢ (their defilements); Tg. Ps.-J. סאובתיהון (their uncleannesses). Vg uses three terms to translate טמא (in order): *inmunditia* (filthiness), *sordes* (dirt, filth), and *polluere* (to pollute, infect, violate).

3. Wright, "Spectrum," 152.

4. Cf. Moore, "Divine." Minimizing the centrality of the defilement-holiness polarity, Morales argues that Leviticus is a priestly depiction of "a sacred journey to Yhwh's abode" (*Leviticus*, 35), arguing that "the shape of the Pentateuch shapes (and forms)

defined or measured,[5] defilement is one of the most serious problems facing *any* community,[6] not just ancient Israel.[7] No community can function very long without dealing with defilement in a communally acceptable way.[8] As Mary Douglas points out, "Sacred things and places are to be protected from defilement" because "holiness and impurity" stand "at opposite poles" on the religio-cultural spectrum.[9] The thing that makes Israel different from other ANE communities is simply the *manner* in which it handles it. Like the chaos-creation polarity in Genesis and the slavery-freedom polarity in Exodus, the defilement-holiness polarity in Leviticus dominates the Pentateuch's central scroll.[10] Nor is its location in the center an accident,[11] for, as Michael Morales points out, there are two concentric circles in play here: (1) the book of Leviticus sits at the heart of the Pentateuch, and (2) the Day of Atonement ritual sits at the heart of Leviticus.[12] Doubtless other factors contribute to this concentricity, but the bottom line is that *Leviticus is the longest, clearest, and most focused discourse on the defilement-holiness polarity in ANE literature.* Its impact simply cannot be overstated, a fact attestable by even the most cursory examination of Second Temple texts like

---

its unifying theme: *Yhwh's opening a way for humanity to dwell in the divine Presence*" (*Leviticus*, 38; emphasis original).

5. Following the lead of others, Klawans distinguishes between two types of impurity: *ritual* impurity and *moral* impurity (*Impurity*, 22).

6. Bildstein observes that "concepts and practices of purity and defilement shape the understanding of human nature, sin, history and ritual," noting that this polarity is "instrumental for articulating difference, hierarchy, and change" (*Purity*, 3).

7. In Anatolia, e.g., Bryce observes that if "normal, legitimate sexual activity leaves a person unclean," then "defilement is much greater for . . . deviant, illegal sexual behavior," noting that "this defilement can spread to others" to the point that "a whole community can be infected by it, and suffer the full force of divine wrath" (*Hittite*, 49).

8. Law codes are universally designed as necessary instruments for maintaining some semblance of law and order in the real (i.e., defiled) world (cf. Westbrook, *History*; Wilcke, *Law*).

9. Douglas, *Purity*, 9.

10. The root טמא appears twenty-six times in Leviticus, its densest concentration occurring in 11:24–40; 13:14–46; 15:5–27; often appearing in synonymous parallel with חלל (to pollute) and in antonymous parallel with טהר (to be pure).

11. Klingbeil, *Ritual*, 155–57; Radday, "Chiasm." The decision of Aaron's sons to dismiss its importance costs them their lives (Lev 10:1–2; cf. McCarter, "Rage").

12. Morales, *Leviticus*, 23–38. Instructions for the יום כפר ritual (*yom kippur* [lit., the day of covering]) are listed in ch. 16 (see below).

CD 4.17–18,[13] 11Q19;[14] 1 Cor 3:16–17,[15] Rev 11:19,[16] and the GNT Letter to the Hebrews,[17] not to mention whole sections of Mishnah, Talmud, and the midrashim.[18]

One of the most intuitive contemporary students of Leviticus is Mary Douglas, a British anthropologist whose 1966 book *Purity and Danger* dramatically changed the whole landscape of Leviticus studies.[19] Writing in reaction to deleterious reports about "primitive peoples' obsession" with purification, she discovered from her fieldwork in the Congo[20] that "far from being aberrations from the central project of religion, rituals of purity and impurity create unity in experience and are positive contributions to atonement."[21] This anthropological reframing of "atonement" has dramatically altered the course of contemporary Leviticus studies,[22]

---

13. Alongside fornication (זנות) and wealth (ההין), Belial nets his victims by persuading them to engage in "defilement of the holy place" (טמא המקדש). Cf. Baumgarten, "Damascus," 1:166. *DSSSE* presumes that המקדש (CD 4.18) refers to "the temple," but n.b. that in Exodus מקדש denotes the "sanctuary" on Yhwh's mountain (Exod 15:17) as well as the מקדש (holy place) (25:8) paralleled by the משכן (tabernacle; lit., dwelling place) (25:9).

14. The longest of the Dead Sea Scrolls, the Temple Scroll (11Q19) is a rewriting of Exodus through Deuteronomy from a priestly puritan perspective (cf. García Martínez, "Temple"; Harrington, "Intermarriage").

15. The apostle Paul asks the Corinthians, "Do you not know that you are God's temple [ναός] and that God's Spirit dwells within you? If anyone destroys God's temple [ναός], God will destroy that person. For God's temple [ναός] is holy [ἅγιος], and you [pl.] are that temple [ναός]" (cf. R. Hays, *First Corinthians*, 56–58).

16. "Then God's temple [ναός] in heaven was opened, and the ark of his covenant was seen within his temple [ναός]." Fee recognizes that "the temple is always for the believing Jew the place of the Divine Presence" (*Revelation*, 159).

17. Scholer points out that the verb τελειοῦν (to complete, make perfect) in Heb 2:10; 5:9; 7:19, 28; 9:9, 11; 11:40; 12:23 "consistently means to have access to the heavenly holy of holies, or to be in the presence of God" (*Priests*, 201).

18. Seder Kodashim (קדשים [holy things]) and Seder Taharot (טהרות [clean things]) together make up twenty-three of Mishnah's sixty-three tractates. Cf. Goldin, "Midrash"; Klawans, *Purity*, 111–211; and Balberg, "Sacrifice." N.b. that Qur'an warns against الرجس (impurity) (Q 22:30), and نجس (defilement) (9:28), and that one of Alla's titles is القدوس (the Holy One) (59:23; 62:1; cf. Isa 1:4; 5:19, 24). Qur'an also mentions the "rituals of Alla" (حومت الله) (Q 22:30), but Islam maintains no cultic mechanism for dealing with "impurity" (cf. Zellentin, *Law*, 282–333).

19. Douglas, *Purity* (see also Douglas, *Leviticus*).

20. Douglas, *Lele*.

21. Douglas, *Purity*, 3.

22. Grabbe singles out Douglas as the "one particular social scientist" who has "had considerable impact on Hebrew Bible studies, esp. in the area of purity and the books of Leviticus and Numbers" ("History," 97).

having essentially freed students from hitherto ineffectual efforts to clear the following hurdles:

1. Some interpreters, particularly those schooled in the Western "intellectualist" tradition, harbor a deep bias against ritual and ritual studies.[23] Pejorative terms like "preliterate," "irrationalist," and "primitivist," though not as prevalent as they used to be, still dot the landscape of "intellectualist" analysis,[24] often exemplifying little more than the prejudices of a *fin de siècle* mindset mired in the quicksand of reductionist interpretation, ideological reaction-formation, and institutionalized classism.[25]

2. Priestly ritual is technical, cryptic, and difficult to interpret.[26] Hebrew priestly texts are, if anything, often more difficult to understand than their ANE counterparts, due in part to the layered religious framework in which they now sit.[27]

3. A vast corpus of ANE priestly literature has come to light in the past century or so,[28] and new discoveries are not infrequent.[29] Relatively few biblical scholars, however, know how to engage this literature from a holistic perspective informed by a critical understanding of the rudiments of social anthropology.[30]

---

23. Tylor (*Primitive*, 101–44), Lévy-Bruhl (*Primitive*, 503–22), Spencer (*Sociology*), and Radcliffe-Brown (*Primitive*, 1–27) are perhaps the best known representatives of this school.

24. Modified cognitive approaches continue to shape the work of Atran (*Gods*, 13–15); Guthrie ("Religion"); Lewis-Williams and Dowson ("Entoptic"); and Luhrmann (*Persuasions*, 3–41).

25. S. Heschel documents an extremist example of this mindset (*Aryan*, 1–25), while Cornell simplistically argues that Islam "generalizes the priesthood by abolishing the hierarchy and making every believer a priest" (*Voices*, 14), even though the fact remains that Qur'an, like many of the rabbinic texts, tends to avoid the word "priest" (كاهن; Heb כוהן). See Wheeler, *Moses*, 57.

26. The classic study of Mesopotamian priesthood is by Renger ("Priestertum"), the classic study of the Hittite cult is by Sturtevant ("Hittite"), and Cody surveys some of the most obvious Hebrew peculiarities ("Priesthood").

27. See Wellhausen (*Geschichte*, 125–74); Gorman ("Ritual"); and Klingbeil (*Ritual*, 226–41). For Gottwald "temple priesthoods are indispensable to political order, but the relationship between rulers and priests is often rocky," esp. when politicians perceive themselves to be "privileged deputies of the gods" (*Politics*, 146).

28. See Roberts, "Environment," 92.

29. See Levine (*Numbers*, 241–75); Renger ("Priestertum"); Klinger (*Kultschicht*); and Wright (*Disposal*).

30. *Exceptions*: Douglas (*Wilderness*); Milgrom (*Leviticus*); Gorman (*Ideology*); Haran (*Temples*); Levine (*Presence*); Olyan (*Inequality*). N.b. that Cryer justifiably

4. In sum, serious study of the defilement-holiness polarity, when divorced from holistic interdisciplinary analysis, tends to suffer the slings and arrows of methodological uncertainty,[31] ideological bias,[32] and reactionary sophism.[33]

Like Exodus, Leviticus divides into two sections. Section 1 (chs. 1–16) is addressed to the priesthood,[34] and section 2 (chs. 17–27) addresses "the people of Israel (by) commanding the pursuit of holiness as the collective goal of religious life."[35] In section 1 the priestly writer lists several types of sacrifices designed to cleanse people from defilement, whether it be cultic or moral.[36] The holocaust offering (Lev 1:3),[37] field offering (Lev 2:1),[38] compensation offering (Lev 3:1),[39] purification offering (Lev 4:3),[40] and reparation offering are the primary types of sacrifice (Lev 5:19),[41] but within the latter three occur several variations designed mainly to differentiate between intentionality and unintentionality. Additionally there are

criticizes those who gravitate to sociology "as a magic wand to make the biblical and other ancient texts intelligible" (*Divination*, 14).

31. O'Brien argues that "due to the scholarship of the past few decades, a post-exilic date for 'P' can no longer be merely assumed. Even if one disagrees with the arguments of Haran, Kaufmann and Milgrom, biblical scholars must consider—at the very least—the possibility of a date for 'P' which is earlier than that proposed by Wellhausen. In the wake of discussion of the term 'sons of Aaron' by scholars like Cody, Haran and Cross, and the suggestion that Chronicles may preserve some reliable traditions, Wellhausen's view that 'sons of Aaron' is an artificial creation must also be questioned" (*Priest*, 23). See Knohl, *Sanctuary*.

32. Blenkinsopp dubs Wellhausen a "Hegelian" in the sense that Wellhausen, like Hegel, believes ideas to have "an almost hypostatic character" (*Pentateuch*, 11–12).

33. See, e.g., Curtiss (*Priests*, 153–67); Abba, "Priest and Levites"; and Rooker (*Leviticus*, 139–66).

34. Milgrom notes that "although the focus of Leviticus is on the priests, only a few laws are reserved for them alone (i.e., 6:1—7:21; 10:8–15; 16:2–28)" (*Leviticus*, 1). Blenkinsopp's assessment is blunt, but correct: "The history of the Israelite priesthood remains very obscure" (*Pentateuch*, 153).

35. Levine, "Leviticus," 312. For Wenham "it would be wrong to describe Leviticus only as a manual for priests. It is equally, if not more, concerned with the part the laity should play in worship" (*Leviticus*, 3).

36. Klawans, *Impurity*, 22.

37. עולה, from עלה (to lift up).

38. קרבן מנחה (lit., offering of a gift).

39. שלמים, from שלם (to compensate, make peace).

40. חטאת. The verb חטא means "to sin" in the G form, but in the D form "to purify" (Ezek 43:20).

41. Following Milgrom (*Leviticus*, 342), Noonan denominates the חטאת sacrifice as the "purification offering" (Lev 4:3) and the אשם sacrifice as the "reparation offering" (5:15) ("Efficacy," 285).

instructions for votive and freewill offerings, priestly ordination (Lev 8–9),[42] various problems associated with improper priestly protocol, (un)clean animals,[43] leprous infections on persons and dwellings, the special needs of women and infants,[44] and complications associated with the proper management of seminal fluid (Lev 15:16–17).[45]

Section 2 focuses on (in)appropriate uses of blood,[46] moral statutes distinguishing Israelites from non-Israelites,[47] and implementation of the sacrifices listed in section 1, plus statutes on planting and harvesting, breeding animals, treating resident aliens and slaves, avoiding sorcerers and mediums, treating worshipers of graven images, handling sacred donations, treating the handicapped, taking care of priests' families, treating the poor and wealthy, handling the dead, observing festivals and Sabbaths, managing the tabernacle, observing the jubilee, maintaining the ancestral covenants, and generally doing business with others in an appropriate way. The rationale behind these statutes originates from one source: the *imago Dei*.

קדשים תהיו You shall be holy
כי קדוש אני for I am holy—
יהוה אלהיכם Yhwh your God. (Lev 19:2)

Two passages in Leviticus examine the defilement-holiness polarity from theological and socioeconomic perspectives. The Day of Atonement ritual is Israel's most potent theological defense against the previous year's pandemic of defilement threatening Yhwh's people (Lev 16:2–34). The Year of Jubilee, on the other hand, applies the defilement-holiness polarity to the

---

42. See Moore, "Role"; Moore, *What Is This Babbler*, 25–41.

43. Douglas contends that "the rule for land animals ... is quite simple when the covenant is seen to be its guiding principle. God is the feudal lord. From this it follows that no one is allowed to harm God's people or use God's things.... The teaching about the sanctity of blood derives from this feudal relationship. God protects the people of Israel, his rites give them covering, and sacrifice is the means he has given to them for expiation" (*Leviticus*, 136).

44. Because it involves the "shedding" of blood, menstruation poses special problems for women.

45. שכבת זרע (lit., coated seed). See Deut 23:10–11.

46. This is particularly important because (a) נפש הבשר בדם הוא (the life of the flesh is in the blood); thus (b) the blood is necessary for המזבח לכפר (the sacrifice of atonement) (Lev 17:11).

47. Most of these statutes focus on the very minimum boundaries necessary for maintaining non-defiling relationships between the sexes, boundaries which, when violated, cause טמא הארץ (defilement of the land) (Lev 18:25).

all-too-common problem of losing one's ancestral inheritance to creditors due to debilitating indebtedness.

Day of Atonement

At the heart of the Day of Atonement ritual are the following instructions:

יבא אהרן אל הקדש	Aaron shall come into the holy place
בפר בן בקר לחטאת	with a young bull for a purification offering
ואיל לעלה	and a ram for a holocaust offering. (Lev 16:3)
עזים וקח שני שעירי	He shall take ... two male goats
לחטאת	for a purification offering
ואיל אחד לעלה	and one ram for a holocaust offering.
והקריב אהרן את פר החטאת	Aaron shall offer the bull as a purification offering
אשר לו וכפר בעדו	for himself, and shall make atonement for himself[48]
ובעד ביתו	and for his family.
ולקח את שני השעירים	He shall take the two goats
והעמיד לפני יהוה	and set them before Yhwh
פתח אהל מועד	at the entrance to the tent of meeting.
ונתן אהרן על שני שירים גורלות	And Aaron shall cast lots over the two goats,
גורל אחד ליהוה	one lot for Yhwh
וגורל אחד לעזאזל	and one lot for Azazel.[49]

---

48. Pemberton points out that there are at least four components to the notion of "atonement": "(a) an action that may calm or restrain anger caused by some offense; (b) an act of cleansing or removal; (c) as an action that seeks reconciliation or cleansing, atonement brings forgiveness to the sinner; and (d) as an extension of the previous ideas, atonement may consecrate people or things to holy status" ("Leviticus," 170).

49. "Azazel" refers to (a) a geographical designation meaning "rugged cliff" or "precipitous place" (see Tg. Ps.-J. Lev 16:10, לשדרא יתיה לממת באתר תקיף וקשי דמדברא צוק) (to send it out to die in a place rough and hard in the rocky desert); Driver, "Pentateuch," 97–98); or (b) it is a combination of two terms: עז (goat) + אזל (to go away, disappear), thus the "(e)scape(d)-goat" (see OG ἀποστεῖλαι αὐτὸν εἰς τὴν ἀποπομπὴν ἀφήσει αὐτὸν εἰς τὴν ἔρημον [to send it into the place of casting out, letting it go into the wilderness]); or (c) the proper name of a well-known wilderness demon (1 En. 8:1; 9:6;

והקריב אהרן את שעיר	And Aaron shall bring near the goat
אשר עלה עליו הגורל ליהוה	chosen by lot for Yhwh
ועשהו לחטאת	and offer it as a purification offering.
והשעיר אשר עלה עליו הגורל לעזאזל	But the living goat chosen by lot for Azazel
יעמד חי לפני יהוה לכפר עליו	he shall put before Yhwh to make atonement over it,[50]
לשלח אתו לעזאזל המדברה	then send it out to Azazel in the wilderness. (Lev 16:7–10)[51]

Defilement is dealt with in different ways by different cultures. In Anatolia, for example, a family suffering from internal conflict can go to a "wise woman" (^{SAL}ŠU.GI) who prepares clay figurines representing the parties in dispute and places them at their feet.[52] She ties colored strips of wool around the necks of the figurines, each representing a different aspect of the defilement responsible for forcing the parties into conflict. Then she cuts away the colored woolen strips (while invoking the name of the appropriate deity), thereby "releasing" the parties in dispute from the defilement crippling them. After this a white sheep is brought in. The parties in dispute each spit into the animal's mouth and the "old woman" says, "Thus have you spit out the defilement." Having thus transferred the defilement into an animate homeopathic substitute, she kills the sheep and buries it. Thus, as the animal's corpse is buried from sight, so is the defilement.

Reading these rituals intertextually it becomes obvious that (a) each claims to be able to remove defilement; (b) each is fundamentally homeopathic in nature; and (c) each utilizes not one, but two ritual methods. The main dissimilarities are that (a) the Hittite ritual does not provide blood for the cleansing of the officiant or her clients; and (b) the Hittite "scape-animal" is killed and buried, not released into the desert. What this means, among other things, is that ANE peoples find defilement to be a problem

---

10:4–8; 13:1; Apoc. Ab. 13:6–14; 14:4–6; 20:5–7; 22:5; 23:11; 29:6–7; 31:51). See Wright, "Azazel"; and Janowski, "Azazel."

50. Lit., to cover it.

51. This central sequence is prefaced with instructions on where to stand and what to wear; and followed by instructions on how to cleanse both priest and tabernacle מטמאת בני ישראל ומפשעיהם לכל חטאתם (from the defilements [טמא] of the children of Israel, and for their transgressions and all their sins) (16:16).

52. This is the ritual of Maštikka, a ^{SAL}ŠU.GI from Kizzuwatna, examined by Rost ("Ritual") and summarized by Vieyra ("Sorcier," 110–12). ANET 35–51 has an English translation. This and similar ritual texts are discussed by Gurney (*Hittite*, 52–58) and Moore (*Balaam*, 23–24).

so serious, it mandates the use of multiple "back-up systems" to ensure its elimination. Whether the threat is to a single family or an entire nation is nothing compared to the challenge of convincing the parties involved that it is in fact eliminated.

Year of Jubilee

Debt slavery is a perennial problem, especially for the poor.[53] Some ANE governments grant debt remission at various times for various reasons.[54] The Hebrews do as well. The Year of Jubilee makes it possible for displaced Hebrews, regardless of extenuating circumstances, to return to their ancestral land and start over. Bankruptcy laws today are based on the same principle of forgiving debt to help debtors start over.[55] That it happens every seven years is doubtless a check against its abuse, thereby ensuring that it leads to a "another, healthier, end," rather than simply "the End."[56]

SUMMARY

Much more might be said, of course, about this centrally important pentateuchal scroll. In a recent volume of essays, for example, some important questions are raised; e.g., (a) "Can Leviticus be read as a separate book?"[57] (b) "Is Leviticus really the heart of the Pentateuch?"[58] and (c) "Is it possible to understand how the statutes in Leviticus are interpreted in the Second Temple period?"[59] These are all valid questions, to be sure, but theologically they are peripheral to the challenge of ascertaining the full impact of the book's single-minded focus on the defilement-holiness polarity.

---

53. *CH* §88 indicates that the median interest rate on grain and silver is 20 percent.

54. Hallo, e.g., details the socioeconomic impact of the seventeenth-century BCE Edict of Ammiṣaduqa (*ANET* 526–28) ("Sharecropping").

55. *Pace* Skeel's claim that "bankruptcy law in the United States is unique in the world" (*Dominion*, 1), perhaps a more accurate assessment is that bankruptcy laws today are in some measure foreshadowed by the debt forgiveness laws in the Bible (particularly the law of Jubilee in Leviticus), the most significant contributor to the Judeo-Christian tradition upon which American socioeconomic values are generally formulated (see Moore, *WealthWatch*, 7).

56. Skeel, *Dominion*, 1.

57. Rendtorff, "Leviticus."

58. Auld, "Leviticus."

59. Harrington, "Leviticus."

4

Numbers: Wilderness or Homeland?

IN LIEU OF DENOMINATING "titles," ANE texts tend to be classified according to their first word(s). In Tanak the fourth book of the Pentateuch begins with the Hebrew word במדבר (*bĕmidbar*) because its first words read, "Yhwh spoke to Moses *in the wilderness*" (*bĕmidbar*) (Num 1:1).[1] OG ignores this tradition and instead entitles it *Arithmoi* (Numbers),[2] probably because of its emphasis on rosters and lists and inventories.[3] Luther calls it *Das vierte Buch Mose* (The fourth book of Moses), but this "title" speaks more to authorship than contents.[4]

HISTORICAL CONTEXT

Although extra-biblical evidence for Moses remains elusive, empirical evidence for ancient Israel's existence is attested by a hieroglyphic phrase carved near the bottom of the Egyptian Merneptah Stela which reads, "Israel is laid waste; its seed is no more."[5] Because of this hard evidence it is difficult to imagine a historical background to Exodus-Numbers that is not influenced in some way by the accomplishments of Egypt's nineteenth

---

1. וידבר יהוה אל משה במדבר.
2. Gk Ἀριθμοῖ (cf. the term "arithmetic").
3. Vg then follows suit by calling it *Numeri* (numbers); hence the title "Numbers" in all ETs.
4. Luther, *Bibel*, 138.
5. Eg *ysr3r fk(w) bn prt.f* (cited in Grabbe, *Dawn*, 150). The Merneptah Stela was first discovered by Petrie (*Thebes*, 28; plates xiii–xiv), and ETs appear in *ANET* 376–78 and *COS* 2:40–41.

dynasty (1293–1187 BCE), especially the reigns of Pharaoh Seti I, his son Ramesses II, and his grandson Merneptah. One of the nineteenth dynasty's most characteristic accomplishments is its reestablishment of traditional polytheism after the maverick reign of Pharaoh Amen-hotep IV (d. 1334 BCE). A Pharaoh of the eighteenth dynasty, Amen-hotep IV comes to power at a time when Egypt's traditional priesthoods control practically everything in the country, a situation which greatly troubles the new Pharaoh, who soon begins to challenge their power. Renouncing traditional polytheism, he introduces a henotheistic religious system centered upon the worship of the Aten (sun disc).[6] At first he champions this cult as an alternative to the stifling legalism of Egypt's traditional priesthoods, but eventually he compels its observance on pain of punishment.

To underline his determination to reform Egyptian religious culture he decides to change his name to Akhenaten (One who is effective on behalf of the Aten) and move the capital to a new city, Akhetaten (The place of the horizon of the Aten). Like David, his strategy is to unite a divided country by moving the capital to a "neutral" location somewhere in the middle (2 Sam 5:5–7). Just as David's move to Jerusalem drains power away from the traditional capitals of Shiloh (north) and Hebron (south), so Akhenaten's strategy drains power away from the northern priesthood of Ra (Heliopolis) and the southern priesthood of Amun (Thebes).[7] Whether his motivation for doing so is political or religious (or both), Egyptian monotheism does not survive his death. In fact, his son and successor Tutankhamun reinstates the old priesthoods and removes all evidence of sun disc worship from official literature and monuments. Historians call this era the "Amarna period" because most of our information about it comes from Akkadian letters accidentally discovered at Tell El-Amarna, the site of ancient Akhetaten (approximately 180 miles south of Cairo).[8]

Presuming the events in Exodus-Numbers to be contextualized by this history, this helps to explain (a) why Mosaic monotheism so aggressively challenges the traditional gods of Egypt, and (b) why Moses' Pharaoh (probably Ramesses II) fights so hard against it. As the biblical text reports, Pharaoh's heart "hardens" at the very thought of freeing the Hebrews (Exod 4:21).[9] The theological question, however, is not whether Yhwh takes delight in hardening Pharaoh's heart, but whether the king's behavior

---

6. Zevit, *Religions*, 44–48.

7. Brazil's decision to move its capital to Brasilia—a city created *ex nihilo* in the jungle—is yet another example.

8. See Redford, "Amarna."

9. חזק, "to harden" (Moore, "Obduracy").

betrays a hypersensitivity to *any* kind of religiopolitical change, especially anti-polytheistic change. Is it merely coincidental that Moses comes along at this precise moment in Egyptian history, or that Exodus credits his victory to Yhwh's defeat of Egypt's (newly-reinstated?) traditional deities?[10]

The point of rehearsing this history here is simply to note that Numbers continues the same theological trajectory as that found in Exodus. As Israel moves from one polytheistic culture (Egypt) to another (Canaan), Yhwh leads his people through several more cosmic confrontations: the wilderness/desert (Mot),[11] the bronze seraph (Ḥoron?) (Num 21:8; 2 Kgs 18:4), Balaam's "gods" (Num 22:22),[12] and the Ba'al of Peor (Num 25:3; 1 Kgs 18:20–40). None of these encounters is any less significant than those occurring in Egypt. On the contrary, these "teaching moment" encounters are quite effective in helping the Hebrews learn how to emulate the *imago Dei*. Compared to the mud pits of Egypt (four hundred years) the wilderness proves to be a much more effective classroom (forty years).

LITERARY STRUCTURE

The OG translators of Numbers call it *Arithmoi* because of its preoccupation with lists and inventories. Preeminent among these stand two census lists in chs. 1 and 26. The first is taken at Sinai and includes a muster of Israel's qualified warriors. The second shows Moses and Eleazar (Aaron's son) starting a brand-new list for a brand-new generation. The Sinai generation begins its journey with promise and potential, but ultimately fails to enter Canaan. The post-Sinai generation picks up the mantle of its parents because whereas the first shrinks back from following Yhwh, the second reaps the benefits of ignoring their bad example. The first dies in the wilderness (save Joshua and Caleb), while the second goes on to inherit the promised land. Numbers accentuates these differences in part by the way it positions these census lists.[13] Another way to view the book's structure is to follow the lead of ch. 33 and telescope all the major events into one master list, an approach which condenses forty years of wandering into a travelogue of forty separate "stages" (Num 33:1),[14] each clustering around one of Israel's major encampments:

10. See Assmann, *Akhenaten*, 43–59.
11. In Canaanite myth Mot is the God of death and desert (P. Watson, "Death"; Healey, "Mot").
12. אלהים (gods/God).
13. Olson, *Framework*, 175.
14. מסעי (lit., the "pulling up" [of tent pegs]).

- In the shadow of Sinai (the *Sinai* encampment) (Num 1:1—10:10)
- A community in conflict (the *Kadesh* encampment) (Num 11:11—20:13)
- Preparing for the promised land (the *Moab* encampment) (Num 20:14—36:13)

IN THE SHADOW OF SINAI (NUM 1:1—10:10)

Michael Blake's novel *Dances with Wolves* narrates the story of Lt. John Dunbar, a Union Army officer yearning to see the American frontier before it vanishes. Moving west to the Great Plains, he marvels at the way the Lakota Sioux can tear down a village, transport it miles away, and reconstruct it in just a few hours. He wonders whether the US Army might learn a thing or two from this. He wonders about their whole way of life, in fact, because in his mind the Sioux have created something precious. Each individual seems to know his/her place in the world, from the smallest child to the fiercest warrior. Each seems to understand that self-defense need not turn warriors into criminals (like the Pawnee) nor settlers into invaders (like the white Europeans). The Sioux seem to know how to balance communal structure with individual spirit, internal dream with external reality. Having just escaped the horrors of the Civil War, Dunbar gravitates to this balance like a child to its mother.

Israel yearns for a similar balance. Having just received the law on Sinai, the question before them now is "What's next?" Will Israel trust in the law and wean themselves away from Egyptian influence? Or will they reject the law, slink back into Egypt, and settle for a life of institutionalized slavery? Yhwh relentlessly puts this choice before them, each conflict testing whether they will move forward or retreat backward. Each battle tests whether they will trust in Pharaoh or their Divine Warrior.[15] Each squabble tests whether they will emulate the covenant ethics of their Emancipator or the survivalist ethics of "the rabble" (Num 11:4).[16] Like the Sioux, Israel has to formulate a "game plan" if it expects to survive the wilderness. Num 1–10 records the details of that "game plan," and like all game plans this one addresses several key concerns: How is Israel going to deal with internal problems like leadership, identity, and stewardship? How will they address external problems like enemies, limited resources, and foreign cults? How

---

15. *CMHE* 91–111.
16. האספסף (the rabble).

will they address these problems in a way firm enough to maintain order, yet flexible enough to allow adaptational change? Most importantly, how will they stay loyal to their Covenant Partner in the process?

The First Census List (Num 1:1–54)

Census lists serve several functions. Clay tablets from Ebla, for example (Syria, twenty-fourth century BCE), lay out dozens of census lists documenting the distribution of food and supplies.[17] Census lists from Alalakh and Ugarit (Syria, fourteenth century BCE), on the other hand, focus on identifying military recruits for enlistment.[18] Such lists betray not only the pervasiveness of famine and war, but the unavoidable truth that realistic preparation is necessary to ensure survival. Israel's census lists emphasize that Yhwh's war strategy is a *holy* war strategy. So important is this strategy, in fact, Yhwh exempts one whole tribe from military service in order to give Israel a better chance at survival. Yhwh singles out the Levites to care for the tabernacle and guard it against potential defilement. Anyone violating its sacral boundaries takes his life in his hands. Anyone challenging the authority of its priesthood risks severe punishment. From the narrator's perspective these boundaries are nonnegotiable because just as it is impossible to imagine Israel emigrating across the desert without a game plan, so is it impossible to imagine this game plan without the Holy One at its center.[19]

The Design of the Camp (Num 2:1–34)

Discipline and order are critical to defense planning, so everybody in the camp must (a) have a job, and (b) know something about how their job interfaces with everyone else's job. Numbers is about premodern survival, not postmodern autonomy.[20] The tabernacle may be modeled after the Egyptian war camp,[21] and many of the ideas in Numbers are later picked up

---

17. The texts discovered at Ebla (Tell Mardikh in NW Syria) constitute the largest single find of third-millennium BCE cuneiform texts so far recovered, approx. 80 percent of which are administrative (Biggs, "Ebla," 263–65).

18. See Vita, "Ugarit," 492–98.

19. *CMHE* 231; Rothenberg, *Timna*, 12–16.

20. J. Leach finds it "intuitively reasonable that those who are cool and calm during the period of impact, and can formulate and carry out a plan, have a better chance of surviving than those who are hostile, bewildered, or otherwise psychologically impaired" (*Survival*, 150).

21. Homan, "Warrior."

and elaborated in the War Scroll from Qumran (1QM), another text written to prepare for holy war. Whether 1QM actually quotes from Numbers is not always clear, but it does use similar terminology in its descriptions of the "banners" and "signs" which distinguish battalions and build esprit de corps (Num 2:2).[22] Like 1QM, however, Numbers reads more like a ballet than a battle strategy, a fact which becomes painfully clear once the opportunity arises to go into actual battle (Num 14:45; Josh 7:4).

The Aaronid Priesthood (Num 3:1–4)

Numbers has a lot to say about leadership—its goals, its challenges, its parameters. Most importantly it stresses that the "sons of Aaron" oversee the Levites in Israel's priestly economy. In fact, the Levites are portrayed as a divine "gift" to the Aaronids (Num 3:9). Kohathite leaders are to report directly to Eleazar, son of Aaron (Num 3:32). Gershonite and Merarite leaders are to report directly to Ithamar, son of Aaron (Num 4:28, 33). All collected monies are to be turned over to Aaron and his sons, who pronounce the priestly blessing and sound the trumpet alarms (Num 3:48; 6:23; 10:8). Only the Aaronids are allowed to touch the holy things inside the tabernacle; the Levites merely carry them after they have been packed up (Num 4:15). Thus, even though two of Aaron's sons die for dismissing cultic boundaries (Lev 10:2), the failure of *some* Aaronids in no way challenges the authority of *all* Aaronids. Aaron still has two more sons (Eleazar and Ithamar), and one of the main purposes of this first main section is to place tabernacle leadership firmly in their hands.

The Levites (Num 3:5–39; 8:5–26)

Because the Levites do most of the heavy lifting it's important to allot to them their own census list. Each of Levi's sons (Gershon, Kohath, and Merari) has responsibility for a specific task. The Levites are to set up the tabernacle at the middle of the camp, the place where Yhwh "meets" Israel. All divine communication is to occur at this tent of "meeting" (Num 1:1),[23] a term elsewhere denoting the "meeting hall" of divine assemblies.[24] On the north side of the tabernacle the sons of Merari take care of the large support

---

22. דגלת (banners); אתת (signs). See 1QM 6.1, 4, 5; 3.13.

23. מועד.

24. E.g., *CAT* 1.2.1.14; cf. *CHME* 322; Kitchen, "Tabernacle"; Rothenberg, *Timna*, 122–30.

structures: the bars and poles and other skeletal equipment. On the south side the sons of Kohath take care of the packed-up interior furniture: the ark, the lampstand, the altars, and the rest of the tabernacle furniture. On the west side the sons of Gershon take care of the tabernacle's coverings and curtains, both exterior and interior. Finally, Moses and Aaron oversee worship on the east side, where messages are received from Yhwh and administrative decisions are made. Because leadership is so important, Numbers devotes a good deal of space to it, repeatedly explaining the exact responsibilities of each Levitical clan (Num 4:1–39; 8:5–26). Thus, even though the entire congregation participates in consecrating the Levites (all Israel lays their hands on them), Aaron and his sons remain firmly in control.

Redemption of the Firstborn (Num 3:40–51)

Behind this priestly economy stands a theological rationale to which Tanak often refers, but never fully explains. This is the rite of the "firstborn" (Exod 13:2).[25] Patrilineal societies celebrate the arrival of firstborn sons because such births guarantee the survival of the family inheritance (thus the special request of Zelophehad's daughters [Num 27:1–12]). Aware of this primogenitural system, ANE priests sometimes gauge the depth of a family's religious devotion by whether or not it will allow its most precious commodity to be sacrificed to this or that deity. King Mesha, for example, publicly sacrifices his firstborn son to Chemosh, the national deity of Moab (2 Kgs 3:27). Mercifully, this practice never finds a home in Israel, even though isolated instances occur here and there (Jer 7:31; 2 Sam 21). The redemption of the firstborn seems to preserve a faint trace of this pre-Yahwistic legacy. From Hurrian contracts we know that debtors can pledge family members to creditors in exchange for food and supplies and other commodities (the so-called *tidennutu* contract),[26] and this suggests that the Israelite *bĕkōrâ* has parallels rooted in the tenets of ANE law. Translated into Hebrew terms, this means that Israel's "creditor" (Yhwh) is the party responsible for taking the Levites "in pledge," i.e., in lieu of Israel's firstborn sons. While this remains only a possible understanding of this custom, Numbers nonetheless assumes that readers have a basic understanding of it.

---

25. בכור (*bĕkōr* [firstborn]). See 22:28; 34:1–20; Num 3:11–13; 8:16–18; 18:15.
26. See Taggar-Cohen, "Levites."

Miscellaneous Concerns (Num 5:1–31)

Maintaining order is impossible without law, but some laws are more helpful in certain circumstances than others (1 Tim 1:8; 1 Cor 6:12). In addition to the laws revealed on Sinai, this section of Numbers addresses several physical, economic and social concerns. In terms of literary form, narrative interspersed with law is one of Numbers' most characteristic features,[27] and while some argue for structuring the book in a way that privileges law over narrative, others find this unnecessarily reductive.[28] In terms of content, no one knows why the narrative singles out these *particular* concerns (leprosy, restitution, adultery), but that these are typical *kinds* of concerns seems more than a little obvious. The critical factor is that each ritual illustrates the necessity of priestly involvement, one of the book's most prevalent themes.

Physical Concerns (Num 5:1–4)

The usual Hebrew term for "leprosy" can refer to various types of skin disease (Num 5:2),[29] but it can also refer to blemishes and defects on cloth and leather, even the walls of buildings. Of course, there is always a debate over whether a cause-effect relationship exists between "illness" and "sin,"[30] but apart from this debate Israel still needs some kind of strategy for dealing with physical illness. Further, since priests are the only group even remotely qualified to address these issues (there are no "medical doctors" in the wilderness), priestly involvement is a given.

Economic Concerns (Num 5:5–10)

Political utopians may imagine forgiveness and reconciliation to be universally normative, but *reparation* is the backbone of most economies, ancient and/or modern (Num 5:15).[31] In Leviticus, the reparation offering is a specific kind of sacrifice for sin, whether it be "intentional" or "unintentional." The only valid question is how such sacrifices *effect* reparation; i.e., whether

---

27. Douglas, *Wilderness*, 83–88.
28. Con. Douglas, *Wilderness*, 144–59.
29. צרוע (leprous); see Kinnier-Wilson, "Medicine," 354–65.
30. Con. the Nazarene rabbi in John 9:1–3, a thirteenth-century rabbi argues that lepers should not consider their illness as something occurring "by chance," but that "the greatness of his sin is the cause of it" (Sefer ha-Chinukh 169.1).
31. אשם (reparation). See Van de Mieroop, "Debt."

or not they are truly fair and just. Payment in full plus one fifth seems to be the equation most frequently favored (Num 5:7; Lev 5:16).

Social Concerns (Num 5:11–31)

In this strange ritual Numbers appears to be adapting a pre-Yahwistic rite to a contemporary situation.[32] Adultery is a perennial social problem in all cultures and this is one of Israel's oldest attempts to deal with it. Much has been written about this ritual of the *soṭah* (straying woman). Some speculate that its purpose is to halt the spread of female "defilement," allegedly because this "problem" has the potential to defile the land and its inhabitants.[33] Others see it as a rite designed to restrict a husband's power by not-so-subtly repositioning it under the authority of the priesthood.[34] Suffice it to say that the *soṭah* ordeal is a very primitive attempt to address a very delicate problem.[35] Historically this is an important text because compared to other ANE texts about adultery, the ordeal described here actually improves (yes, improves) a woman's chances for finding justice.[36] Whether or not it might also be a "patriarchal mechanism for protecting masculine identity" is impossible to ascertain.[37]

The Nazirite Vow (Num 6:1–21)

This ritual links to the preceding one because it too requires priestly involvement. Whereas the Aaronids and the Levites have their own specialized ministries, the Nazirites are laypeople who simply want to "separate" themselves for Yhwh (Num 6:2).[38] Whereas the previous ritual focuses on

32. Van der Toorn, "Ordeal," 5:40.
33. Frymer-Kensky, "*Sotah*."
34. Haberman, "Adulteress," 12–42.
35. Wells responds to E. Otto's observation ("Aspekte") that the use of cultic rituals to decide difficult cases in Mesopotamia dramatically declines in the OB period, concluding that by the Neo-Babylonian and Persian periods, the use of rituals and ordeals dissipates in Babylonia, but not in Assyria ("Verdicts").
36. E.g., the Hittite Code (§197) permits husbands simply to execute their wives if they catch them *in flagrante* (Van der Toorn, "Ordeal").
37. Con. Haberman, "Adulteress," 36. Qur'anic law specifies that if "chaste women" (المحضنت) are accused of adultery their accusers must produce four witnesses, and if not, she is to be acquitted. Further, if a husband accuses his wife of adultery without witnesses he must make five vows to Alla, but his wife may also make five vows (Q 24:4–9). N.b. that (a) this is not a ritual, and (b) there is no third party involved (like a priest).
38. להזיר (to make separate, via a נדר [vow]).

some bizarre ingredients ("water of bitterness," "one-tenth ephah of barley flour"), the main ingredient here is money. That is, Nazirites become Nazirites only after they hand over a sizeable portion of their capital: one male lamb, one ewe lamb, one ram, one basket of unleavened bread, several cakes of choice flour mixed with oil, several unleavened wafers spread with oil, one grain offering, and several drink offerings.[39] And this pertains only to the *consecration* ritual. Should they want a *cleansing* ritual too, the price goes up: two turtledoves (or pigeons) plus one more male lamb. Many have speculated about the contents of this vow, with its idiosyncratic renunciation of grapes, corpses, and haircuts, but why these particular items are prohibited remains a mystery.[40]

The Dedication Offering (Num 7:1–88; 8:1–4)

Another component of Israelite ritual involves the dedication of two key pieces of sacred furniture: the altar (Num 7:1–88) and the lampstand (8:1–4). In addition, Israel has to consecrate the Levites for service (8:5–26), make preparations for Passover (9:1–14), and hammer out the silver trumpets (10:1–10). The cost of all this is significant, of course, so the only way this "game plan" will work is if everybody chips in to support it. Thus, on the day of the altar's "anointing" and "dedication" (7:10),[41] Israel responds to the challenge. Though written in rather artificial prose, this passage documents the first offering taken to support the Levites.

The Passover Celebration (Num 9:1–14)

With Passover, however, Israel faces a problem. Put bluntly, "How are unclean and absentee Hebrews to celebrate Passover?" Put theologically, "How does the imperative to avoid defilement reconcile with the imperative to create holistic community?" Where, exactly, is the line between cultic purity and corporate unity? Instead of wrestling with this question by himself,

---

39. Chepey observes that whereas various Jewish sects of the Second Temple period express devotion to God via specific beliefs and restrictions for membership, Nazirites "are know from all walks of Jewish life, whether man, woman, or child, possibly slave as well as free, rich or poor, common as well as the socially elite," identified only by the "simple desire to express personal devotion to the God of Israel" (*Nazirites*, 199).

40. Qur'an indicates that Muslims are to avoid three items: carrion, blood, and swine (Q 6:145), items also prohibited in Torah as טמא (defiling) (Num 19:13; Lev 3:17; 11:7).

41. משח (anoint); חנכה (*ḥanukka* [dedication]).

Moses takes it directly to Yhwh, and Yhwh responds: *holistic community takes precedence over cultic purity* (Num 9:10–12). Whatever this might ultimately mean, it immediately means that outlanders can celebrate Passover with indigenous Hebrews. Why? Because Yhwh's desire is to establish not an exclusive priesthood, but an inclusive community. The priesthood is simply a means to this end. In other words, *mission* is more important than *method*. To underline this principle, Moses issues a law punishing any "clean" Hebrew's unexcused absence from Passover. The purpose of priestly regulation is to serve the creation, not become an end in itself. As the Nazarene prophet puts it, "The Sabbath is made for man, not man for the Sabbath" (Mark 2:27). Outlanders and "unclean" Hebrews are to be welcomed at Passover because the Creator wants to avoid creating a two-tiered community. Yhwh wants "one statute for all."[42]

The Cloud and the Fire (Num 9:15–23)

Hovering over the tabernacle the Spirit of Yhwh manifests itself in a cloud by day and a pillar of fire at night. Whenever the cloud moves, Israel moves. Whenever the pillar stops, Israel stops. Cloud imagery is deeply rooted in ANE literature. Ba'al, for example, is called the "cloud rider" in Canaanite poetic texts.[43] Psalm 18 preserves the essence of this imagery in an old hymn now thoroughly Yahwicized:

ויט שמים וירד	He stretches the heavens, and descends,
וערפל תחת רגליו	a thick cloud under his feet.
וירכב על כרוב	He rides on a cherub
ויעף וידא על כנפי רוח	and flies swiftly upon the wings of the wind.
	(Ps 18:9–10)

Elsewhere in Tanak, clouds refer to God's "clothing," "veil," and the "dust of God's feet."[44] The advantage of such imagery is its ability to reveal and conceal at the same time, an aspect of deity Rudolf Otto calls the *mysterium tremendum*.[45]

42. Num 9:14 reads, חקה אחת יהיה לכם ולגר ולאזרח הארץ (There will be one statute for you, for both the outlander and the native of the land).

43. Ug *rkb 'rpt* (*CAT* 1.2.4.8); cf. רכב בערבת (rider on the clouds) (Ps 68:5) (W. Herrmann, "Clouds").

44. לבש (garment) (Job 38:9); סכותה בענן (lit., wrapped in a cloud/veil) (Lam 3:44); ענן אבק רגליו (lit., a cloud is the dust of his feet) (Nah 1:3).

45. R. Otto, *Holy*, 23–63.

The Silver Trumpets (Num 10:1–10)

Whereas contemporary alarm systems use, say, colors to indicate various danger levels, Israel uses trumpet blasts. When both trumpets "blare," this is the signal for the assembly to gather at the tent of meeting (Num 10:3).[46] When one trumpet "blares," only the leaders are to gather (10:4). When one trumpet "sounds an alarm," the east camps (Aaron and Moses and company) are to begin moving out (10:5).[47] A second alarm signals the south camp, and so forth, until all the tribes successfully muster. Only the Aaronids are permitted to blow the silver trumpets.

Interspersed Thematic Summaries

Interspersed throughout these lists and laws stand several short summaries, each providing in its own way a telling glimpse into the narrator's worldview. These include Israel's obedience to the exemption of the Levites (Num 1:54), Israel's submission to the encampment pattern (2:34), Moses' delivery of firstborn offerings to Aaron (3:49–51), Moses' warning to the Kohathites (4:20), Israel's obedience to the leprosy law (5:4), the priestly blessing (6:22–27), the description of the revelation process (7:89), Moses' construction of the lampstand "according to the pattern" (8:4), and Israel's reliance on the pillar of fire/cloud (9:15–23). Taken altogether, these summaries emphasize Yhwh's holiness, Israel's obedience, and Aaronid authority.

COMMUNITY IN CONFLICT (NUM 11:11–20:13)

Jaime Escalante is a mathematician from Bolivia. Emigrating to the States, he takes a high-paying job with an aerospace company, but then quits it to start teaching high school in a gang-infested section of East Los Angeles. Instead of complaining, however, he takes a group of his brightest students and teaches them advanced calculus. When they score a high grade on the AP exam, the Educational Testing Service cannot believe it and promptly accuses them of cheating. Rallying behind their teacher, they consent to take a second exam and dramatically repeat the same high scores. When the word gets out about this accomplishment, Escalante and his students

---

46. תקע (to blare a sound).
47. תקע תרוע (to blare an alarm).

become internationally famous, and their story is eventually made into a film every teacher should see: *Stand and Deliver*.[48]

One of the most pivotal scenes in the film is a confrontation in a faculty meeting between Escalante and the head of the math department. Asked what she might do to save the school's accreditation, the department head says, "Nothing." She responds this way because she has come to believe that her students are too illiterate, her school too poorly funded, and her colleagues too poorly trained to accomplish anything approximating real education in the lives of these teenagers. She believes that it's more important to *protect* students from failure than *prepare* them for success. Escalante, however, demands that his colleagues stop complaining and start teaching. He insists that they start raising student expectations. He suggests that they go to professional meetings and acquire the training they need to do their jobs better. He demands the opportunity to teach trigonometry and calculus, not just remedial arithmetic.

Israel faces the same type of conflict. When the cloud starts moving, Israel dutifully breaks camp and starts walking. Everyone does their assigned job. Everything seems to be going well . . . until Sinai disappears over the horizon and they suddenly realize that they are on their own for the first time in four centuries. Then the "rabble" start murmuring,[49] and the "congregation" starts bullying Moses. Their first complaint focuses on food because these former slaves remember (a) the alleged variety of food they used to enjoy in Egypt, and (b) the "fact" that everything in Egypt used to come "free of charge" (Num 11:5).[50] As institutionalized slaves they learn to rely on Egypt for everything. Now Yhwh wants them to rely upon him, and many are resistant. Change is not easy for slaves. Mission is not easy for fatalists (like the math department head). Like frightened children, they cry out in fear. Like angry adolescents, they rebel against authority.

Departure from Sinai (Num 10:11–36)

It's easy to overlook the obvious, but its important to recognize that Israel is trying to do something few nations have ever done. Viewed theologically, this second section of Numbers is a cautionary tale. By emphasizing the anonymity of death, the absence of proper burial, and the matter-of-fact

---

48. Menéndez, *Stand and Deliver*.
49. Coats, *Rebellion*, 1–29.
50. חנם (for nothing) (Moore, *Retribution*, 25–29).

way Yhwh abandons these rebels to their fate, Numbers serves as a warning to future generations (1 Cor 10:1–13; Heb 3:7–19).[51]

Moses Laments (Num 11:1–15)

Up to this point Israel's "faith" is vicariously lived through its leaders, Moses, Aaron and Miriam. Moses successfully delivers Israel from Egyptian slavery. Aaron faithfully mediates the holy presence to Israel. Miriam dramatically leads Israel in worship as a prophetess of Yhwh (Exod 15:20).[52] Israel "trusts" in Yhwh because of what its leaders are doing. Now, only a few days out from Sinai, Yhwh tests this "faith," and Israel disappointingly responds by choosing cold cuts over covenant, garlic over grace, and fish over faith. Israel's problem, of course, has nothing to do with food; in fact, the keyword here is not "food," but "crave" (Num 11:4).[53] In the D form this verb can mean "to wish for" or "to desire,"[54] but here in its reflexive form it denotes a *continual* "wishing/desiring." Israel's "desire," in other words, teeters dangerously on the edge of addiction. They continue to "crave" something they once had, but now do not. Just as no amount of talk therapy can "cure" a drug addiction, so no amount of "food" can satisfy this "craving." Demanding meat instead of manna, Israel is given meat in such abundance, it makes them gag and choke. Amazingly, it takes only one day in the wilderness for Israel's true identity to emerge, thus leading to the naming of this place the "Graves of Addiction" (Num 11:34).[55]

All this profoundly upsets Moses. Frustrated and angry, he pours out his heart before Yhwh in a torrent of questions. Like Jeremiah, he laments the "impossibility" of his ministry, the hiddenness of the deity, the poignant loneliness resulting from having to lead such a spiteful people.[56] Only one of his questions relates to the problem at hand ("Where am I going to find meat for this people?"), but before the "where" question, he must first ask the "why" questions: (a) "Why do you treat your servant so badly?" and (b)

---

51. See Leveen, "Falling."

52. נביאה (prophetess).

53. התאוו תאוה (lit., they craved a craving).

54. See, e.g., Ps 132:13, "Yhwh has chosen Zion; he has desired it [אוה] for his dwelling."

55. קברות האתאוה (*kibroth-hatta'avah* [graves of addiction]).

56. At one of his very lowest points Jeremiah cries out, "Woe is me, my mother, that you ever bore me, a man of strife and contention to the whole land! I have not lent, nor have I borrowed, yet all of them curse me" (Jer 15:10) (Moore, *What Is This Babbler*, 90–92).

"Why do I have to carry this *burden*?" (Num 11:11).[57] This latter term is particularly poignant because it can mean either "burden" or "oracle," depending on context, an ironic choice given the fact that it falls from the lips of Israel's greatest prophet (Deut 34:10).[58] In short, Moses begins to wonder how long he can carry the "burden" of what he calls an "infantile" people (Num 11:12).[59]

Gift of the Spirit (Num 11:16-30)

Then, suddenly, God shows up, and in a way so unexpected it catches everyone by surprise. Truth be told, this is not the first leadership crisis for Moses. In Exod 18, before the revelation of the law on Sinai, his Midianite father-in-law critiques his management skills by encouraging him to delegate some of his tasks to others (Exod 18:13-26). Here Yhwh does something similar, and reading these responses intratextually produces the following reflections: (a) both passages presume the utter necessity of delegation; (b) both passages set up a simple system for delegation; and (c) both emphasize that delegation should be transferred to already recognized leaders.[60] Yet the differences balance out the similarities because (a) Moses responds in Exodus to a suggestion from a relative (Jethro),[61] while in Numbers he takes the initiative upon himself; (b) Exodus distinguishes between "major" and "minor" judicial cases (Exod 18:22), while Numbers marginalizes such distinctions, even when Joshua tries to segregate those "prophesying at the tent of meeting" from those "prophesying in the camp" (i.e., Eldad and Medad) (Num 11:26-28); (c) Exodus presents the new system of delegation without objection, while in Numbers both Joshua and Miriam raise objections; (d) Exodus shows God playing an indirect role, while in Numbers God directs the process personally, taking some of the spirit "given" to Moses and redistributing it to seventy others; and (e) Exodus focuses on the creation of a functioning judicial system, while Numbers focuses on something a bit deeper. In Numbers, Yhwh gives Israel a gift it neither deserves nor expects, but Moses is so delighted by the outcome, he wishes that all of Yhwh's people might have it.

---

57. משא (load, burden, oracle; from נשא [to lift]).
58. Both meanings of משא seem polysemantically active in Jer 23:33.
59. יונק (lit., sucking child). See Brueggemann (*Imagination*, 11-27).
60. The same principle is operative in 1 Tim 3:2-7.
61. Jethro's name in Qur'an is Shuʿayba (شعيب), who is believed to be a prophet sent to Midian by Alla (Q 7:85; 11:84, 95; 29:36).

Historical analysis of this text might suggest that leadership after the giving of the law on Sinai is somehow different from leadership beforehand. If so, this would suggest that there is a correlation between *degrees of pressure* and *degrees of response*. In other words, because Moses appears to be under greater pressure in Numbers, this may be why the Spirit chooses to move now instead of earlier.

Challenging Prophetic Authority (Num 12:1–16)

Whereas the first challenge comes from the "rabble," the second comes from Moses' own siblings, Miriam and Aaron.[62] Ostensibly the reason for this has to do with Moses' marriage to an Ethiopian woman, but this "problem" quickly fades from view because the real issue here is prophetic authority. Up to this point Numbers says little about it because Israel's "game plan" is preoccupied by matters of priestly structure and accountability. This changes in ch. 11 when the Spirit descends and seventy lay elders start "prophesying."[63] One of the lessons here is that priestly ritual in and of itself cannot sustain people in "the wilderness." Another way to express this is that wilderness wanderers need more than just structure to flourish and grow. They also need the power of the Spirit, and since the word is the Spirit's primary conduit,[64] something eventually has to be said about the purpose, function, and authority of prophecy (Num 11:25).[65] So just as Moses dismisses Joshua's criticism of Eldad and Medad (Num 11:28), Yhwh dismisses Miriam's criticism of "my servant Moses" (Num 12:8).[66] In ch. 11 Yhwh addresses Moses' "burden" by redistributing the Spirit at the tent of meeting. Here in ch. 12

---

62. Jeremiah's first lament bewails the fact that his own family is opposed to him (Jer 11:18—12:6).

63. התנבא (the verb נבא in the reflexive form). Whether the elders begin "raving" (like Saul in 1 Sam 10:10) is not clear.

64. Not the *only* conduit, just the primary one (2 Tim 3:16–17).

65. Yhwh later tells Moses, "I will raise up for them a prophet like you from among their own people; I will put my words in the mouth of this prophet, who shall speak to them everything that I command. Anyone who does not heed the words that this prophet speaks in my name, I myself will hold him accountable. But any prophet who speaks in the name of other gods, or who presumes to speak in my name a word that I have not commanded, that prophet shall die. You may say to yourself, 'How can we recognize a word that Yhwh has not spoken?' If a prophet speaks in the name of Yhwh, but the 'prophecy' does not take place or prove true, it is a word which Yhwh has not spoken. The prophet has spoken it presumptuously" (Deut 18:18–21).

66. On the special significance of the epithet עבד יהוה (servant of Yhwh), see Helmer Ringgren, "עֶבֶד," *TDOT* 10:394–95; Noth, *Numbers*, 92–93; and Levine, *Numbers*, 1:328–33.

he calls Aaron and Miriam to the same tent of meeting to explain the nature of prophecy. With most prophets God speaks in "dreams" and "riddles," but not so with Moses. With him God speaks plainly and clearly. Moses is the prophet par excellence.[67] Whereas Aaronid ritual provides *priestly structure*, Mosaic prophecy infuses that structure with *spiritual substance*. By publicly challenging Moses, Miriam challenges not just her little brother, but Israel's greatest prophet.[68] Yhwh strikes her with leprosy and exiles her from the camp because she needs to realize the significance of the boundary she has crossed. Just as Yhwh disciplines Aaron for his part in the Meribah affair (Num 20:22–29), so he disciplines Miriam for challenging Moses' prophetic authority. Soon Moses, too, will be disciplined (Num 20:12), but to focus on punishment instead of prophecy here is to miss the theological point. These texts are not designed to emphasize Yhwh's "judgmental nature," nor are they designed to criticize androcentrism and/or misogyny.[69] The point here is that priests and prophets must learn how to work together if the wilderness is to be survived.

The Twelve Scouts (Num 13:1—14:10a)

Having survived two major crises, Israel now lunges its way toward a third. Twelve men are chosen to slip into Canaan and scout out the land, but when they report back to Moses, ten suggest that they give up their journey and go back to Egypt.[70] Their argument is much like that of the department head in *Stand and Deliver*. The Canaanites are just "too strong." Their cities are "too well fortified" (Num 13:28).[71] Yes, the land flows with "milk and honey," they admit, but the "descendants of Anak" still occupy the land (Num 13:28),[72] and they make them feel like "grasshoppers" by comparison. Like Jaime Escalante, however, Joshua and Caleb reject this fatalism. Yes, they argue, the land is populated by strong people, but if one looks carefully, one can see that no divine "shadow" hovers over them to protect them,

---

67. Brueggemann, *Imagination*, 11–27.

68. Thus Moses' final epitaph reads, "Never was there a prophet like Moses" (Deut 34:10).

69. *Pace* Graetz, "Miriam."

70. In Numbers it's Yhwh's idea to send out scouts (Num 13:2); in Deuteronomy, it's the congregation's idea (Deut 1:22).

71. Ironically, the Amarna letters give credence to this assessment (see Moran, *Amarna*, 232–37).

72. ילדי הענק; Syr ܒܢܝ ܓܢܒܪܐ (sons of the mighty); translated υἱοὺς γιγάντων (sons of giants) in OG Deut 1:28.

thus rendering them naked and vulnerable (Num 14:9).[73] Since this word denotes the "shadows" of protector deities elsewhere,[74] this idiom means more than simply "We've got them where we want them." What it more likely implies is that Israel's Divine Warrior has gone before them to clear their cosmic way. The awful "dread" of Yhwh can and will paralyze their enemies' cosmic defenses (Josh 2:9).[75] All Israel has to do, really, is "mop up." Joshua and Caleb reject the fatalism of their colleagues because underneath it lies the false premise that Yhwh wants Israel to take the land on their own power, without divine help.

When the congregation gets wind of this debate, they immediately start to panic. A good way to gauge the depth of this panic is to compare the verbs used here with the verbs used in previous conflict narratives. Whereas earlier Miriam "speaks" against Moses (Num 12:1),[76] here the congregation "lifts up its voice" (14:1),[77] "weeps" (14:1),[78] and "murmurs" (14:2)[79] against the two brothers, even threatening to "stone" them (14:10).

Prophetic Intercession (Num 14:10b–45)

That's when Yhwh shows up again, more determined than ever. Proposing to destroy the entire camp, he invites Moses to become a "new Abraham," the father of a "new Israel." Whether or not this proposal is intended to be taken seriously is difficult to say, but what *can* be said is that Yhwh's lament resonates deeply with Moses' earlier complaint (Num 11:11–15). Apparently the text intends through this resonance to highlight several facets of Yhwh's relationship to Moses. Both Yhwh and Moses suffer from the "burden" of spiritual leadership (11:11).[80] Yhwh responds to Moses' "burden" by redistributing his Spirit to seventy elders. Moses responds to Yhwh's "burden" by pleading Israel's case before him. This is a classic case of *prophetic intercession*, one of several found in Tanak.[81] As Israel's intercessor, Moses puts three propositions before Yhwh, and though this dialogue

---

73. צל (shadow).
74. See the parallel between צל (shadow) and סתר (shelter) in Ps 91:1.
75. אימה (dread).
76. דבר (to speak).
77. ויתנו את קולם (lift up their voice).
78. בכה (to weep).
79. לון (to murmur).
80. משא (burden/oracle); see Fretheim, *Suffering*, 121.
81. E.g., Exod 32:11–14; 1 Sam 5:1—7:1; 2 Sam 21:1–14; 24:1–25; 1 Kgs 16:29—18:45.

may seem artificial, the arguments themselves succeed in (a) turning away Yhwh's wrath and (b) establishing Moses' prophetic authority.

First, Moses argues that if Yhwh is to remain Israel's Protector, his "shadow" must continue hovering over them (Num 14:4).[82] For Moses this truth seems self-evident, based as it is on Yhwh's previous promises. Even Egypt knows that unlike the Canaanite deities (whose "shadows" are nowhere to be seen [14:9]),[83] Yhwh's "shadow" has genuine cosmic power. Moses therefore asks Yhwh why he would even think of removing it. *Second*, should Yhwh annihilate his people "as one man," such an atrocity would call into question the covenant commitments he made to them at Sinai. *Third*, Yhwh's problem seems clear to Moses. Somehow he must find a way to forgive human sin without compromising his holiness. However difficult the challenge, Yhwh needs to find that delicate balance between absolute holiness and covenant loyalty.[84]

Listening to Moses' arguments, God decides to "change his mind." Instead of exterminating Israel *en masse*, he compromises, deciding to let the Sinai generation perish while the post-Sinai generation survives in Canaan.[85] This behavior does not imply that Yhwh is capricious, or that the future is somehow "up for grabs," or that Yhwh does not truly know the future.[86] It simply means that just as human sovereigns have the freedom to do whatever they want, so does the Divine Sovereign.[87] Regrettably, Israel misses the significance of this truth and decides to invade Canaan without the Divine Warrior's help. Moses warns against such "presumption" (14:44),[88] but Israel decides (again) not to listen to him.

Institutionalizing Forgiveness (Num 15:1–41)

In order to limit the number and severity of future rebellions, ch. 15 follows up with several layers of priestly instruction, addressing (a) what kinds of sacrifices to offer, (b) how to handle "borderline" cases, and (c) how to use visual aids to reinforce priestly statutes. Underneath these statutes lies the priestly presumption that Israel well understands the difference between "intentional" and "unintentional" sin. The latter is forgivable. The former

82. עמד (to stand).
83. צלם (their shadow).
84. For Christians this balance can be found in only one place—Christ Jesus.
85. Sakenfeld, "Forgiveness."
86. Con. Boyd, *Possible*, 3–16.
87. Willis, "Repentance."
88. עפל (to presume).

is not. Unintentional sin can be expiated through animal sacrifice because such "gifts" create financial deterrents against joining this or that rebellion. In addition to Israel's other sacrifices (Lev 1–7), Moses now adds a couple more: grain and bread dough offerings. The principle, however, is simple: the more sacrifices one has to make, the more money one has to lose for choosing conflict over covenant.

But what about those borderline cases where the law needs "explaining" (Num 15:34)?[89] In cases like these Numbers suggests a synthesis of (a) logical analogy and (b) legal precedent. What to do about a man gathering firewood on the Sabbath, for example, can be resolved by giving intratextual attention to another, similar case. In Lev 24:10–23 a man who is Egyptian/Hebrew breaks one of the Ten Commandments (blaspheming the name). But does this law apply to all people or just undefiled native Hebrews? Here in Numbers someone breaks another of the Ten Commandments, the command to sanctify the Sabbath. By analogy, therefore, since the first sin is punishable by death, so must the second. Punishment must be the same for both because both are examples of "intentional" sin. Both involve an intentional violation of revealed law. The first occurs in someone who is half Hebrew, and the second raises questions about the definition of "work," but these are extenuating circumstances and, as such, should not be allowed to determine legal principle.

To help Israel remember this principle, Moses provides a simple visual aid. All educators know the value of visual aids. In lieu of overhead projectors or PowerPoint slides, though, Israel uses colored fringes on garments, leather phylacteries, kosher food, and/or snippets of Scripture on doorposts. Visual aids bring clarity to the learning process because they are so effective at jogging the memory and (re)conditioning the mind.[90] The purpose of this particular visual aid is the same as for all visual aids: (a) to help Israel see who Yhwh is and (b) to help Israel realize that obedience to the law is essential to emulation of the *imago Dei*.

Organized Rebellion (Num 16:1–50)

In this chapter the virus of rebellion infects Israel's leadership. From Numbers' perspective, the leader of this rebellion is Korah, son of Izhar, son of Kohath, son of Levi. According to the "game plan" laid out in ch. 4, Korah's job is like that of every other Kohathite—to carry the packed-up ark and other holy objects from camp to camp. Among the Levitical clans, the

---

89. פרש (to explain; lit., to unravel; see Fishbane, *Interpretation*, 98–100).
90. Crenshaw, *Education*, 85–113.

Kohathites are the servants who work most closely with the "holy things"; so closely, in fact, the law warns them not even to look at them lest they be tempted to touch them (Num 4:20). That Korah now wants to make his next "career move" is therefore not all that surprising. Even though he has been warned, he still wants to move up the priestly ladder and do what the Aaronids do. But instead of going to Moses directly and making his case (like, say, the daughters of Zelophehad [4:20]), Korah gathers an army of 250 men and challenges Moses' leadership authority. This is shocking, of course, but care needs to be taken in interpreting this text because Korah's name does not even appear in Moses' later review of these events (Deut 11:6), an omission which suggests that Dathan and Abiram (the Reubenites) may be playing a more intentional role here than Numbers wants to let on.[91] Perhaps the Reubenites get involved because they are angry at Moses for replacing them (Jacob's firstborn) with another leader (Moses is Levite). Could this be why they "recruit" Korah to voice their grievances against Moses and Aaron?

Yhwh's response, at any rate, leaves no doubt about his position on the matter. This is not a text about "murmuring" or "complaining." This is a text about *rebellion*, so no punishment involving leprosy, or long-term generational death, or "putting out the eyes" (as the Reubenites fear [Num 16:4]) will be enough to stop it from recurring. So the ground opens up and swallows Korah's entire "congregation" into Sheol.[92] Recording these awful events, the text takes great pains to note that Yhwh's response, terrible as it is, is not a response to murmuring against Moses. No, these rebels die because they "despise" Yhwh (16:30).[93]

Aaron's Budding Staff (Num 17:1–13)

Reviewing these chapters, it becomes more and more obvious that rebellion is a persistent allergic reaction to priestly authority, particularly Aaronid priestly authority. Thus Yhwh decides to validate the authority of the Aaronid priesthood with a rather unforgettable visual aid. Each tribe writes the name of an ancestral leader on a staff and deposits it in the tent of meeting overnight. Aaron's name goes onto Levi's staff. The next morning Aaron's staff is bursting with life, while the other eleven remain lifeless and inert. Just as Moses' staff turns into a snake before Pharaoh, so Aaron's staff turns

---

91. See Goodnick, "Korah."

92. The group in rebellion includes "two hundred fifty Israelite men, leaders of the congregation, chosen from the assembly, well-known men" (Num 16:2).

93. נאץ (to despise).

into a budding almond tree before Israel. What this symbolizes, of course, is Yhwh's desire for all Israel to accept the authority of the Aaronid priesthood.[94]

Responsibilities of Priests and Levites (Num 18:1–32)

This chapter follows up by detailing the authority of the Aaronids vs. the Levites. Aaronid priests are to focus on the "area behind the curtain"; i.e., the tabernacle proper. For their work, they are to be paid in kind, not in land. All the sacrifices generated by the grain, purification, and reparation offerings are to be theirs. All the consecrated oil, wine, and produce are to be theirs. All the first fruits and "devoted" offerings are to be theirs (Num 18:14).[95] All the firstborn creatures are to be theirs. All the fat of the firstborn cows, sheep, and goats is to be given to Yhwh, while the meat is to be given to the Aaronid priests. All firstborn human beings and unclean animals are to be theirs as well, though the text is quick to add that each human being is readily redeemable for a nominal fee (five shekels of silver) (3:40–51). The bulk of the Levites' support, however, is to come from Israel's tithe (18:21).[96] Out of these offerings the Levites themselves are to "tithe a tithe," thus demonstrating by example the genius of the Israelite economy (18:26).[97] In addition to this, the Levites are to receive forty-eight cities for houses, flocks, and herds (35:1–8).

The Ritual of the Red Heifer (Num 19:1–22)

Since death is one of the worst types of defilement, it needs its own ritual. In many ways the ritual Israel adopts, the ritual of the red heifer, is the most bizarre ritual in Numbers, certainly as bizarre as the ritual of the *soṭah* (Num 5:11–31).[98] Eventually the priests offer a supplement to this ritual in order to cleanse Israel of all contact with the Midianites (31:21–24),[99] but the general presumption is readily stated: "Defilement is lethally contagious."[100] Like all

---

94. Van der Toorn suggests that the "almond rod" Jeremiah sees in a vision may well be Aaron's budding rod on display in the temple ("Staff").

95. חרם (devoted things); Norbert Lohfink, "חרם," *TDOT* 5:180–99.

96. מעשר (lit., one tenth).

97. Cf. Köstenberger and Croteau, "Tithing."

98. See above.

99. See Wright, "Purification."

100. Douglas, *Wilderness*, 24.

ancient peoples, Israel abhors and fears the netherworld.[101] This passage thus itemizes a few things no Israelite should ever touch, including (a) a human corpse; (b) the tent in which a corpse is found; (c) anything sitting within this tent (e.g., any liquid sitting in an unsealed jar); (d) a human bone (even if found in an open field); and (e) graves. Those who violate any of these taboos must undergo a complicated purification process involving specially prepared "purification water" (19:9).[102] Like the "water of bitterness" in ch. 5, the red heifer ritual uses specially prepared water, the "water of cleansing" produced by mixing water with the ashes of a ritually burnt red heifer. The question, of course, is how any priest can participate in the production of this concoction without himself becoming defiled.[103] Nevertheless, whether it has origins in pre-Yhwistic resurrection myth,[104] or whether the storage place of the red heifer's ashes have been archaeologically recovered,[105] this is one of Israel's key rituals.

Moses Disobeys God (Num 20:1–13)

This is another chapter about death, beginning with Miriam's death and ending with Aaron's. In between the narrator addresses one of the Pentateuch's great mysteries: "Why does Yhwh forbid Moses from entering the promised land?" The answer to this question comes in the text's reflection on the scouts narrative (Num 13–14). Put simply, if Joshua and Caleb are to be the only survivors of the Sinai generation (Num 14:22), then everyone else has to die, including Moses.[106] Aaron dies at Mt. Hor (Num 20:28), Miriam dies at Kadesh (20:1), and Moses dies in Moab (Deut 34:5). It's doubtful whether Numbers seeks to elevate Aaron at Moses' expense,[107] because the text correlates Moses' disobedience with Israel's negative attitude toward Yhwh's "holiness" (Num 20:12).[108] Yet it's important to emphasize that prophets are

---

101. See Saul's conversation with the ghost of Samuel in 1 Sam 28:3–20. T. Lewis observes that there is "an ongoing battle throughout ancient Israel's history between adherents of what becomes normative Yahwism and those who practice death cult rituals" (*Cults*, 2).

102. מי נדה (water of cleansing).

103. R. Harris, "Heifer."

104. Wefing, "Ritual."

105. Browning, "Ashes."

106. Moses later tries to shed some of the blame: "Yhwh was angry with me because of you" (Deut 4:21; see Milgrom, "Magic").

107. *Pace* W. Propp, *Water*, 27.

108. להקדישני (lit., to make me [appear] holy; cf. Deut 32:51).

always held to a higher standard. Absolute obedience is the cardinal value of prophetic Yahwism. In the story of the Judahite "man of God," for example, Yhwh commands his prophet to fast, but when this command is disobeyed via an "innocent" meal with a "colleague," Yhwh immediately strikes him dead (1 Kgs 13:1).[109] Here in Numbers another prophet disobeys, striking a rock instead of speaking to it. Certainly this is not "murmuring" or full-blown "rebellion," yet Yhwh's response is consistent with the established principle: prophetic disobedience is not tolerated.

PREPARING FOR THE PROMISED LAND (NUM 20:14—36:13)

With their parents dying and Sinai fading from memory, the post-Sinai generation faces a difficult question: How can a "weary" (Num 20:14),[110] ragtag group of refugees "inherit" (14:24)[111] the promised land when (a) "Israel" no longer exists (at least not in its earlier form at Sinai), and (b) the promised land looks like it's already been promised to someone else (Anakim, Amalekites, Hittites, Jebusites, Amorites, Canaanites)? This question takes on new urgency with the taking of the second census in ch. 26. This new list bears witness to the sad truth that the Sinai generation has intentionally, defiantly, and persistently rejected Yhwh's plan to "bless all the families of the earth" (Gen 12:3). Like Esau, they sell their birthright for a bowl of soup. Like David, they betray an innocent man to lay claim to his wife. Like Judas, they betray their master with a kiss. This final section of Numbers begins with the post-Sinai generation waiting on Edom's doorstep for another Exodus miracle, but from Edom's perspective it's just too dangerous to allow refugee groups like the Hebrews to traipse across their land. Such groups (called *ḫabirū* in the Amarna correspondence)[112] have a long history of agitation and troublemaking in this part of the world.[113] Edom therefore refuses to stamp Israel's passport.

From Israel's perspective, however, Edom stands as one more "uncrossable" boundary in their journey to the promised land. In Exodus the "uncrossable" boundary is the Red Sea (Exod 14:10–25). In Joshua it's another body of water, the Jordan River (Josh 3:1–17). In Numbers it's the "uncrossable" boundaries of Edom and Moab. Whereas most of Israel's

109. איש אלהים (man of God; cf. 13:24; Moore, *Faith*, 237–42).
110. כל התלאה (all the weariness).
111. ירש (to inherit, [dis]possess).
112. See, e.g., *amēluḫa-bi-ri* (EA 286.19; cf. Lemke, "Ḫabiru").
113. Moran, *Amarna*, 326–34; Snell, *Flight*, 58–62.

conflicts to this point focus on internal concerns (Aaronids vs. Levites, Miriam vs. Moses, two vs. ten scouts, Korah's rebellion), its final challenges become more international than tribal, more political than priestly, more cosmic than mundane. No longer does Israel have only to deal with human power and human strongholds. Now it has to face the terrifying power of the unseen world—seraphim snakes, Balaam's *ĕlōhîm* (gods), and the Baʿal of Peor.

Conflicts in Edom (Num 20:14—21:9)

Edom's rebuff leads to two more incidents in quick succession: Aaron's death and the attack of the seraphim snakes. No connection seems immediately obvious between these incidents, yet each resonates audibly with the other. Aaron does not simply "die" on Mt. Hor, at least not in the way Miriam "dies" in the wilderness of Zin (Num 20:1).[114] No, Moses "strips" him of his priestly garments (20:26)[115] and leaves him to "perish" naked and alone on a strange mountain in a strange land (20:29).[116] With such brusque prose the narrator duly reports Aaron's punishment for his role in the Meribah and golden calf incidents (Exod 17:7; 32:4). Yet there is something else going on here. Numbers preserves not one, but two leadership transitions: (a) the Aaron-Eleazar transition and (b) the Moses-Joshua transition. In the latter, Moses does not "strip" anyone of anything. He rather "supports" Joshua by publicly acknowledging his authority (Num 27:23).[117] In the former, Israel's first high priest "perishes" outside the promised land. In the latter, Israel's quintessential prophet passes his mantle to the next generation.

Reading these stories intratextually makes it easier to understand why the next story appears where it does. Just as Moses "strips" Aaron, so Yhwh "strips" Israel, launching against them a squadron of "seraphim snakes" (Num 21:6).[118] Following Vg and OG, most ETs read "fiery serpents" or the like,[119] but it's important to remember that seraphim are essentially cosmic creatures.[120] Whatever the theological significance of this incident,

---

114. מות (to die).

115. פשט (to strip).

116. גוע (to perish).

117. סמך (to lean on, support).

118. הנחשים השרפים (seraphim snakes).

119. OG τοὺς ὄφεις τοὺς θανατοῦντας (deadly snakes); Vg *ignitos serpentes* (fiery serpents).

120. N.b. the seraphim covering the deity in Isa 6:2 (שרפים), as well as the "flying seraph" (שרף מעופף) in 14:29.

historians can make a strong case for its antiquity because of the many bronze snakes found at sites like Mevorakh and Hazor, not to mention the magnificently preserved bronze snake from a thirteenth-century BCE "tabernacle" at Timna.[121] When Hezekiah later destroys a metallic snake in the temple (2 Kgs 18:4),[122] this raises the questions, Why does Yhwh not do the same thing here in the wilderness? Why does he not simply destroy these seraphim snakes? Why does he instead make snakebitten Israelites stare at a metallic image of that which has bitten them? The answer has to do with the homeopathic principle of *reciprocity*. Just as Hittite priestesses burn wax "tongues" to stop wagging tongues[123] and Philistine diviners use gold "tumors" to stop cancerous tumors (1 Sam 6:5), so Moses makes a metallic snake to cure snakebite.[124] This story, in other words, has more to do with the anthropological principle of *reciprocity* than Yhwh's power over Ḥoron[125] or Moses' prowess as an exorcist.[126] Moses simply constructs an image of "the affliction" in order to bring healing to "the afflicted." To remove the source of the affliction would inappropriately short-circuit Israel's opportunity to learn something important. By forcing Israel to stare at the image of their affliction—even while the seraphim snakes are biting them—is to remind them that healing is contingent and salvation conditional. Like every other visual aid, this one is designed to help Israel remember who they are and who Yhwh is. So effective is the impact, in fact, the Nazarene prophet refers to it centuries later in a comparison of the hideous/healing power of the metallic seraph snake with the hideous/healing power of the Cross (John 3:14).[127]

Conflicts in Moab (Num 21:10—25:18; 31:1–12)

Edom's rebuff is not the last Transjordanian challenge Israel has to face. Others occur in the general vicinity of Moab: (a) Sihon, (b) Og, (c) Balaam, (d) Ba'al Peor, and (e) Midian. Easily dispatching the first two of these challenges, Israel defeats the militias of Sihon and Og. Later it is described

---

121. Rothenberg, *Timna*, 129–30.

122. נחש הנחשת (lit., snaky snake); OG τὸν ὄφιν τὸν χαλκοῦν (copper snake); Vg *serpentem aeneum* (bronze serpent); Syr ܚܘܝܐ ܕܢܚܫܐ (snake of divination).

123. *ANET* 350.

124. See Moore, *Balaam*, 60–64.

125. *Pace* Gray, "Ḥoron." Ḥoron is a minor Canaanite deity associated with snakebite rituals.

126. *Pace* Joines, "Serpent."

127. Cf. Wis 16:5–7.

as Yhwh "hardening the spirit" of Sihon and "giving" Og into Israel's hand (Deut 2:30–33). The last of these challenges, Midian, is a bit more tricky because Israel's relationship to Midian is profoundly ambivalent.[128] That this material comes packaged in a mottled mixture of prose-plus-legal material is not atypical for Numbers,[129] but this only highlights the fact that the middle two conflicts are the most challenging to interpret (Balaam and Ba'al Peor). Prior to this the narrator inserts a transitional segment comprised of several old war songs (Num 21:10–35). Each of these songs has its own tradition history, but strung together they create a transitional bridge between the encounters in Edom and the encounters in Moab. The purpose of this bridge is to show Israel transforming from a group of squabbling tribes into a more-or-less united confederation. Were this not the case it would be difficult to imagine why Moab would suddenly feel "great dread" when Israel arrives on its border (22:3).[130] As Israel changes, so does the tone of the book. Gone now is the constant bickering, the persistent fatalism, the pallid fear. Israel becomes a nation ready to handle anything thrown at them.

But what Moab decides to throw is a magician, not a militia. King Balak hires a magico-religious specialist to "curse" Israel, a common first volley in ANE skirmishes.[131] War generals hire magico-religious specialists like Balaam because they want to trick their opponents' deities into abandoning their clients. The usual procedure is to invite an enemy's gods to a specially prepared feast. Those deities who "take the bait" also take their "shadows" with them, leaving their human clients naked and exposed (14:9).[132] Balaam tries to do this with Yhwh. He wants to trick Yhwh into abandoning Israel, and when things go awry, this makes for some great satire, the purpose of which is not simply to poke fun at Balaam, but to satirize *all* the Balaams of the world who think they can "trick" God.[133]

What makes this incident even more fascinating is the fact that this portrait of Balaam is not the only one presently known. Here in Numbers Balaam enacts a fairly complex role set comprised of divinatory, prophetic, and exorcistic elements, all cleverly packaged into one hilarious "burlesque."[134] Elsewhere, however, Balaam enacts straightforward roles as "diviner,"

---

128. Moses' wife Zipporah is Midianite, as is her father Jethro, priest of Midian.
129. Douglas, *Wilderness*, 144–50.
130. ויגר מואב מפני העם מאד (And Moab was in great dread of the people).
131. Moore, *Balaam*, 29.
132. Moore, *Balaam*, 29.
133. Hackett, "Observations"; Jemielity, *Satire*, 21–49.
134. Rofé, בלעם, 51.

"curser," "answerer," "madman," and "seer."[135] Thus, like the multiple self-portraits of Van Gogh or Rembrandt, Balaam's portrait changes over time as various writers from various traditions accentuate various aspects of his character. The Balaam *cycle* (Num 22–24), however, serves several literary functions. *First*, like the plagues narrative in Exodus, this text preserves Numbers' "final showdown" between "Yhwh and the gods," a contest Yhwh wins when Balaam finally stops looking for "omens" (Num 24:1).[136] *Second*, the Balaam cycle proclaims to friend and foe alike that no power in heaven or earth can hurt Israel, whether human or suprahuman (Num 21:10–35; 22:1—24:24). Isaiah proclaims this same message to the Babylonian exiles (Isa 44:1–8), and Paul addresses a similar message to the Roman church (Rom 8:38–39). *Third*, Israel is to be led someday by a charismatic messiah (Num 24:17–24). This passage may well be Numbers' best-known, most-cited text. Some of the covenanters at Qumran, for example, quote it to identify their Teacher of Righteousness as the fulfillment of their messianic hopes.[137] The Nazarenes see in their founder the "bright and morning star" (Rev 22:16).[138] Rabbi Akiba proclaims Simon bar Koziba as *Bar Kokhba* (son of the star, d. 135 CE), citing Num 24:17 as "proof."[139] Centuries later the controversial European leaders Shabbetai Tzevi and Jacob Frank lead messianic movements in the seventeenth and eighteenth centuries CE.[140] Today Rabbi Menahem Schneersohn (d. 1994) remains the messianic hope of many Ḥasidim.[141]

After the Balaam encounter, things turn from bad to worse. Whereas the Dead Sea is the lowest point on earth, so Baʻal Peor is the lowest moral point in Tanak. Whereas the Moab-Israel conflict ends in stalemate, the Midian-Israel conflict ends in defilement and apostasy. Because of what Israel does at Baʻal Peor Yhwh sends a plague so virulent, it makes Moses afterwards issue strict instructions on how to (re)purify Israel from Midianite "defilement" (Num 31:13–24).[142] The Baʻal Peor cult itself remains

---

135. In order, Josh 13:22; 24:9; Mic 6:5; 2 Pet 2:15; *DA* 1.1 (see Moore, *Balaam*, 110–16).

136. נחשים (omens); cf. 21:6. In Deut 23:5 Moses says that Yhwh (a) refuses to listen to Balaam, (b) turns the curse into a blessing, and (c) does all of this out of love for his people.

137. CD 7.18; see J. Collins, *Scepter*, 7–26.

138. See Moore, "Jesus Christ."

139. "When R. Aqibah saw Bar Koziba he said, 'This is the king, the messiah'" (היינו מלכא משיחא) (Lam. Rab. 2.2.4). Cf. Yadin, *Bar Kokhba*, 22–34.

140. Salkin, "Frankists."

141. Dein, "Lubavitch," 385–97.

142. Cf. Josh 22:17.

something of a mystery, some hypothesizing it to be an orgiastic cult dedicated to an Anatolian-type "lord of fire,"[143] others doubting whether it has anything to do with orgiastic activity at all, Anatolian or otherwise.[144] Whatever its secrets, Numbers depicts Israel's "yoking" of itself to Ba`al Peor as something profoundly horrid (Num 25:3),[145] an opinion reflected in other biblical passages referring to the incident. The psalmist, for example, notes how the participants of the Peor cult "eat sacrifices for the dead" (Ps 106:28). Hosea remembers the Peor incident as a time when Israel "consecrates itself" to something "vain" and "detestable."[146] Joshua speaks simply of "the Peor iniquity" (Josh 22:17).[147]

As the priest responsible for stopping the Peor plague, Phineas secures for himself a revered place in Israelite history (Num 25:7). Granted, the solution he offers is grisly and violent (impalement of a copulating couple), but what's most important to note here is that Phineas is an *Aaronid* priest.[148] Thus, when Phineas "intercedes" (Ps 106:30)[149] with Yhwh on behalf of Israel, the (re)telling of this story constantly reminds Israel of its debt to the Aaronids. Whether or not human sacrifice is *required* to stop the plague is a question complicated by the fact that this is not the only time in Tanak when someone "impales" a cultic violator (Num 25:4).[150] By "piercing" these violators (Num 25:8),[151] Phineas stops a horrendous plague generated by horrendous sin. In other words, Aaronid zeal is the focus of this story, not human sacrifice (Num 25:11).[152] Because they are responsible for "tricking" Israel (Num 25:18),[153] Yhwh's decision to "harass" Midian is therefore just and fair (Num 25:17).[154] When Israel goes on to seek "revenge" against Midian (Num 31:2),[155] the appearance of a much harsher verb spotlights Israel's ambivalence toward things Midianite. On the one hand, Moses' wife

---

143. Mendenhall, *Tenth*, 109.

144. Levine, *Numbers*, 2:294–97.

145. צמד (to yoke).

146. "They consecrate [נזר (to make separate, abstain, vow)] themselves to a shameful thing [בשת] and become detestable [שקוצים] like that which they love [כאהבם]" (Hos 9:10).

147. עון פעור.

148. I.e., not a Levite or a Reubenite (Levine, *Numbers*, 297–300).

149. פלל (to intercede).

150. יקע (to impale); cf. 2 Sam 21:6, 9.

151. דקר (to pierce).

152. קנא (zeal).

153. נכל (to trick, deceive).

154. צרר (to harass).

155. נקם (to avenge).

Zipporah is the daughter of a Midianite priest, a man Moses deeply respects. On the other hand, Midian tries to "trick" Israel through the hiring of Balaam (Num 22:7) and the "yoking" of Israel's male population to Ba`al Peor (25:1-4). So when Israel tries to soften its response to these tragedies, Moses angrily reacts (31:14-18).[156] None of this behavior is explainable apart from a clear understanding of the delicate balance between priestly theology and prophetic theology.[157]

Cases Involving Women (Num 27:1-11; 30:1-16; 36:1-13)

At first glance the final chapters of Numbers seem to follow no discernible outline or literary pattern. Traditions about leadership awkwardly bump into statutes about stewardship. Paragraphs about female vow taking suddenly collide with strategies about war booty. That these are not simply tacked-on appendices, however, becomes clear when the narrative draws parallels between the attitude of Gad-Reuben-Manasseh (Num 32:8-9) and the fatalism of the ten cowardly scouts (13-14). Evidently the refusal of the Gad-Reuben-Manasseh alliance to cross the Jordan covertly links the flaws of the Sinai generation with the flaws of the post-Sinai generation.[158] Yet it's striking that this section, like the book of Proverbs, begins and ends with material about godly women (Prov 1, 8-9; 31:10-31). Literary critics call this type of parallelism *inclusio*; i.e., a feature in which a common theme frames otherwise miscellaneous material. By using *inclusio* narrators can subtly prioritize the issues on their agenda. This in turn implies that of all the issues on *this* narrator's agenda, female inheritance rights are important. Should women be excluded from inheriting land just because they are women? If not, then which provisions should be made to protect *their* inheritance rights?

As with previous "difficult cases," Moses takes this one directly to Yhwh, and the answer he receives is immediate. *Daughters without fathers and brothers can indeed inherit ancestral land* (Num 27:1-11). This ruling shows both Yhwh's wisdom and Moses' flexibility, yet if left unchecked can easily lead to the unraveling of Manasseh's tribal integrity. Thus several of Zelophehad's relatives convince Moses to delimit it, so that Numbers ends with Zelophehad's daughters inheriting property *on the condition* that they marry men within their own tribe, Manasseh (36:1-13). Thus the statutes regulating female vow taking rest on the same patrilineal presumptions with

---

156. Cf. 1 Sam 15:1-35 for a parallel.
157. Cf. Gammie, *Holiness*, 9-44; Moore, *Faith*, 237-48.
158. Olson, *Framework*, 175.

regard to the same patrilineal boundaries (30:1–16). Vows are essential to everyday commerce, but the transactions they validate remain subject to patrilineal approval.

This section therefore highlights the following four themes: (a) equitable justice for all Israelites (including those who find themselves landless through no fault of their own); (b) legislative flexibility in the face of unexplored legal territory (the decision to award land to the daughters of Zelophehad); (c) endogamous marriage (to protect Manasseh's tribal integrity); and (d) a system of checks and balances to protect daily business transactions. Moses highlights these themes because Israel will soon have to face these issues in Canaan with a vengeance.[159] That so many of them focus on women is not lost on the rabbis, who continue these discussions in the third order of the Mishnah, Nashim.[160]

Cases Involving Leadership (Num 27:12–23; 34:16—35:8)

Yhwh prohibits Moses from entering the land for two reasons, one active and one passive. Moses (a) actively participates in the rebellion at Meribah, and (b) passively fails to "show my holiness before the eyes of Israel" (Num 27:14). The first feels more familiar, perhaps, because Yhwh overtly punishes Moses for what he calls his "faithlessness" (20:12).[161] The text later calls this "rebellion" (27:14),[162] but the portrait here contrasts sharply with Moses' recollection in Deuteronomy, where Moses blames the people for the incident (Deut 3:26).[163] The second, passive reason is doubtless less familiar to readers because (a) it highlights a basic flaw in Moses' theological thinking, and (b) most postmoderns, as a general rule, have little appreciation for (or understanding of) the defilement-holiness polarity. In short, Moses does not simply fail to trust Yhwh at Meribah; he fails to exalt Yhwh's "holiness" (20:12). Leadership is many things, but from a priestly perspective it's basically about consecrating the name of God, the Holy One of Israel, the "Holy One in your midst." "Consecration of the name" stands at the very center of priestly holiness theology.[164] Thus when Moses asks the thirsty crowd, "Shall we bring forth water for you?," he crosses the line from sacred to the

---

159. Kunin, *Incest*, 53–61.
160. נשים (*nashim* [women]); cf. Steinsaltz, *Talmud*, 280–81.
161. לא אמן (not believe, trust).
162. מרה (to rebel).
163. ויתעבר יהוה בי למענכם (Yhwh was angry with me on your account; see below).
164. Moses later elaborates this "name" theology in more detail (Deut 12:5; see below).

profane.¹⁶⁵ By failing "to show my holiness before their eyes" he fails to do the job for which he was originally commissioned.

But there is another question here. Why does the mantle of leadership pass to Joshua instead of, say, Eleazar (Aaron's son)? The Aaronids control all religious practice connected to the tabernacle, to be sure, so why does Moses not put Eleazar in charge of the camp? Perhaps the answer to this question lies not in what the text says, but in what it does not say. Note, for example, the conspicuous absence of Aaronid priests in the incident where "the rabble" threaten Joshua and Caleb (Num 13-14). Note also the absence of Aaronid participation in the incident where Moses delegates miraculous spiritual power to seventy lay elders (11:16-30). It would be inappropriate to conclude too much from these silences, and it certainly would be inappropriate to argue for the "superiority" of prophetic leadership over priestly leadership. Yet prophetic leadership is, in fact, a check and balance against the tendency among priesthoods to degenerate into oligarchical aristocracies.¹⁶⁶ This holds true even though Numbers never imagines Joshua as a "prophet" like Moses (Deut 18:15).¹⁶⁷ Moses' sibling conflict with Miriam makes it clear that the deity speaks "face to face" with only one prophet (Num 12:8),¹⁶⁸ and the book of Joshua makes it clear that the source of Joshua's authority is faithful interpretation of the law, not charismatic experience (Josh 1:7-8).¹⁶⁹

Cases Involving Offerings (Num 28:1—29:40)

The offerings in Num 28:1-8 echo the offerings in Exod 29:38-46, with a few minor differences. *First*, Numbers prescribes this offering at the "appointed time" (Num 28:2),¹⁷⁰ while Exodus speaks of it as a "daily" offering (Exod 29:38).¹⁷¹ *Second*, Numbers calls it a "fire offering" (Num 29:13),¹⁷² while Exodus calls it a "holocaust offering" (Exod 29:42).¹⁷³ *Third*, Numbers augments the daily offering with two more, the Sabbath offering and the monthly offering. The rest follow the list laid out in Lev 23—Passover

---

165. Eliade, *Sacred*, 8-18.
166. Cf. VanderKam, *Priests*, 1-42.
167. נביא (prophet).
168. Cf. Moore, "Miriam's."
169. Cf. Schniedewind, *Word*, 1-37.
170. מועד (appointed time).
171. תמיד (daily).
172. אשה (fire).
173. עלה (holocaust).

offering, offerings for the festival of weeks, offerings for the festival of trumpets, offerings for the day of atonement, and offerings for the festival of booths. The Pentateuch preserves three different descriptions of Israel's feasts. Deuteronomy 16 highlights the pilgrimages to the feasts, Num 28-29 the offerings at the feasts, and Lev 23 the feasts themselves. According to Baruch Levine, whether any of these texts are dependent on each other seems far less likely than the possibility of there being some type of common reliance on the traditions underlying Lev 23.[174] This must remain speculative, though, because ascertaining the tradition-histories behind priestly texts is notoriously difficult. The fact that there are several *types* of offerings, however, points to a singular truth—Israel's deep need for divine forgiveness.

Cases Involving Civil Justice (Num 35:1-34)

Asylum is a very old solution to a very old dilemma.[175] Unlike modern Western cultures, where crime victims can appeal to magistrates and courts, ancient tribal cultures allow "avengers of blood" to execute justice and reestablish societal equilibrium (Num 35:9).[176] One does not have to see the *Godfather* films to realize that such a system can easily spin out of control. As a check against vendetta, the law therefore provides "cities of refuge" to regulate and control this primitive form of tribal justice. Several biblical passages mention these cities (Exod 21:13; Deut 4:41-43; 19:1-13; Josh 20). Some, like Numbers, lump them in with the forty-two Levitical cities (making a total of forty-eight cities). Others focus on the crimes for which a refugee might seek asylum, carefully distinguishing between "intentional" (murder) and "unintentional" (manslaughter) killings. Others give the names and locations of these cities: Bezer, Ramoth, and Golan in Transjordan; Kadesh, Shechem, and Hebron in Cisjordan. Continued questioning about them leads Talmud to suggest that if a refugee is a teacher, he can take his students with him into his city of refuge. If a student, he can have a teacher brought there to him.[177] To discourage blood avengers from harassing these cities Talmud bans certain trades like textile making, rope making, and weapons making.[178] To make escape easier some rabbis suggest

---

174. Levine, *Numbers*, 2:394.
175. Snell, *Flight*, 31-62.
176. גאל הדם (avenger of blood).
177. b. Mak. 10a.
178. b. Mak. 10a; see also t. Mak. 3:9.

that road signs be put up at intersections showing directions to the nearest refuge city.[179]

Cases Involving War (Num 31:1—32:42; 33:50—34:15)

Israel's war against Midian destroys some of its most intransigent enemies: (a) the "five kings of Midian" (Evi, Rekem, Zur, Hur, and Reba); (b) Balaam ben Beor; and (c) the women responsible for "tricking" Israel into worshiping Ba'al Peor. This last task, however, collapses into internal struggle as some of Israel's warriors try to bring Midianite women home as wives and servants.[180] This option, however, violates the fundamental principle of holy war, which by definition requires "complete devotion" of *everything* to Yhwh.[181] Since those who ignore this imperative often pay dearly for it,[182] Moses insists that Israel obey the divine imperative with regard to the Midianite women. The only compromise he makes is to spare the virgin Midianite women, presumably because of their absence at Peor. Intrigued by this compromise, some rabbis later question how exactly these "virgins" are to be identified. One suggests that the way to find out is to parade each Midianite woman before the high priest, and if his "forehead plate" turns pale green, this indicates her non-virginal status (!).[183] After a lengthy list of distribution equations the narrative goes on to note that Reuben, Gad, and Manasseh decide to settle in Gilead, not Canaan. Wary of the Reubenites (see Num 13–14, 16), Moses nevertheless accepts this decision, but only on the condition that these three tribes first help the other tribes secure their tribal inheritances. Contemporary archaeologists tend to be skeptical about these traditions, however, because (a) there is no corroborative archaeological evidence for these Israelite tribes ever having been in Transjordan, and (b) the present archaeological evidence suggests that the only destructions in this period occur farther north.[184]

---

179. b. Mak. 10b; t. Mak. 3:5.
180. Cf. Deut 21:10–14.
181. I.e., חרם (complete devotion; cf. von Rad, *Theology*, 1:17).
182. Cf. Josh 7:1; 1 Sam 15:11–23.
183. b. Yebam 60b; see Exod 28:36, ציץ (forehead plate).
184. Dever, "Conquest," 3:547–49.

SUMMARY

The book of Numbers covers a lot of ground. The wilderness-promised land polarity frames the book's overall identity, but within this framework stand several themes.

Cosmic Victory

Numbers documents the ongoing conflict between Yhwh and the gods of the nations. Famous for humbling Egypt's deities, Yhwh takes the cosmic war to the wilderness in Numbers, successfully projecting his "dread" (Num 22:3)[185] over Transjordan and his "terror" over Canaan (Josh 2:9).[186] When Joshua and Caleb testify to the Canaanites' cosmic nakedness, this contrasts sharply with the reality of Yhwh's "shadow" hovering over the tabernacle. Yhwh therefore rebuffs the maneuverings of Balaam and scoffs at the crude temptations of his flatfooted "gods." He surgically removes the cancer at Peor with a plague-forged scalpel. He launches a squadron of seraphim snakes even as he challenges their victims to trust in the power of their Divine Healer.

That Numbers would so intentionally focus on Yhwh's cosmic power is not unusual given the *Zeitgeist* of the premodern world of the ancient Near East. What *is* unusual, however, is the Sinai generation's unwillingness to follow Yhwh, yet his determination to fight for them anyway. It's practically impossible to imagine Ba'al or Marduk or Osiris or Ishtar or any other deity doing such a thing. Why? Because unlike these gods, Yhwh is a covenant-making, covenant-keeping, covenant-sustaining God, and though it's difficult at times to carry this "burden" (Num 11:11), he never abandons it. He never succumbs to cheap magical tricks. He never removes the "shadow" of his protection.[187] Israel's faithlessness never dissuades him from following the "game plan" begun with his promises to Abraham.

Fatalism vs. Faith

Israel's fatalism is understandable. After all, who really prefers the "faith zone" to the "comfort zone"? Who prefers the strange hotel lobby to the familiarity of hearth and home? Translating these polarities into the language

---

185. גור (to dread).
186. אימה (terror).
187. At least not until Ezek 11:22–23.

of Numbers, "Who prefers cold bland manna to hot beef stew?" Were food not to have been the trigger, the "rabble" would doubtless have found some other pretext for harassing Moses. Fatalism, however, as Numbers takes great pains to point out, is simply a synonym for faithlessness. In Numbers Israel struggles to trust Yhwh in the midst of challenge after relentless challenge. When things look hopeless, as they often do in the wilderness, Israel has to decide whether fatalism is preferable to faith, whether the challenge before them is cosmic (Baʿal Peor) or political (Korah, Dathan, Abiram) or missional (the scouts) or financial (Midianite war-booty) or domestic (ritual of the *soṭah*) or painfully familial (Miriam's rebuke). Only when the post-Sinai generation starts trusting in Yhwh does the tone of the book begin to change.

Leadership

Israelite leadership in Numbers breaks down into three categories: *priestly* (Aaronids, Levites), *prophetic* (Moses, Joshua) and *lay* (seventy elders, Nazirites). Each serves a vital function within Yhwh's "game plan." Priestly leadership grabs the lion's share of attention as the text lays out the structure of the camp and the duties of tribe and clan. Aaronid leadership stands at the top of the priestly hierarchy while the Levites serve by hauling the tabernacle and its furniture from place to place. Prophetic leadership complements this work, especially with regard to prophetic intercession. Lay leadership manifests itself in the distribution of the Spirit to seventy Israelite elders, the appointment of tribal leaders, and the Nazirite ritual.

Education

The wilderness is Yhwh's classroom, a place where conflicts appear not as defeats, but as "teaching moments." This seems clear from the fact that several crises conclude with sections preserving statutes based on fundamental principles designed to help Israel avoid similar conflicts in the future. Preeminent among these are the priority of spiritual mission over priestly method (Num 11:26-29), the principle of financial deterrence (15:1-21), the principles of analogy and precedent (15:22-31), the principle of reciprocity (21:1-9), the principle of legal flexibility (27:1-11), the principle of *ḥerem* (total devotion) (31:13-24), the principle of covenant loyalty (32:1-32), the principle of asylum (35:9-34), and the challenge to maintain tribal integrity (36:1-12). To illustrate these principles the narrative lists several visual aids, including Aaron's budding staff, the fringed garments, the cloud over the tabernacle, and the metallic seraph snake.

Priestly Theology

John Gammie observes that "biblical holiness" breaks down into three categories: (a) as ritual cleanness in the priestly literature; (b) as the cleanness of social justice in the prophets, and (c) as the cleanness of individual morality in the wisdom literature.[188] Numbers preserves laws and rituals rooted almost exclusively in the first of these categories, including especially the ritual of the *soṭah*, the ritual of the red heifer, and the Nazirite vow. Like all rituals, these function within a well-defined system based on the axiom that "defilement is lethally contagious."[189] Yet underneath it all lies the conviction that Yhwh of Hosts is absolutely, mysteriously, and ineffably holy. Several seraphim ceaselessly chant this truth in Isaiah ("holy, holy, holy" [Isa 6:3]), and Moses experiences it at the burning bush ("take off your sandals" [Exod 3:5]). The red heifer ritual presumes it because its purpose, like all priestly ritual, is to cleanse that which has become defiled. This emphasis on ritual and sacrifice comes out of the primitive belief that defilement is as real as holiness is ideal. When someone violates a holy boundary, be it spatial or temporal, priestly ritual is the only way to reconnect the violator to the Holy One. Accordingly, priestly theology is the only way for believers to understand how important it is to steer clear of defilement if they want to experience Yhwh's presence.

Prophetic Theology

Prophetic theology is muted, but not absent in Numbers because Moses is the prophet par excellence and prophetic intercession is an important check against the excesses of priestly oligarchy. When Israel's tendency is to pull centripetally inward, the Spirit pushes centrifugally outward. When Aaronids become hyper-exclusivist, Moses reminds them of Yhwh's desire to be globally inclusive; e.g., in the statute permitting aliens and defiled worshipers to celebrate Passover together with the rest of the congregation (Num 9:1–14). Thus one of Numbers' most important directives is that all wilderness wanderers learn how to live healthy spiritual lives balanced between priestly structure *and* spiritual mission.

188. Gammie, *Holiness*, 195–98.
189. Douglas, *Wilderness*, 24.

5

Deuteronomy: Conflict or Covenant?

ORIGINALLY ENTITLED SIMPLY "THE Words" (*haděbarîm*),[1] "Deuteronomy" is a transliteration of Vg *Deuteronomium*, which is itself a transliteration of OG Δευτερονόμιον, a compound word (δευτερος + νομος) meaning "second law," or better, "summary of the law" (Deut 17:18).[2] It's hard to overestimate the importance of this scroll, not just for understanding the Pentateuch, but for understanding Tanak as a whole. Moshe Weinfeld finds in Deuteronomy "the turning point of Israelite religion" because it represents, in his opinion, a "secularized" revision of the Israelite cult.[3] Walter Brueggemann calls it "the theological center of the OT,"[4] and Bill Arnold calls it "a compendium of the most important ideas of the OT."[5] Mark Hamilton calls it "the linchpin of the OT,"[6] while Siegfried Hermann calls it "the center of biblical theology."[7] Recognizing the influence of Deuteronomy on the Former Prophets,[8]

---

1. The first two words are אלה דברים (These are the words [Deut 1:1]), the first of four phrases introducing the major sections of the book, the others being 4:44–45; 29:1; and 33:1.

2. משנה התורה הזות על ספר (a copy of this law on a scroll). OG reads δευτερονόμιον τοῦτο εἰς βιβλίον; cf. Vg *deuteronomium legis huius in volumine*; Syr ܢܡܘܣܐ (the law) is a transliteration of νόμος (law).

3. Weinfeld thinks that "the very purpose of Deuteronomy is to curtail and circumvent the cult" and that it pursues this through its "open dependence on the wisdom tradition" ("Deuteronomy," 2:175, 181–82).

4. Brueggemann, *Canon*, 37.

5. Arnold, *Deuteronomy*, 1.

6. M. Hamilton, "Deuteronomy," 203.

7. S. Herrmann, "Restauration."

8. The "former prophets" (הנבים הראשנים) (Zech 7:4, 7, 12) include Joshua, Judges,

Martin Noth suggests that instead of simply being a summation of the law, Deuteronomy is for all intents and purposes a theological introduction to Joshua-Kings.[9] Agreeing with Noth, Weinfeld imagines a "deuteronomistic" trajectory developing in three stages: (a) the book of Deuteronomy, (b) DH (Joshua-Kings), and (c) the prose sermons of Jeremiah.[10] This he bases on his thesis that "deuteronomic composition is the creation of scribal circles which begin their literary project some time prior to the reign of Josiah."[11]

LITERARY-HISTORICAL CONTEXT

Since this is the only book claiming to have been "written" by Moses (Deut 3:19),[12] Deuteronomy (or significant parts thereof) is (a) widely held to be the "scroll of the law" discovered in the temple during the reign of Josiah (d. 609 BCE) (2 Kgs 22:8)[13] and (b) likely serves as the primary impetus for the Josianic reformation.[14] Another reason for associating Deuteronomy with this reformation is the unusually close parallels between the curse sequences in Deut 28 and the curse sequences in the NA Vassal Treaties of Esarhaddon.[15] John Collins thus argues the majority opinion that Deu-

---

1–2 Samuel, and 1–2 Kings.

9. Noth argues that "given that the books Genesis-Numbers ... look completely different from Joshua-Kings, we can only conclude that the books Genesis-Numbers, or at any rate the form of these books that antedate the Priestly work, are no part of Dtr's work" (*Studien*, 13).

10. Following Duhm (*Jeremia*), Mowinckel subdivides Jeremiah into four "sources": A—the words of the historical prophet; B—words from the scribe Baruch; C—sermonic prose from a later writer using Dtr vocabulary and style; and D—the "book of Consolation" (Jer 30–31) (*Jeremia*). Sharp prefers to call the C material "deutero-Jeremianic prose" (*Jeremiah*, 17).

11. Weinfeld, *School*, 9 (following Kaufmann, *Religion*, 157). This hypothesis sharply challenges the Wellhausenian view that the priestly literature (P) is *younger* than the deuteronomic literature (D). Monroe challenges Weinfeld's reconstruction, positing instead an early account with parallels in priestly ritual texts followed by a later, postmonarchic, deuteronomistic version recasting Josiah as the only Judahite king fully able to appreciate the obligations and limitations of the Mosaic Code (*Reform*). Elrefaei documents the ins and outs of this debate (*Wellhausen*).

12. ויכתב משה את התורה הזות (and Moses wrote down this law).

13. ספר התורה (scroll of the law). Actually this scroll is discovered by workers, who take it to Hilkiah the high priest, who takes it to Shaphan the scribe, who reads it to King Josiah, who tears his clothes when he hears it.

14. Cf. Wette, *Versuch*, 175–79 (cf. discussion in Moore, *Faith*, 260–62). Some would counter that this scroll is a *reflection* of the Josianic reformation, not its *cause*.

15. For photographs, transliterations, and translations of VTE cf. Wiseman, "Esarhaddon," 29–99. Steymans lists some of these parallels in detail: (a) the same curse

teronomy "draws on history as a motivational tool and reinforces the commandments with curses and blessings corresponding to that of the ancient vassal treaties."[16]

For Diana Edelman, "it is common for textbooks to describe the book of Deuteronomy as a lawcode (chaps. 12–26) framed secondarily by narratives (chaps. 1–11 and 27–34)," arguing that this "understanding derives from the partial overlap in material in chaps. 12–26 with what has been identified as legal formulations in Exodus and Leviticus."[17] Without going into all the reasons behind this hypothesis, the pages below focus rather on Moses' words to the post-Sinai generation through a theological lens ground by the conflict-covenant polarity. This is hardly the first attempt to read Deuteronomy this way. Raymond Brown, for example, similarly interprets it in his TBST commentary, subdividing it into five sections:[18]

- Introducing the covenant (1:1—4:43)
- Expounding the covenant (4:44—11:32)
- Applying the covenant (12:1—26:19)
- Confirming the covenant (27:1—30:20)
- Sharing the covenant (31:1—34:12)

MOSES' FIRST SPEECH (DEUT 1:1—4:43)

Moses' first speech picks up Israel's history at the point where Israel pulls up stakes to leave Mt. Horeb (Num 10:11–13).[19] Having just received the law it is quite telling that Israel's first instinct is not to pray or serve each other on the upcoming journey, but to "quarrel" (Deut 1:12).[20] Moses reminds

---

motifs occur in the same sequence in VTE §§39, 40, 42 and Deut 28:27–30 (skin-disease, darkness, and violated wife); and (b) the same *kinds* of motifs occur in VTE §§63–64 and Deut 28:23–24 (sky and earth made of metal, rain turns into coal and ashes) (*Deuteronomium*). The question as to whether Deuteronomy is *literarily* dependent on VTE, however, remains a matter of debate. Whereas Frankena ("Esarhaddon"), Weinfeld ("Traces"), and Steymans (*Deuteronomium*) argue *for* literary dependence, McCarthy (*Treaty*, 111, 113, 135), Hillers (*Treaty*, 83–89), and Crouch (*Assyrians*, 47–92) argue *against* it (cf. Moore, Review of *Deuteronomium*; and Lauinger, "Treaty").

16. J. Collins, *Hebrew Bible*, 164–65.

17. Edelman, "Introduction," 1.

18. Brown, *Deuteronomy*. The polar star for this approach comes from Deut 4:23: "Be careful to keep the covenant which Yhwh your God has made with you."

19. Sinai is always called Horeb in Deuteronomy (G. Davies, "Sinai").

20. MT ריבכם (your quarreling, sg.); OG τὰς ἀντιλογίας ὑμῶν (your quarrels, pl.);

them that because of this behavior the job of leadership is a "heavy burden,"[21] and that this is why he is forced to choose leaders from every tribe (except Levi) to help out. Arriving at Kadesh, twelve men are chosen to scout the land, but even after they return with a positive assessment (Deut 1:25),[22] the quarreling does not stop—in fact, it gets worse.[23] In other words, the chaos generated by incessant internal conflict threatens to destroy all the positive gains made since the call of Moses and, indeed, since the call of Abraham.

MOSES' SECOND SPEECH (DEUT 4:44—11:32)

In his second speech Moses reminds Israel that Yhwh makes covenants not only with their ancestors, "but with all of us alive here today" (Deut 5:3). The Horeb covenant he then fleshes out by attending carefully to the principles in the Decalogue (i.e., Ten Commandments), differing only slightly from the Exodus version in its rationale for keeping the Sabbath (Deut 15:12–15). Moshe Weinfeld explains: "Sabbath is a day of identification with the creator who rests from his work in order to contemplate on the one hand (Exodus version), and a day of identification with the slave and servant who need to rest, on the other (Deuteronomic version)."[24]

Chapter 6 features the Shema, the closest thing in the Pentateuch to a short credo:[25]

שמע ישראל	Hear, O Israel!
יהוה אלהינו	Yhwh is our God,
יהוה אחד	Yhwh alone!
ואהבת את יהוה אלהיך	And you shall love Yhwh your God

Syr ܡܘܒܠܝܟܘܢ ܘܡܣܒܝܟܘܢ ܘܕܝܢܝܟܘܢ (your donations and your burdens and your judgments, pl.); Tg. Ps.-J. "How can I alone sustain the labor, your sensuality, your evil thoughts, your words of strife [מילי דגנבון, pl.]?"

21. Deut 1:12 and Num 11:17 both use the term משא (burden, oracle).

22. Cf. Num 13:28.

23. Cf. Asaph's summary in Ps 78:12–17: "In the sight of their ancestors he worked marvels in the land of Egypt, in the fields of Zoan. He divided the sea and let them pass through it, and made the waters stand like a heap. In the daytime he led them with a cloud, and all night long with a fiery light. He split rocks open in the wilderness, and gave them drink abundantly as from the deep. He made streams come out of the rock, and caused waters to flow down like rivers. Yet they sinned still more against him, rebelling against the Most High in the desert."

24. Weinfeld, *Deuteronomy 1–11*, 302 (see above on Exod 20).

25. Von Rad identifies longer credos in Deut 26:5–9 and Josh 24:2–13 ("Hexateuch").

בכל לבבך with all your heart,

בכל נפשך with all your soul,

ובכל מאדך and with all your strength. (Deut 6:4–5)[26]

Reminding them of the scouts' positive assessment of the land,[27] he warns them not to abandon their Emancipator after they take possession of it, and especially not to worship the lifeless deities of its inhabitants. Should Israel give in to the social pressure and conform to Canaanite religious culture, Yhwh will treat this as an unwarranted "test" of the covenant and respond accordingly. Thus the best way to avoid such a scenario is to avoid contact with the land's inhabitants as much as possible.[28]

Chapter 7 goes into greater detail. *First*, there is only one God and only one covenant.[29] To negotiate covenants with other nations, however well-intended, is categorically forbidden. This includes intermarriage because this exposes the children of such unions to idolatrous defilement before they can even tell the difference between right and wrong, much less recognize Yhwh as the one true God.[30] *Second*, they need to stop defining themselves as "grasshoppers." Should they be threatened by the land's inhabitants, Yhwh will keep his covenant promise to protect them. Previewing the blessings at the end of the third speech (Deut 28:1–14), ch. 7 closes with lavish promises of blessing for personal, social, and economic health (7:12–14).[31]

Chapter 8 goes deeper. Moses tells them that the reason why Yhwh allows them to experience hunger in the wilderness is (a) to humble them and (b) to teach them that "man does not live by bread alone, but by every word from the mouth of God" (8:3).[32] Yhwh disciplines his people for the same

---

26. When asked about "the greatest commandment" the Nazarene prophet unhesitatingly responds by citing this credo (Mark 12:29).

27. Expounding the scouts' report—essentially negative in Numbers—Moses specifically mentions the "houses already stocked with supplies," the "cisterns already dug," and the "vineyards and olive groves already planted" (Deut 6:10–11).

28. To say that this is a major theme in Deuteronomy is the "mother of all understatements."

29. The Moabite covenant mentioned in Deut 28:69 (ET 29:1) is essentially the Sinai covenant more methodically applied (D. Christensen, *Deuteronomy 1—21:9*, 221, pace Weinfeld, "Deuteronomy," 2:168).

30. Cf. 2 Cor 6:14. N.b. that Jeremiah later encourages intermarriage (Jer 29:6).

31. Braulik carefully chronicles the supple relationship between "blessing" and "covenant" in Deuteronomy ("Gottesbund").

32. This is the first text the Nazarene prophet quotes to the devil during his desert fast (Matt 4:4).

reason a parent disciplines a child—to help them reach maturity.³³ Yhwh is excited about their prospects because after forty years in the wilderness they finally stand on the edge of a beautiful land filled with flowing streams, abundant fruits and vegetables, and valuable metals like iron and copper.³⁴ The worry, however, is that reception of these blessings might lead them into a mindset where they start believing that *they* are the ones responsible for it all:

ואמרת בלבבך	Do not say in your heart,
כחי ועצם ידי	"My power and the might of my own hand
עשה לי את החיל הזה	have made this wealth for me."³⁵
וזכרת את יהוה אלהיך	But remember Yhwh your God
כי הוא הנתן כח לעש חיל	for he is the one who gives you the ability to make wealth
למען הקים את בריתו	so that he may affirm his covenant³⁶
אשר נשבע לאבתיך	which he swore to your ancestors. (Deut 8:17–18)³⁷

Chapter 9 follows up with a warning to Israel not to imagine their "righteousness" as being in any way responsible for their inheritance of the land.³⁸ Israel's "righteousness" hardly obligates Yhwh to give them anything,³⁹ but there is another, darker concern. Yhwh dispossesses the peoples of Canaan because (a) they are covered in sin and paralyzed by "wickedness" (9:4)⁴⁰

---

33. Cf. Heb 12:7–11.

34. Moses revisits this fertility/prosperity imagery in Deut 11:10–12, adding that should they abandon the covenant and turn to other gods Yhwh will shut off this fertility/prosperity (11:13–18).

35. Cf. Moore, *WealthWatch*, 223–31.

36. MT קום in the Š form; OG στήσῃ τὴν διαθήκην αὐτοῦ (make his covenant stand); Vg *impleret pactum suum* (implement his pact); Tg. Ps.-J. לקיימא ית קיימיה דקימם לאבהתכון (to confirm that which he established with your fathers; lit., to establish that which is established which he established with your fathers).

37. Fee challenges any attempt to interpret this passage as a "biblical rationale" for the "prosperity gospel" (*Disease*, 3). Qur'an remembers that when "Alla sets forth the example of a society safe and at ease, gathering its provision in abundance from all directions," and "its people reject Alla's favors," he will respond to such ingratitude by "letting them wear [فاذقها] (lit., taste)] the garb of hunger" (لباس‌الجوع) (Q 16:112).

38. Isa 64:6 warns returning exiles that their self-declared "righteousness" is so "defiled" (טמא), it looks like a "menstrual rag" (בגד עדים).

39. Cf. Isa 57:12–14.

40. ברשעת הגוים האלה יהוה מורישם (for the wickedness of these nations Yhwh is

and because (b) the oath he swore to Israel's ancestors—Abraham, Isaac, and Jacob—obligates him to keep his promises (9:5):[41]

וידעת כי לא בצדקתך	Understand that it is not because of your righteousness[42]
יהוה אלהיך נתן לך הארץ הטובה הזאת	that Yhwh your God gives you this good land,
לרשתה	to inherit it.
כי עם קשה ערף אתה	For you are a stiff-necked people. (Deut 9:6)[43]
ממרים הייתם עם יהוה	You have been rebellious against Yhwh[44]
מיום דעתי אתכם	from the day he has known you. (Deut 9:24)

The remainder of the chapter engages Israelite history from this *Realpolitik* perspective, spotlighting the fact that Israel's rebellious spirit can be so inflexible, Moses sometimes "fears" that Yhwh will abandon his covenant and "exterminate" them (9:19).[45] In chs. 10 and 11 Moses tells the story of the re-chiseling of two stone tablets upon which the Ten Commandments are rewritten (10:1),[46] along with the creation of the ark, the placement inside it of these inscribed tablets, and his eighty days of fasting on their behalf (forty days each trip) (Deut 10:3–5, 10). Then he asks the crucial, all-important question:

ועתה ישראל מה יהוה אלהיך שאל מעמך	Now Israel, what does Yhwh your God ask of you,
כי אם ליראה יהוה אלהיך	except to fear Yhwh your God,

---

dispossessing them; repeats verbatim in 9:5). Heb ירש can mean either "(dis)inherit" or "(dis)possess."

41. Cf. Heb 6:17–18.

42. Kissane observes that "the book of Job is a discussion of the problem of retribution—the apparent contradiction between the doctrine of the justice of God and the facts of human experience" (*Job*, xv).

43. The "stiff-necked" metaphor recurs in 9:13 and elsewhere (e.g., Exod 32:9; 33:3; 34:9). Cf. Deut 10:16, ערפכם לא תקשו עוד (do not stiffen your neck any longer).

44. מרה (to rebel); Syr ܡܡܪܡܪܝܢ (contentious); OG ἀπειθοῦντες (disobedient); Vg *rebelles*. N.b. that the verb ידע (to know) bookends this text.

45. יגר (to be afraid); שמד (to exterminate). Cf. Exod 32:10.

46. Cf. Exod 34:1.

ללכת בכל דרכיו	to walk on all his paths,
לאהבה אתו ולעבד יהוה אלהיך	to love him and serve Yhwh your God[47]
בכל לבבך ובכל נפשך	with all your heart and all your soul,
לשמר את מצות יהוה אלהיך	to keep the commandments of Yhwh your God
ואת חקתיו	and his statutes
אשר אנכי מצוך היום לטובלך	which I am commanding you today for your good? (Deut 10:12–13)[48]

Moses reminds his audience that Yhwh plans to continue to protect them from *external* (Egyptian Pharaoh) as well as *internal* conflict (the Reubenites Dathan and Abiram),[49] warning them that if they choose to disobey the law they will lack the strength to do what needs to be done to "inherit the land" (Deut 11:8).[50] Foreshadowing the blessings and curses at the end of the third speech (chs. 27–28), he then concludes:

ראה אנכי נתן לפניכם היום	Look, I set before you today
ברכה וקללה	a blessing and a curse:
את הברכה אשר תשמעו	the blessing if you obey[51]
אל מצות יהוה אלהיך	the commandments of Yhwh your God
אתכם היום אשר אנכי מצוה	which I am commanding you today;
והקללה אם לא תשמעו	and the curse if you do not obey
אל מצות יהוה אלהיך	the commandments of Yhwh your God
וסרתם הדרך	and turn away from the path

---

47. אהב (love); cf. Deut 5:10; 6:5; 7:9, 13; 10:15, 19; 11:1; 13:3; 30:6). N.b. that it is not "to love and serve," but "to love *him* [אתו] and serve." Moran points out that "love" is often a sociopolitical notion shared between ANE monarchs and vassals to strengthen alliances and treaties ("Deuteronomy"; cf. Moore, *What Is This Babbler*, 140–55), and Spicq calls Deuteronomy "the biblical document *par excellence* about 'love'" (*Agapè*, 89).

48. Enkidu's courtesan articulates a very different conception of the "good life": "O come, Enkidu, into Sheepfolded Uruk, where young men wear bright sashes, where every day is a feast day, where the drums rumble, where the courtesans (are fair) of form.... O Enkidu, this is the good life" (*hadû balaṭa* [GE 1.226–33]; cf. Moore, *WealthWatch*, 64).

49. N.b. that Korah the Kohathite is not mentioned (con. Num 16:1).

50. ירש (inherit, possess, occupy); Norbert Lohfink, "ירש," *TDOT* 6:368–96.

51. שמע (Syr ܫܡܥ) means either "hear" or "obey," depending on context. Here OG reads ἀκούσητε (hear) while Vg reads *oboedieritis* (obey).

אשר אנכי מצוה אתכם היום   which I am commanding you today
ללכת אחרי אלהים אחרים   to walk after other gods
אשר לא ידעתם   which you do not know. (Deut 11:26–28)[52]

MOSES' THIRD SPEECH (DEUT 12:1—26:19)

Moses' third speech is by far the longest section of the book, preserving what many hold to be a close facsimile to the "book of the law" discovered in the temple and presented to Josiah.[53] Analyzing its structure, Duane Christensen observes that far from being random, each section of the speech is an exposition (in order) of the Ten Commandments:[54]

1. Preamble/introduction (Deut 11:29—12:1)

2. "No other gods before me" (5:7-10)—worship at the central sanctuary (12:2—13:19)

3. "Taking Yhwh's name in vain" (5:11)—a holy people set apart for God (14:1–21)

4. "Remember the Sabbath" (5:12-15)—cult and society in sacred rhythm (14:22—16:17)

5. "Parental respect" (5:16)—authority in ancient Israel (16:8—18:22)

6. "Do not murder" (5:17)—murder, justice, and war (19:1—21:9)

7. "Do not commit adultery" (5:18)—marriage, family, and sex (21:10—24:4)

8. Theft, false testimony, coveting (5:19-21)—humanitarian concerns (24:5—25:16)[55]

---

52. In Hosea Yhwh laments that his people no longer "know" him (ידע [Hos 2:8; ET 2:10]; cf. Moore, *WealthWarn*, 94).

53. "When the king heard the words of the book of the law [ספר התורה] he tore his clothes" (2 Kgs 22:11). Cf. Moore, *Faith*, 260-62.

54. D. Christensen, *Deuteronomy 1—21:9*, 221.

55. For obvious reasons the following discussion cannot address in detail every law and statute in Deut 12-26.

No Other Gods before Me (Deut 12:1—13:19)

At the core of this first exposition stands a simple contrast between two words: "places" and "place." Whereas the nations worship false gods at various "places," the one true God is to be worshiped at only one "place"—the "place where he causes his name to dwell."[56] Prior to this statute sacrifices and gifts are brought to Yhwh's "house" (Exod 23:19),[57] but Deuteronomy submits what Gerhard von Rad calls a "theological corrective"[58] dissociating the person of the deity from any and all earthly "places."[59] Yhwh dwells in heaven. Only his name inhabits an earthly "place."[60] As Weinfeld recognizes, this corrective represents one of Deuteronomy's key contributions to biblical theology because it so thoroughly replaces "the ancient popular belief that the deity actually dwells within the sanctuary."[61] Agreeing with this assessment, Michael Hundley lays out what he sees to be two possible interpretations: "Is the Temple for the Name (a) merely a forwarding station that sends human concerns to God in heaven, or (b) is the Name some form of representative presence, perhaps approaching hypostasis?"[62]

The point here, of course, is that regardless of the answer to this question, the deeper conflict here is profoundly cosmic; i.e., the conflict between Yhwh and the gods of Canaan. Not only is the first commandment the foundation of the other nine, but the decision to obey it obliges Israel to follow Yhwh's example in deposing idolatrous imposters. Not only are their "dwellings" to be destroyed, but also the human voices used to seduce his people into breaking covenant. Moses warns Israel that there will be different voices vying for their attention in the days to come—diviners, prophets, "children of Belial"—but that the least expected (and most effective) will come from their own family and friends. *Question:* "Why does Yhwh allow all this to go on?" *Answer:* "To 'test' the sincerity of Israel's covenant 'love'" (Deut 13:4).[63]

---

56. Deut 12:5 *et passim*. Most see this as a reference to the tabernacle/temple.

57. בית יהוה אלהיך (house of Yhwh your God).

58. Von Rad, *Deuteronomium-Studien*, 25–30.

59. Richter, *Name*, 127.

60. Exactly what this means is not crystal clear; cf. the suggestions of I. Wilson (*Fire*), Richter (*Name*), and Hundley ("Name," 533–55). Qu'ran, of course, teaches that "the messiah, Jesus, son of Mary, is no more than a messenger of Alla. . . . So believe in Alla and his messengers and do not say trinity [ثلاثة (lit., three)] . . . for Alla alone is the one God" (Q 4:171).

61. Weinfeld, "Deuteronomy," 2:175; cf. Hurowitz, "Storm."

62. Hundley, "Name," 533–34.

63. נסה (to test; n.b. this is the same term used to describe the "testing" of Abraham

A Holy People Set Apart for God (Deut 14:1–21)

Ever sensitive to the danger of defilement, Moses warns Israel not to eat anything deemed "abhorrent," listing several examples. Recognizing the widespread appeal of death cults, he prohibits specific types of body markings and shavings designed to satisfy requirements for membership in such cults.[64] John Betlyon notes that "the deuteronomistic legal material and the Holiness Code stand out in the ancient Near East for their prohibitions against conjuring or consulting the spirits of the dead."[65]

Cult and Society in Sacred Rhythm (Deut 14:22—16:17)

Sensitive to reality, Moses gives permission to anyone living far away from the central sanctuary to exchange livestock for money and use it to buy meat slaughtered at the "place where he causes his name to dwell." Every third year Israel is to bring its tithe and distribute it to the Levites. Every seventh year all Israelite debts are to be forgiven. Payment can be required from foreigners, but not fellow Israelites. Why? Because Yhwh wants to make sure that the poor do not "fall between the cracks." There will always be needy neighbors,[66] but those who *have* must give liberally (not cynically) to help those who *have not*. When slaves are set free they are to be given what they need to become independent. Why? Because Israel was once in bondage to Egypt, and Yhwh graciously freed *them*. So, as the Sabbath provides a sacred rhythm to weekly living, so the festivals of Passover, Weeks (Pentecost), and Tabernacles provide a sacred rhythm to yearly occasions.

Authority in Ancient Israel (Deut 16:8—18:22)

Even as parents are to be obeyed, so must recognized community leaders be accorded the same respect.[67] Granted, political and judicial leaders must

---

[Gen 22:1]); אהב (to love) (13:4; ET 13:3). Qur'an claims that "we took from the prophets their covenant [ميثقهم, from وثق (to trust in, depend upon)] . . . from Noah, Abraham, Moses, and Jesus, son of Mary" (Q 33:7).

64. Cf. Jer 16:5; Amos 6:7. T. Lewis defines "death cult" as "those acts directed toward the deceased functioning either to placate the dead or to secure favors from them for the present life" (*Cults*, 2).

65. Betlyon, Review, 109. T. Lewis observes that Deuteronomy represents a clear "attempt to combat a cult of the dead" (*Cults*, 175). Cf. Deut 18:9–14; 1 Sam 28:3–25; 2 Sam 12:15–24; 18:18; 2 Kgs 9:34–37; 13:20–21; 21:6; 23:24.

66. "The poor you have with you always" (Matt 26:11 // Mark 14:7 // John 12:8).

67. Cf. Rom 13:1.

earn the respect of their communities by refusing to show partiality or take bribes. But if someone is accused of a capital offense, and evidence is brought against them by two or three witnesses, they are to be judged, convicted, and sentenced, so that "you shall purge the evil in your midst" (Deut 17:7). If a given case proves too difficult to judge, then it is to be transferred to a higher court whose decision is final. If the justice system so created is thus respected, then "all the people will fear" and justice will occur.

If the populace decides to coronate a king, there are rules he must respect.[68] He must not be a foreigner. He must not sate himself with excessive wealth or numerous wives. Most importantly, he must keep a "copy of the law" (Deut 17:18)[69] and "read it every day for the rest of his life" (17:19). Perfectly willing to sound like a broken record, Moses warns Israel repeatedly "not to imitate the abhorrent practices of the nations" (18:9),[70] especially practices like child sacrifice, divination, sorcery, augury, soothsaying, and necromancy.[71] There is only one source from which messages from the unseen world are acceptable; viz., the words spoken by "a prophet in your midst, among your brothers, like me" (18:15).[72]

Murder, Justice, and War (Deut 19:1—21:9)

When it comes to murder, the keywords are "intentional" vs. "unintentional." If a man unintentionally kills someone (manslaughter), then that killer can flee to a city of refuge.[73] But if a man flees to a refuge city after intentionally killing someone (murder), then the leaders of his village can have him extradited and handed over to the "avenger of blood" (Deut 19:6).[74] As for the judgement process itself, false witnesses are to be punished with the same penalty as that to which they would subject the innocent. In wartime two scenarios are to be distinguished: (a) war against distant towns and villages and (b) war against Canaanite villages designated for repossession.

---

68. This section of the book is often cited to "prove" that Deuteronomy cannot be a premonarchic text.

69. משנה התורה; OG δευτερονόμιον; Vg *deuteronomium*.

70. לא תלמד לעשות כתועבת (lit., you shall not learn to do such abhorrent things); OG βδελύγματα (detestable things); Vg *abominationes* (abominations).

71. Cf. Kuemmerlin-McLean, "Magic."

72. נביא מקבך מאחיך כמני. Cf. Petersen, *Roles*; R. Wilson, *Prophecy*; Stökl, *Prophecy*; Moore, *WealthWarn*, 56–121.

73. Eventually there are six cities of refuge, as indicated in Num 35:6–28 (cf. Kislev, "Refuge").

74. גאל הדם. Cf. Moore, "הגאל."

In the first Israel is to execute the men, but take the women, children, and livestock as spoil. In the second, however, Israel is to destroy everyone and everything. Why?

למען אשר לא ילמדו אתכם	So that they may not teach you
לעשות ככל תועבותם	to do all their abhorrent things
אשר עשו לאלהיהם	which they do for their gods,
וחטאתם ליהוה אלהיכם	and you thus sin against Yhwh your God.
	(Deut 20:18)

Exemptions from battle are few: (a) a new house not yet dedicated, (b) a new vineyard not yet harvested, (c) a marriage not yet consummated,[75] and (d) a fearful spirit.

Marriage, Family, and Sex (Deut 21:10—24:4)

As mentioned above, Deuteronomy preserves a law prohibiting a man with two wives from preferring the firstborn of the favored wife over his biological firstborn.[76] Other laws in this section include the following: If a man takes a wife as a prisoner of war and she proves unacceptable, he cannot sell her into slavery. If a son ignores the discipline of his father the latter can take him before the town council and have him executed. If someone is hung on a tree to die, the corpse must be taken down and buried within twenty-four hours. Parapets must be built onto the roofs of two-story buildings to protect guests from falling off and injuring themselves. Cross-dressing is forbidden. If a man falsely accuses his wife of promiscuity, the tokens of her virginity are to be provided to protect her from punishment, and the husband shall pay her father one hundred shekels of silver. If, on the other hand, her virginity cannot be proven, she is to be executed. If a virgin engaged to be married is raped in town, both she and the rapist are to be executed—the virgin because she does not cry out for help, and the man because he has violated his neighbor's fiancée. If the same crime occurs outside of town, however, only the rapist is to be executed, the presumption being that even if she cries out, nobody will hear it.

Ammonites and Moabites are prohibited from attending Yhwh's assembly, as are genitally injured men and bastards. Edomites and Egyptians,

---

75. Deut 24:5 allows a newly married man one year of leave with his new wife before returning to service.

76. Cf. above discussion on patriarchal prejudice, particularly in the Joseph novella.

however, are not to be so harshly treated—Edomites because they are kin, and Egyptians because of Israel's sojourn in Egypt as a resident alien. Finally, if a man divorces his wife and she remarries, but then becomes a widow or a divorcee, she cannot remarry her first husband.

Humanitarian Concerns (Deut 24:5—25:16)

The final section of the third speech deals mainly with socioeconomic concerns. For example, when a creditor takes a pledge from a debtor he cannot run roughshod over him, but must treat him with dignity and respect. A creditor cannot take the millstone of a miller who needs it to make a living. No one can kidnap and sell a fellow Israelite. When collecting a debt, a creditor cannot go into the debtor's home, but must wait outside for the debtor to bring payment out to him. A creditor cannot take a poor debtor's coat overnight, but must return it to him so that he does not become ill. Widows are not obligated to part with their clothing to pay off debts. Resident aliens and orphans must be similarly treated. Employers must pay their employees their wages every day before sunset. No field shall be harvested so thoroughly that the poor cannot find enough grain or olives or grapes to make a meal.[77] No family should have to endure the loss of their ancestral name. Thus if a brother dies, the living brother is obligated to take the widow into his family and support her, and any child born of that union must take the name of the deceased husband.

MOSES' FOURTH SPEECH (DEUT 26:1—28:68)

Chapters 26-28 are comprised of three sections: (a) a creedal statement summarizing Israelite history in just a few sentences, (b) a list of blessings to be conferred upon those who keep the covenant, and (c) a list of curses to be conferred upon those who do not.[78]

---

77. Ruth the Moabite takes advantage of this statute to safeguard the stability of her mother-in-law, Naomi (Ruth 2:2).

78. Many ANE treaties conclude with blessings and curses similar to those found in Deut 27-28; e.g., *KAI* 222.21-42; 224.1-24; VTE 414-93, 519-29; and *KBo* 1.54'-69' (cf. Barrett, *Deuteronomy*, 160-201).

SUMMARY: MOSES' FIFTH SPEECH (DEUT 29:1–33:29)

To call this section a "speech" is misleading because it is little more than a loose summary of Mosaic traditions sutured together to fashion a satisfying ending to the book of Deuteronomy as well as the Pentateuch proper. Chapters 29 and 30 are sermonic reviews, but the remaining chapters serve different roles. Chapter 31 is an address to Joshua to prepare him for leadership after he crosses the Jordan. Chapter 32 is a "song" (Deut 31:30)[79] reviewing Israelite history from a *Realpolitik* perspective. Chapter 33 is a series of blessings on each of the twelve tribes,[80] and ch. 34 is Moses' final epitaph. The temptation is great to follow Moses here and focus on the ominous:

ויאמר יהוה אל משה	Yhwh said to Moses,
הנך שכב עם אבותיך	"Soon you will lie down with your ancestors.
וקם העם הזה וזנה	Then this people will rise up and prostitute themselves
אחרי אלהי נכר הארץ	to strange gods in the land....
ועזבני והפר את בריתי	They will abandon me and break my covenant
אשר כרתי אתו	which I cut with them.
והרה אפי בו ביום ההוא	On that day my anger will burn against them,
ועזבתים והסתרתי פני מהם	I will abandon them and hide my face from them,
והיה לאכל ומצאוהו	so that those who find them will devour them,
רעות רבות וצרות	inflicting great grief and distress,
ואמר ביום ההוא	and on that day they will ask,
הלא על כי אין אלהי	'Have these troubles not come upon us
בקרבי מצאוני הרעות האלה	because our God is no longer in our midst?'"
	(Deut 31:16–17)

Of course, all this eventually comes true, but the matter-of-fact tone here at the end of the Pentateuch is enough to catch anyone off guard, and seems to go a step or two beyond *Realpolitik*: "As soon as you die, Moses, everything will unravel. Not only will Israel break my covenant, but they will prostitute themselves to other gods." Hosea is famous for manipulating the

---

79. שירה (song).

80. De Geus points out that Tanak preserves two versions of the twelve tribes' confederacy: (a) "system A" includes Levi and the tribe of Joseph; (b) "system B" excludes Levi and substitutes Ephraim and Manasseh for Joseph. The listing in Deut 33 follows the format of "system A" ("Gad," 2:864).

"prostitution" motif (Hos 2:4) and Jeremiah uses the term זנה (to prostitute) to (a) identify Israel's infidelity and (b) link it to the collapse of the Judahite economy (Jer 2:20).[81] The same can be said for the final speech in DH. To the question "Why has Yhwh allowed foreigners to destroy the temple?," the narrator answers:

> This occurred because the people of Israel sinned against Yhwh their God, who had brought them up out of the land of Egypt from under the hand of Pharaoh king of Egypt. They worshiped other gods and walked in the customs of the nations whom Yhwh drove out before the people of Israel. . . . They built for themsleves high places in all their towns. . . . They set up pillars and sacred poles on every high hill and under every green tree. . . . Yhwh warned Israel and Judah by every prophet and every seer . . . but they were stubborn and would not listen, like their ancestors. . . . They despised his statutes and his covenant that he made with their ancestors. . . . Therefore Yhwh was very angry with Israel and removed them from his sight. (2 Kgs 17:7–18)

---

81. Cf. Moore, *WealthWarn*, 89–97; Moore, *Faith*, 343–50.

Concluding Remarks

THE PENTATEUCH IS A masterpiece for several reasons, but not least because it so thoroughly engages Israel's most basic theological polarities: *chaos-creation* (Genesis), *slavery-freedom* (Exodus), *defilement-holiness* (Leviticus), *wilderness-homeland* (Numbers), and *conflict-covenant* (Deuteronomy). Echoes of these polarities reverberate throughout the rest of Tanak into Mishnah, Talmud, GNT, other midrashim, and the Judeo-Christian tradition generally, not to mention its later echoes in Qur'an and the hadiths. One simply cannot understand the nature of ancient or contemporary religious conflict apart from a clear grasp of these basic polarities. They huddle together at the center not only of biblical theology, but of Western cultural thought. Much, much more may be said, of course, but because this is a "short theological introduction," we will stop here. The title of the present volume, *Chaos or Covenant*, is a well-meaning, albeit feeble attempt to try and capture the meaning of the Pentateuch in just a couple of words. This is impossible, of course, but nonetheless it is hoped that this volume will help beginning students understand this library a bit more clearly, and colleagues more readily distinguish what is more important in the Pentateuch from what is less so.

Bibliography

Abba, Raymond. "Priests and Levites." *IDB* 3:876–89.
Abrahams, Israel, and Cecil Roth. "Cassuto, Umberto." *EncJud* 4:510–11.
Abusch, Tzvi. "Sacrifice in Mesopotamia." In *Sacrifice in Religious Experience*, edited by Albert I. Baumgarten, 39–48. Numen Book Series. Leiden: Brill, 2002.
Alexander, T. Desmond. "Are the Wife/Sister Incidents of Genesis Literary Compositional Variants?" *VT* 62 (1992) 145–53.
———. *From Paradise to the Promised Land: An Introduction to the Pentateuch*. 4th ed. Grand Rapids: Baker, 2022.
———. Review of *The Pilgrimage Pattern in Exodus*, by Mark S. Smith. *JETS* 42 (1999) 493–94.
Allen, James P. *Genesis in Egypt: The Philosophy of Ancient Egyptian Creation Accounts*. New Haven, CT: Yale University Press, 1988.
Alter, Robert. *The Art of Biblical Narrative*. 2nd ed. New York: Basic, 2011.
———. "Introduction to the Old Testament." In *The Literary Guide to the Bible*, edited by Robert Alter and Frank Kermode, 11–35. Cambridge, MA: Harvard University Press, 1987.
Alster, Bendt. "Tammuz." *DDD* 828–34.
Anderson, Bernhard W. *Creation versus Chaos: The Reinterpretation of Mythical Symbolism in the Bible*. Repr., Philadelphia: Fortress, 1987.
———. "From Analysis to Synthesis: The Interpretation of Genesis 1–11." *JBL* 97 (1978) 23–39.
———. "A Stylistic Study of the Priestly Creation Story." In *Canon and Authority: Essays in Old Testament Religion and Theology*, edited by George W. Coats and Burke O. Long, 148–62. Philadelphia: Fortress, 1977.
Anderson, Bradford A. *An Introduction to the Study of the Pentateuch*. T&T Clark Approaches to Biblical Studies. London: Bloomsbury, 2017.
Anderson, James M. *Daily Life during the Spanish Inquisition*. Westport, CT: Greenwood, 2002.

Anderson, Robert T., and Terry Giles. *The Samaritan Pentateuch: An Introduction to Its Origin, History, and Significance for Biblical Studies*. SBLSBS 79. Atlanta: Society for Biblical Literature, 2012.

Apollodorus. *The Library*. Translated by James George Frazer. 2 vols. London: Heineman, 1921.

Aquinas, Thomas. *Summa Theologiae: Prima Secundae, 1–70*. Translated by Laurence Shapcote, OP. Latin-English Opera Omnia. Green Bay, WI: Aquinas Institute, 2017.

Arnold, Bill T. *Deuteronomy 1–11*. NICOT. Grand Rapids: Eerdmans, 2022.

Assmann, Jan. *From Akhenaten to Moses: Ancient Egypt and Religious Change*. Cairo: American University Press, 2014.

Astruc, Jean. *Conjectures sur les mémoires originaux dont il paraît que Moyse s'est servi pour composer le récit de la Genèse*. Paris: Cuvelier, 1753.

Atran, Scott. *In Gods We Trust: The Evolutionary Landscape of Religion*. Evolution and Cognition. New York: Oxford University Press, 2002.

Auerbach, Erich. *Mimesis: The Representation of Reality in Western Literature*. Translated by Willard R. Trask. Princeton: Princeton University Press, 1953.

Augustine. *De Genesi ad litteram*. Paris: Desclée, De Brouwer, 1936.

Auld, Graeme. "Leviticus at the Heart of the Pentateuch?" In *Reading Leviticus: Responses to Mary Douglas*, edited by John F. A. Sawyer, 40–51. LHBOTS 227. Sheffield: Academic, 1996.

Avruch, Kevin. "Reciprocity, Equality, and Status-Anxiety in the Amarna Letters." In *Amarna Diplomacy: The Beginnings of International Relations*, edited by Raymond Cohen and Raymond Westbrook, 154–64. Baltimore: Johns Hopkins University Press, 2000.

Baden, Joel S. *The Book of Exodus: A Biography*. LGRB. Princeton: Princeton University Press, 2019.

———. *The Composition of the Pentateuch. Renewing the Documentary Hypothesis*. AYBRL. New Haven, CT: Yale University Press, 2012.

———. *J, E, and the Redaction of the Pentateuch*. FAT 68. Tübingen: Mohr Siebeck, 2009.

———. *The Promise to the Patriarchs*. New York: Oxford University Press, 2013.

Baden, Joel S., and Jeffrey Stackert. "Introduction: Convergences and Divergences in Contemporary Pentateuchal Research." In *The Oxford Handbook of the Pentateuch*, edited by Joel S. Baden and Jeffrey Stackert, 1–22. Oxford Handbooks. Oxford: Oxford University Press, 2021.

Bailey, Randall C. Review of *The Pentateuch*, by Michael D. Guinan, OFM. *CBQ* 55 (1993) 111–13.

———. Review of *The Pentateuch: Introducing the Torah*, by Thomas B. Dozeman. *JETS* 61 (2018) 268–71.

Balberg, Mira. "The Animalistic Gullet and the Godlike Soul: Reframing Sacrifice in Midrash Leviticus Rabbah." *AJSR* 38 (2014) 221–47.

Baltzer, Klaus. "Considerations Regarding the Office and Calling of the Prophet." *HTR* 61 (1968) 567–81.

Bandstra, Barry. *Genesis 1–11: A Handbook on the Hebrew Text*. Waco: Baylor University Press, 2008.

Baptist, Edward E. *The Half Has Never Been Told: Slavery and the Making of American Capitalism*. New York: Basic, 2014.

Barrett, Rob. *Disloyalty and Destruction: Religion and Politics in Deuteronomy and the Modern World*. LNTS 511. New York: T&T Clark, 2009.

Barth, Karl. *Die Lehre von der Schöpfung*. Vol. 3.1 of *Die kirchliche Dogmatik*. Berlin: Siebenstern, 1965.

Barton, John. "Law and Narrative in the Pentateuch." *CV* 51 (2009) 126–40.

———. *The Nature of Biblical Criticism*. Louisville: Westminster John Knox, 2007.

Batto, Bernard F. "The Combat Myth in Israelite Tradition Revisited." In *Creation and Chaos: A Reconsideration of Hermann Gunkel's* Chaoskampf *Hypothesis*, edited by JoAnn Scurlock and Richard H. Beal, 217–36. Winona Lake, IN: Eisenbrauns, 2013.

———. *In the Beginning: Creation Motifs in the Ancient Near East and the Bible*. Winona Lake, IN: Eisenbrauns, 2013.

———. "Mythic Dimensions of the Exodus Tradition." In *Israel's Exodus in Transdisciplinary Perspective: Text, Archaeology, Culture and Geoscience*, edited by Thomas E. Levy et al., 187–96. Quantitative Methods in the Humanities and Social Sciences. New York: Springer, 2015.

Baumgarten, Joseph M. "Damascus Document." *EDSS* 1:166–70.

Beckert, Sven, and Seth Rockman. "Introduction: Slavery's Capitalism." In *Slavery's Capitalism: A New History of American Economic Development*, edited by Sven Beckert and Seth Rockman, 1–27. Early American Studies. Philadelphia: University of Pennsylvania Press, 2016.

Berg, Herbert. *The Development of Exegesis in Early Islam: The Authenticity of Muslim Literature from the Formative Period*. Routledge Studies in the Qur'an. Richmond, UK: Curzon, 2000.

Berlin, Adele. Review of *Before Abraham Was: The Unity of Genesis 1–11*, by Isaac M. Kikawada and Arthur Quinn. *BA* 50 (1987) 252–53.

Bernstein, Moshe. "'Rewritten Bible': A Generic Category Which Has Outlived Its Usefulness?" *Textus* 22 (2005) 169–96.

Betlyon, John. Review of *Cults of the Dead in Ancient Israel and Ugarit*, by Theodore J. Lewis. *CBQ* 53 (1991) 108–10.

Biggs, Robert D. "Ebla Texts." *AYBD* 2:263–70.

Bildstein, Moshe. *Purity, Community, and Ritual in Early Christian Literature*. Oxford Studies in the Abrahamic Religions. New York: Oxford University Press, 2017.

Bird, Phyllis A. "'Male and Female He Created Them': Gen 1:27b in the Context of the Priestly Account of Creation." *HTR* 74 (1981) 129–59.

Blake, Michael. *Dances with Wolves*. New York: Ballentine, 1988.

Bleich, David. *Subjective Criticism*. Baltimore: Johns Hopkins University Press, 2019.

Blenkinsopp, Joseph. *Creation, Un-Creation, Re-Creation: A Discursive Commentary on Genesis 1–11*. New York: T&T Clark, 2011.

———. *The Pentateuch: An Introduction to the First Five Books of the Bible*. AYBRL. Repr., New Haven, CT: Yale University Press, 2000.

———. "The Structure of P." *CBQ* 58 (1976) 275–92.

———. *Treasures Old and New: Essays in the Theology of the Pentateuch*. Grand Rapids: Eerdmans, 2004.

———. "Was the Pentateuch the Civic and Religious Constitution of the Jewish Ethnos in the Persian Period?" In *Persia and Torah: The Theory of the Imperial Authorization of the Pentateuch*, edited by James W. Watts, 41–62. SymS 17. Atlanta: SBL, 2001.

Bloch, René. *Jüdische Drehbühnen: Biblische Variationen im antiken Judentum.* Tria Corda 7. Tübingen: Mohr Siebeck, 2013.

———. "Leaving Home: Philo of Alexandria on the Exodus." In *Israel's Exodus in Transdisciplinary Perspective: Text, Archaeology, Culture and Geoscience*, edited by Thomas E. Levy et al., 357–64. Quantitative Methods in the Humanities and Social Sciences. New York: Springer, 2015.

Boehm, Omri. *The Binding of Isaac: A Religious Model of Disobedience.* LHBOTS 468. London: T&T Clark, 2007.

Bowler, Kate. *Blessed: A History of the American Prosperity Gospel.* Oxford: Oxford University Press, 2013.

Boyd, Gregory A. *God of the Possible: A Biblical Introduction to the Open View of God.* Grand Rapids: Baker, 2000.

Braulik, Georg. "Gottesbund und Gnade im Deuteronomium." *BZ* 67 (2023) 1–42.

Brett, Mark G. *Genesis.* OTR. London: Routledge, 2000.

Brickell, Henry M., and Regina H. Paul. *Curriculum and Assessment Policy: 20 Questions for Board Members.* Toronto: Scarecrow Education, 2005.

Briggs, Richard S. and Joel N. Lohr, eds. *A Theological Introduction to the Pentateuch: Interpreting the Torah as Christian Scripture.* Grand Rapids: Baker, 2012.

Brown, Raymond. *The Message of Deuteronomy.* TBST. Downers Grove, IL: IVP Academic, 2021.

Browning, Daniel C. "The Strange Search for the Ashes of the Red Heifer." *BA* 59 (1996) 74–89.

Brueggemann, Walter. *The Creative Word: Canon as a Model for Biblical Education.* Philadelphia: Fortress, 1982.

———. *The Prophetic Imagination.* Philadelphia: Fortress, 1978.

———. *Theology of the Old Testament: Testimony, Dispute, Advocacy.* Minneapolis: Fortress, 1997.

Bryan, Betsy M. "The Egyptian Perspective on Mitanni." In *Amarna Diplomacy: The Beginnings of International Relations*, edited by Raymond Cohen and Raymond Westbrook, 71–84. Baltimore: Johns Hopkins University Press, 2000.

Bryce, Trevor. *Life and Society in the Hittite World.* Oxford: Oxford University Press, 2002.

Burchard, Christoph. "Joseph and Aseneth." *OTP* 2:177–247.

Byron, John. *Cain and Abel in Text and Tradition: Jewish and Christian Interpretations of the First Sibling Rivalry.* TBN 14. Leiden: Brill, 2011.

Campbell, Dennis R. M. "On the Theogonies of Hesiod and the Hurrians: An Exploration of the Dual Natures of Teššub and Kumarbi." In *Creation and Chaos: A Reconsideration of Hermann Gunkel's* Chaoskampf *Hypothesis*, edited by JoAnn Scurlock and Richard H. Beal, 112–26. Winona Lake, IN: Eisenbrauns, 2013.

Caquot, André. Review of *Deuteronomy and the Deuteronomic School*, by Moshe Weinfeld. *RHR* 185 (1974) 96–97.

Carimokam, Sahajeh. *Muhammad and the People of the Book.* Bloomington, IN: XLibris, 2010.

Carr, David M. *The Formation of Genesis 1–11: Biblical and Other Precursors.* Oxford: Oxford University Press, 2020.

———. *The Formation of the Hebrew Bible: A New Reconstruction.* Oxford: Oxford University Press, 2011.

———. *Genesis 1–11.* IECOT. Stuttgart: Kohlhammer, 2021.

Carroll, Michael P. "Leach, Genesis, and Structural Analysis: A Critical Evaluation." *American Ethnologist* 4 (1977) 663–77.
Cazelles, Henri. "Statut public et droit privé dans la Tôrâh." In *Birkat Shalom: Studies in the Bible, Ancient Near Eastern Literature, and Post-Biblical Judaism Presented to Shalom Paul on the Occasion of His Seventieth Birthday*, edited by Chaim Cohen et al., 3–10. Winona Lake, IN: Eisenbrauns, 2008.
Chalier, Catherine. *Il nous créa à Son Image: Un commentaire de la Genèse*. Montrouge, Fr.: Bayard, 2023.
———. *Reading the Torah: Beyond the Fundamentalist and Scientific Approaches*. Translated by Michael B. Smith. Pittsburgh: Duquesne University Press, 2017.
Chaloupka, Libor. "The Daughters of Humans and the Sons of God (Gen 6:1–4)." *CV* 58 (2016) 366–77.
Chepey, Stuart. *Nazirites in Late Second Temple Judaism: A Survey of Ancient Jewish Writings, the New Testament, Archaeological Evidence, and Other Writings from Late Antiquity*. AJEC 60. Leiden: Brill, 2005.
Childs, Brevard S. *The Book of Exodus: A Critical, Theological Commentary*. OTL. Louisville: Westminster John Knox, 1974.
———. *Introduction to the Old Testament as Scripture*. Philadelphia: Fortress, 1979.
Chirichigno, Gregory C. *Debt-Slavery in Israel and the Ancient Near East*. JSOTSup 141. Sheffield: Sheffield Academic, 1993.
Christensen, Duane L. *Deuteronomy 1—21:9*. 2nd ed. WBC 6A. Grand Rapids: Zondervan, 2001.
Christensen, Duane L., and Marcel Narucki. "The Mosaic Authorship of the Pentateuch." *JETS* 32 (1989) 465–71.
Christensen, Wendy. *Empire of Ancient Egypt*. GEP. New York: Facts on File, 2004.
Clifford, Richard C. *Creation Accounts in the Ancient Near East and in the Bible*. CBQMS 26. Washington, DC: Catholic Biblical Association, 1994.
———. "Towards a Precise Translation of Psalm 115:1." *BZ* 56 (2022) 293–301.
Clines, David J. A. *The Theme of the Pentateuch*. 2nd ed. JSOTSup 10. Sheffield: Academic, 1996.
———. "Theme in Genesis 1–11." *CBQ* 38 (1976) 483–507.
Clines, David J. A., and J. Cheryl Exum. "The New Literary Criticism." In *The New Literary Criticism and the Hebrew Bible*, edited by J. Cheryl Exum and David J. A. Clines, 11–25. Sheffield: Academic, 1993.
Coats, George W. *Exodus 1–18*. FOTL 2A. Grand Rapids: Eerdmans, 1999.
———. *The Moses Tradition*. JSOTSup 161. Sheffield: Academic, 1993.
———. *Rebellion in the Wilderness: The Murmuring Motif in the Wilderness Traditions of the Old Testament*. Nashville: Abingdon, 1968.
Cody, Aelred. "An Excursus on Priesthood in Israel." In *Ezekiel: With an Excursus on Old Testament Priesthood*, 256–63. Wilmington, DE: Glazier, 1984.
Cohen, Arthur Allen. *The Myth of the Judeo-Christian Tradition and Other Dissenting Essays*. New York: Schocken, 1971.
Collins, C. John. "Noah, Deucalion, and the New Testament." *Bib* 3 (2012) 403–26.
Collins, John J. *Introduction to the Hebrew Bible*. 3rd ed. Minneapolis: Fortress, 2018.
———. *The Invention of Judaism: Torah and Jewish Identity from Deuteronomy to Paul*. Berkeley: University of California Press, 2017.
———. "Israel." In *Religions of the Ancient World: A Guide*, edited by Sarah Iles Johnston, 181–88. Harvard University Press Reference Library. Cambridge, MA: Harvard University Press, 2004.

———. *The Scepter and the Star: The Messiahs of the Dead Sea Scrolls and Other Ancient Literature.* AYBRL. New York: Doubleday, 1995.
Collins, Steven, and Latayne C. Scott. *Discovering the City of Sodom: The Fascinating, True Account of the Discovery of the Old Testament's Most Infamous City.* New York: Howard, 2013.
Cornell, Vincent J. *Voices of Islam.* Westport, CT: Praeger, 2007.
Crenshaw, James. *Education in Ancient Israel: Across the Deadening Silence.* AYBRL. New York: Doubleday, 1998.
Cross, Frank Moore. "The Tabernacle: A Study from an Archaeological and Historical Approach." *BA* 10 (1947) 45–68.
Crouch, Carly L. *Israel and the Assyrians: Deuteronomy, the Succession Treaty of Esarhaddon, and the Nature of Subversion.* ANEM 8. Atlanta: SBL, 2014.
Crüsemann, Frank. *Die Tora: Theologie und Sozialgeschichte des alttestamentlichen Gesetzes.* Munich: Kaiser, 1992.
Cryer, Frederick. *Divination in Ancient Israel and Its Ancient Near Eastern Environment: A Sociohistorical Investigation.* Sheffield: JSOT, 1994.
Curtiss, Samuel I. *The Levitical Priests: A Contribution to the Criticism of the Pentateuch.* Edinburgh: T&T Clark, 1877.
Damrosch, David A. "Leviticus." In *The Literary Guide to the Bible*, edited by Robert Alter and Frank Kermode, 66–77. Cambridge, MA: Harvard University Press, 1987.
Davidson, Robert. *Genesis 1–11.* CBC. Cambridge: Cambridge University Press, 1973.
Davies, Eryl W. *Biblical Criticism: A Guide for the Perplexed.* New York: Bloomsbury T&T Clark, 2013.
Davies, Graham I. "Sinai, Mount." *AYBD* 6:47–49.
———. "Wilderness Wandering." *AYBD* 6:912–14.
Day, John. *From Creation to Babel: Studies in Genesis 1–11.* LHBOTS 592. London: Bloomsbury Academic, 2011.
———. *God's Conflict with the Dragon and the Sea: Echoes of a Canaanite Myth in the Old Testament.* Cambridge: University of Cambridge, 1985.
Dein, Simon. "What Really Happens When Prophecy Fails: The Case of Lubavitch." *SocR* 62 (2001) 383–402.
Dershowitz, Alan. *Terror Tunnels: The Case for Israel's Just War against Hamas.* New York: Rosetta, 2014.
Dever, William G. "Israel, History of: Archaeology and the Israelite 'Conquest.'" *AYBD* 3:545–58.
Dillard, Raymond B., and Tremper Longman III. *An Introduction to the Old Testament.* Grand Rapids: Zondervan, 1994.
Dillmann, August. *Die Genesis.* Leipzig: Hirzel, 1892.
Doedens, Jaap J. T. *The Sons of God in Genesis 6:1–4: Analysis and History of Exegesis.* OtSt 76. Leiden: Brill, 2019.
Douglas, Mary. *In the Wilderness: The Doctrine of Defilement in the Book of Numbers.* New York: Oxford University Press, 2001.
———. *The Lele of the Kasai.* Repr., London: Routledge, 2003.
———. *Leviticus as Literature.* New York: Oxford University Press, 1999.
———. *Purity and Danger: An Analysis of Concept of Pollution and Taboo.* Routledge Classics. London: Kegan Paul, 1966.
Dozeman, Thomas B. *Exodus.* ECC. Grand Rapids: Eerdmans, 2007.

———. "Exodus." In *The Old Testament and Apocrypha*, edited by Gale A. Yee et al., 137–78. Fortress Commentary on the Bible. Minneapolis: Fortress, 2014.

———. *God at War: Power in the Exodus Tradition*. New York: Oxford University Press, 1996.

———. *The Pentateuch: Introducing the Torah*. Introducing Israel's Scriptures. Minneapolis: Fortress, 2017.

Dozeman, Thomas B., et al. *The Pentateuch: International Perspectives on Current Research*. FAT 78. Tübingen: Mohr Siebeck, 2011.

Driver, Godfrey R. "Three Technical Terms in the Pentateuch." *JSS* 1 (1956) 97–105.

Duhm, Bernard. *Das Buch Jeremia*. Tübingen: Mohr, 1901.

Dumbrell, William J. *The Faith of Israel: Its Expression in the Books of the Old Testament*. Grand Rapids: Baker, 1988.

Edelman, Diana. "Introduction." In *Deuteronomy in the Making: Studies in the Production of Debarim*, edited by Diana Edelman, 1–10. BZAW 533. Berlin: de Gruyter, 2021.

Edelman, Diana V. "Preface." In *Opening the Books of Moses*, edited by Diana V. Edelman et al., viii. BibleWorld. London: Routledge, 2014.

Eichrodt, Walter. *Theology of the Old Testament*. Translated by J. A. Baker. 2 vols. OTL. Philadelphia: Westminster, 1967.

Eissfeldt, Otto. *The Old Testament: An Introduction*. Translated by Peter R. Ackroyd. Oxford: Basil Blackwell, 1965.

Eliade, Mircea. *The Sacred and the Profane: The Nature of Religion*. New York: Harcourt, Brace, Jovanovich, 1959.

Elledge, Casey D. "Re-Writing the Sacred: Some Problems of Textual Authority in Light of the Rewritten Scriptures from Qumran." In *The Function of "Canonical" and "Non-Canonical" Religious Texts*, edited by James H. Charlesworth and Lee Martin McDonald, 87–103. JCT 7. London: T&T Clark, 2010.

Elrefaei, Aly. *Wellhausen and Kaufmann: Ancient Israel and Its Religious History in the Works of Julius Wellhausen and Yehezkel Kaufmann*. BZAW 490. Berlin: de Gruyter, 2016.

Engel, Beverly. *Breaking the Cycle of Abuse: How to Move beyond Your Past to Create an Abuse-Free Future*. Hoboken, NJ: Wiley and Sons, 2005.

Engnell, Ivan. *Gamla Testamentet: En traditionshistorisk inledning*. Stockholm: Svenska kyrkans diakonistyrelses, 1945.

Espak, Peeter. *The God Enki in Sumerian Royal Ideology and Mythology*. Philippika: Altertumswissenschaftliche Abhandlungen/Contributions to the Study of Ancient World Cultures 87. Wiesbaden: Harrassowitz, 2015.

Estelle, Bryan D. *Echoes of Exodus: Tracing a Biblical Motif*. Downers Grove, IL: IVP Academic, 2018.

Farber, Zev. Review of *Making a Case*, by Sarah J. Milstein. *RBL* 11 (2023). https://www.sblcentral.org/API/Reviews/1000578_72683.pdf.

Fee, Gordon D. *The Disease of the Health and Wealth Gospels*. Vancouver: Regent College Publishing, 1985.

———. *Revelation: A New Covenant Commentary*. NCCS. Cambridge: Lutterworth, 2013.

Feinman, Peter. "Where Is Eden? An Analysis of Some of the Mesopotamian Motifs in Primeval J." In *Creation and Chaos: A Reconsideration of Hermann Gunkel's Chaoskampf Hypothesis*, edited by JoAnn Scurlock and Richard H. Beal, 172–89. Winona Lake, IN: Eisenbrauns, 2013.

Feldman, Ariel et al. *Scripture and Interpretation: Qumran Texts That Rework the Bible*. BZAW 449. Berlin: de Gruyter, 2014.

Firestone, Reuven. "Difficulties in Keeping a Beautiful Wife: The Legend of Abraham and Sarah in Jewish and Islamic Tradition." *JJS* 42 (1991) 196–214.

———. "Prophethood, Marriageable Consanguinity, and Text: The Problem of Abraham and Sarah's Kinship Relationship and the Response of Jewish and Islamic Exegesis." *JQR* 83 (1993) 331–47.

Fishbane, Michael. *Biblical Interpretation in Ancient Israel*. Clarendon Paperbacks. Oxford: Clarendon, 1985.

———. *Biblical Myth and Rabbinic Mythmaking*. New York: Oxford University Press, 2005.

Fleming, Daniel E. *Time at Emar: The Cultic Calendar and the Rituals from the Diviner's House*. MC 11. Winona Lake, IN: Eisenbrauns, 2000.

Flury-Scholch, André. *Abrahams Segen und die Völker: Synchrone und diachrone Untersuchungen zu Gen 12,1–3 unter besonderer Berücksichtigung der intertextuellen Beziehungen zu Gen 18; 22; 26; 28; Sir 44; Jer 4 und Ps 72*. FB 115. Würzburg: Echter, 2007.

Fokkelman, Jan P. "Genesis." In *The Literary Guide to the Bible*, edited by Robert Alter and Frank Kermode, 36–55. Cambridge, MA: Harvard University Press, 1987.

Ford, William A. *God, Pharaoh, and Moses: Explaining the Lord's Actions in the Exodus Plagues Narrative*. PBM. Milton Keynes, UK: Paternoster, 2006.

Fortna, Robert Tomson. *The Gospel of Signs: A Reconstruction of the Narrative Source Underlying the Fourth Gospel*. Cambridge: Cambridge University Press, 1970.

Foster, Benjamin. "In Search of Akkadian Literature." In *Before the Muses: An Anthology of Akkadian Literature*, 1–47. Bethesda, MD: CDL, 2005.

Fowler, Henry W., and Francis G. Fowler. *The Works of Lucian of Samosata*. Oxford: Clarendon, 1905.

Fowler, Robert M. *Let the Reader Understand: Reader-Response Criticism and the Gospel of Mark*. Harrisburg, PA: Trinity International, 1996.

França, Rafael. "O Deus Moisés e o profeta Arão." *Reflexus* 12 (2018) 279–98.

Frankena, Rintje. "The Vassal-Treaties of Esarhaddon and the Dating of Deuteronomy." *OWN* 25 (1965) 122–54.

Frei, Peter. "Zentralgewalt und Lokalautonomie im Achämenidenreich." In *Reichsidee und Reichsorganisation im Perserreich: Zweite, bearbeitete und stark erweiterte Auflage*, edited by Peter Frei and Klaus Koch, 5–131. OBO 55. Göttingen: Vandenhoeck & Ruprecht, 1996.

Freidenreich, David M. "The Use of Islamic Sources in Saadia Gaon's *Tafsīr* of the Torah." *JQR* 93 (2003) 353–95.

Fretheim, Terence E. *Abraham: Trials of Family and Faith*. Studies on Personalities of the Old Testament. Charleston: University of South Carolina Press, 2007.

———. *Creation, Fall, and Flood: Studies in Genesis 1–11*. Minneapolis: Augsburg, 1969.

———. *The Pentateuch*. IBT. Nashville: Abingdon, 1996.

———. *The Suffering of God: An Old Testament Perspective*. OBT. Philadelphia: Fortress, 1984.

Frick, Frank S. "The Political and Ideological Interests of Female Sexual Imagery in Hosea 1–3." In *To Break Every Yoke: Essays in Honor of Marvin L. Chaney*, edited by Robert B. Coote and Norman K. Gottwald, 200–208. SWBA. Sheffield: Phoenix, 2007.

Friedman, Richard Elliott. *The Bible with Sources Revealed: A New View into the Five Books of Moses*. New York: Harper Collins, 2009.
———. "Tabernacle." *AYBD* 6:292–300.
Frymer-Kensky, Tikva. "The Atrahasis Epic and Its Significance for Our Understanding of Genesis 1–9." *BA* 40 (1977) 147–55.
———. "The Strange Case of the Suspected *Sotah*." *VT* 34 (1984) 11–26.
———. *In the Wake of the Goddesses: Women, Culture, and the Biblical Transformation of Pagan Myth*. New York: Random House, 1993.
Gadamer, Hans-Georg. *Truth and Method*. Translated by Joel Weinsheimer and Donald G. Marshall. New York: Bloomsbury Academic, 2013.
Gaiser, Frederick. "Sarah, Hagar, Abraham—Hannah, Peninnah, Elkanah: Case Studies in Conflict." *WW* 34 (2014) 273–84.
Gall, August F. von. *Der hebräische Pentateuch der Samaritaner*. 4 vols. Giessen, Germ.: Töpelmann, 1914–18.
Gammie, John. *Holiness in Israel*. OBT. Philadelphia: Fortress, 1989.
García Martínez, Florentino. "Temple Scroll." *EDSS* 2:927–33.
Gerstenberger, Erhard S. *Israel in the Persian Period: The Fifth and Fourth Centuries BCE*. Translated by Siegfried S. Schatzmann. BibEnc 8. Atlanta: Society of Biblical Literature, 2011.
———. *Theologies in the Old Testament*. Translated by John Bowden. London: T&T Clark, 2002.
Gertoux, Gérard. *Abraham and Cherlaomer: Chronological, Historical, and Archaeological Evidence*. Morrisville, NC: Lulu, 2015.
Gese, Hartmut. "Die Religionen Altsyriens, Altarabiens, und der Mandäer." In *Die Religionen Altsyriens, Altarabiens, und der Mandäer*, edited by Hartmut Gese et al., 1–232. DRM 10.2. Stuttgart: Harrassowitz, 1970.
Geus, Cornelius Hendrick Jan de. "Gad." *AYBD* 2:865–65.
Gilan, Amir. "Once upon a Time in Kiškiluša: The Dragon-Slayer Myth in Central Anatolia." In *Creation and Chaos: A Reconsideration of Hermann Gunkel's Chaoskampf Hypothesis*, edited by JoAnn Scurlock and Richard H. Beal, 98–111. Winona Lake, IN: Eisenbrauns, 2013.
Glazov, Gregory Y. *The Bridling of the Tongue and the Opening of the Mouth in Biblical Prophecy*. JSOTSup 311. Sheffield: Sheffield Academic, 2001.
Goldin, Judah. "Midrash and Aggadah." *ER* 9:6013–19.
Goldingay, John. *Genesis*. BCOT. Grand Rapids, Baker, 2020.
Good, Edwin S. *Genesis 1–11: Tales of the Earliest World*. Stanford, CA: Stanford University Press, 2011.
Gooder, Paula. *The Pentateuch: A Story of Beginnings*. Biblical Studies. London: Bloomsbury Academic, 2005.
Goodnick, Benjamin. "Korah and his Aspirations." *JBQ* 28 (2000) 177–81.
Gordis, Robert L. *The Judeo-Christian Tradition: Illusion or Reality?* New York: Judaica, 1965.
Gordon, Cyrus, H. "Biblical Customs and the Nuzu Tablets." *BA* 3 (1940) 1–12.
Gorman, Frank H., Jr. *The Ideology of Ritual: Space, Time and Status in the Priestly Theology*. Sheffield: JSOT, 1990.
———. "Ritual Studies and Biblical Studies: Assessment of the Past, Prospects for the Future." *Semeia* 67 (1994) 13–36.
Gossai, Hemchand. *Barrenness and Blessing: Abraham, Sarah, and the Journey of Faith*. Eugene, OR: Cascade, 2008.

Gottwald, Norman K. *The Hebrew Bible: A Brief Socio-Literary Introduction*. Minneapolis: Fortress, 2009.

———. *The Politics of Ancient Israel*. Louisville: Westminster John Knox, 2001.

———. "Social Class as an Analytical and Hermeneutical Category in Biblical Studies." *JBL* 112 (1993) 3–22.

Grabbe, Lester L. *The Dawn of Israel: A History of Canaan in the Second Millennium BCE*. London: T&T Clark, 2023.

———. "History of Religion." In *The Oxford Handbook of Ritual and Worship in the Hebrew Bible*, edited by Samuel E. Balentine, 93–108. New York: Oxford University Press, 2020.

———. "The Last Days of Judah and the Roots of the Pentateuch: What Does History Tell Us?" In *The Fall of Jerusalem and the Rise of Torah*, edited by Peter Dubovský et al., 19–46. FAT 107. Tübingen: Mohr Siebeck, 2016.

Graetz, Naomi. "Miriam: Guilty or Not Guilty?" *Judaism* 40 (1991) 184–92.

Gray, John. "The Canaanite God Ḥoron." *JNES* 8 (1949) 27–34.

Graybill, Rhiannon. *Texts after Terror: Rape, Sexual Violence, and the Hebrew Bible*. Oxford: Oxford University Press, 2021.

Greifenhagen, Franz Volker. "Egypt in the Symbolic Geography of the Pentateuch: Constructing Biblical Israel's Identity." PhD diss., Duke University, 1998.

Grenz, Stanley J. *Welcoming but Not Affirming: An Evangelical Response to Homosexuality*. Louisville: Westminster John Knox, 1998.

Gröger, Martin. *Wellhausens Wegbereiter: Studien zur alttestamentlichen Hermeneutik im 19. Jahrhundert*. BHT 202. Tübingen: Mohr Siebeck, 2021.

Gross, Walter. *Bileam: Literar- und formkritische Untersuchung der Prosa in Num 22–24*. SANT 38. Munich: Kösel, 1974.

Guinan, Michael D. *The Pentateuch*. MBS. Collegeville, MN: Liturgical, 1990.

Gunkel, Hermann. *Genesis: Übersetzt und erklärt*. Göttingen: Vandenhoeck & Ruprecht, 1901.

———. "Die Komposition der Josephsgeschichte." *ZDMG* 76 (1922) 55–71.

———. *Schöpfung und Chaos in Urzeit und Endzeit: Eine religionsgeschichtlich Untersuchung über Gen. 1 und Ap. Jon 12*. Göttingen: Vandenhoeck & Ruprecht, 1895.

Gurney, O. R. *Some Aspects of Hittite Religion*. Oxford: Oxford University Press, 1977.

Guthrie, Stewart Elliott. "Religion as Anthropomorphism." In *Faces in the Clouds: A New Theory of Religion*, 177–204. Oxford: University Press, 1993.

Gutiérrez, Gustavo. *A Theology of Liberation: History, Politics, and Salvation*. Translated by Caridad Inda and John Eagleson. 15th anniv. ed. with new introduction. London: SCM, 1988.

Habel, Norman. "The Form and Significance of the Call Narratives." *ZAW* 77 (1965) 297–323.

Haberman, Bonna D. "The Suspected Adulteress: A Study of Textual Embodiment." *Proof* 20 (2000) 12–42.

Hackett, Joanne A. "Some Observations on the Balaam Tradition at Deir ʿAllā." *BA* 49 (1986) 216–22.

Hallo, William W. "Sharecroping in the Edict of Ammi-ṣaduqa." In *Ḥesed ve-Emet: Studies in Honor of Ernest S. Frerichs*, edited by Jodi Magness and Seymour Gitin, 205–16. BJS 320. Atlanta: Scholars, 1998.

Hamilton, Mark W. "Deuteronomy." In *The Transforming Word: A One-Volume Commentary on the Bible*, edited by Mark W. Hamilton, 203–36. Abilene: ACU Press, 2009.

———, ed. *The Transforming Word: A One-Volume Commentary on the Bible*. Abilene: ACU Press, 2009.

Hamilton, Victor P. *Handbook on the Pentateuch: Genesis, Exodus, Leviticus, Numbers, Deuteronomy*. Grand Rapids: Baker Academic, 2005.

Haran, Menachem. *Temples and Temple Service in Ancient Israel: An Inquiry into Biblical Cult Phenomena and the Historical Setting of the Priestly School*. Winona Lake, IN: Eisenbrauns, 1985.

Hardmeier, Christof. "The Achilles Heel of Reader-Response Criticism and the Concept of Reading Hermeneutics of Caution." In *Literary Construction of Identity in the Ancient World: Proceedings of the Conference Literary Fiction and the Construction of Identity in Ancient Literatures; Options and Limits of Modern Literary Approach*, edited by Hanna Liss and Manfred Oeming, 121–34. Winona Lake, IN: Eisenbrauns, 2010.

Harrington, Hannah K. "Intermarriage in the Temple Scroll: Strategies of Neutralization." In *Current Issues in Priestly and Related Literature: The Legacy of Jacob Milgrom and Beyond*, edited by Roy E. Gane and Ada Taggar-Cohen, 463–81. RBS 82. Atlanta: SBL, 2015.

———. "Interpreting Leviticus in the Second Temple Period: Struggling with Ambiguity." In *Reading Leviticus: Responses to Mary Douglas*, edited by John F. A. Sawyer, 214–29. LHBOTS 227. Sheffield: Academic, 1996.

Harris, Paul. *Profane Egyptologists: The Modern Revival of Ancient Egyptian Religion*. New York: Routledge, 2018.

Harris, Rachel T. "The Ritual of the Red Heifer." *JBQ* 26 (1998) 198–200.

Hays, Christopher B. *Hidden Riches: A Sourcebook for the Comparative Study of the Hebrew Bible and Ancient Near East*. Louisville: Westminster John Knox, 2014.

Hays, Richard B. *First Corinthians*. IBC. Louisville: Westminster John Knox, 2011.

Healey, John F. "Mot." *DDD* 598–603.

Heard, R. Christopher. *The Dynamics of Diselection: Ambiguity in Genesis 12–36 and Ethnic Boundaries in Post-Exilic Judah*. Semeia 39. Atlanta: Society of Biblical Literature, 2001.

———. "Genesis." In *The Transforming Word: A One-Volume Commentary on the Bible*, edited by Mark W. Hamilton, 107–42. Abilene: ACU Press, 2009.

Heller, Bernard. "The Judeo-Christian Tradition Concept: Aid or Deterrent to Goodwill?" *Judaism* 2 (1953) 133–39.

Helyer, Larry. "The Separation of Abram and Lot: Its Significance in the Patriarchal Narratives." *JSOT* 26 (1983) 77–88.

Hendel, Ronald S. *The Book of Genesis: A Biography*. LGRB. Oxford: Princeton University Press, 2013.

———. *The Epic of the Patriarch: The Jacob Cycle and the Narrative Traditions of Canaan and Israel*. HSM 42. Atlanta: Scholars, 1987.

———. "The Exodus in Biblical Memory." *JBL* 120 (2001) 601–22.

———. Review of *Sodom and Gomorrah*, by Weston Fields. *JBL* 118 (1999) 126–28.

———. *The Text of Genesis 1–11: Textual Studies and Critical Edition*. New York: Oxford University Press, 1998.

Hepner, Gershon. "Abraham's Incestuous Marriage with Sarah: A Violation of the Covenant Code." *VT* 53 (2003) 143–55.

Herrmann, Siegfried. "Die konstruktiv Restauration: Das Deuteronomium als Mitte biblischer Theologie." In *Probleme biblischer Theologie: Gerhard von Rad am 70. Geburtstag*, edited by Hans Walter Wolff, 155–70. Munich: Kaiser, 1971.

Herrmann, Wolfgang. "Rider on the Clouds." *DDD* 703–5.

Heschel, Abraham Joshua. *The Sabbath: Its Meaning for Modern Man*. New York: Farrar, Strauss, and Giroux, 1951.

Heschel, Susannah. *The Aryan Jesus: Christian Theologians and the Bible in Nazi Germany*. Princeton: Princeton University Press, 2008.

Hess, Richard S., and Toshio Tsumura, eds. *I Studied Inscriptions from before the Flood: Ancient Near Eastern, Literary, and Linguistic Approaches to Genesis 1–11*. SBTS 4. Winona Lake, IN: Eisenbrauns, 1994.

Hillers, Delbert R. *Treaty Curses and the Old Testament Prophets*. BibOr 16. Rome: Pontifical Biblical Institute, 1964.

Hoffmeier, James K. *Ancient Israel in Sinai: The Evidence for the Authenticity of the Wilderness Traditions*. Oxford: Oxford University Press, 2005.

Holladay, Carl R. *Historians*. Vol. 1 of *Fragments from Hellenistic Jewish Authors*. Chico, CA: Scholars, 1983.

Hollis, Susan T. *The Ancient Egyptian "Tale of Two Brothers": The Oldest Fairy Tale in the World*. OSCC 7. Norman: University of Oklahoma Press, 1990.

———. "Ancient Israel as the Land of Exile and the 'Otherworld' in Ancient Egyptian Folktales and Narratives." In *Boundaries of the Ancient Near Eastern World: A Tribute to Cyrus H. Gordon*, edited by Meir Lubetski et al., 320–27. LHBOTS 273. Sheffield: Sheffield Academic, 1998.

Holtz, Shalom E. Review of *Inventing God's Law: How the Covenant Code of the Bible Used and Revised the Laws of Hammurabi*, by David P. Wright. *CBQ* 72 (2010) 820–22.

Homan, Michael W. "The Divine Warrior in His Tent." *BRev* 16 (2000) 22–36.

Hopper, Stanley R. "The 'Terrible Sonnets' of Gerard Manley Hopkins and the 'Confessions' of Jeremiah." *Semeia* 13 (1978) 29–73.

Houston, Walter J. "The Character of Yhwh and the Ethics of the Old Testament: Is *Imitatio Dei* Appropriate?" In *Patronage in Ancient Palestine and in the Hebrew Bible: A Reader*, edited by Emanuel Pfoh, 423–44. SWBA, 2nd ser., 12. Sheffield: Sheffield Phoenix, 2022.

———. *Pentateuch*. London: SCM, 2013.

Hughes, Aaron W. *Abrahamic Religions: On the Use and Abuse of History*. New York: Oxford University Press, 2012.

Hummel, Horace. Review of *Handbook on the Pentateuch: Genesis, Exodus, Leviticus, Numbers, Deuteronomy*, by Victor P. Hamilton. *Con* 10 (1984) 32.

Humphreys, W. Lee. *The Character of God in the Book of Genesis: A Narrative Appraisal*. Louisville: Westminster John Knox, 2001.

Hundley, Michael. "To Be or Not to Be: A Reexamination of Name Language in Deuteronomy and the Deuteronomistic History." *VT* 59 (2009) 533–55.

Hunt, Lynn. "The Problem with Presentism Is That It Blurs Our Understanding of the Past." In *Presentism: Examining Historical Figures through Today's Lens*, edited by Sabine Cherenfant, 12–16. New York: Greenhaven, 2019.

Hurowitz, Victor P. "From Storm God to Abstract Being: How the Deity Became More Distant from Exodus to Deuteronomy." *BR* 14 (1998) 40–47.

———. *I Have Built You an Exalted House: Temple Building in the Bible in Light of Mesopotamian and Northwest Semitic Writings.* JSOTSup 114. Sheffield: JSOT, 1992.

Jacobs, Mignon R. "The Conceptual Dynamics of Good and Evil in the Joseph Story: An Exegetical and Hermeneutical Inquiry." *JSOT* 27 (2003) 309–38.

Janowski, B. "Azazel." *DDD* 128–31.

Janzen, Waldemar. *Exodus.* BCBC. Scottdale, PA: Herald, 2000.

Jeansonne, Sharon Pace. *The Women of Genesis: From Sarah to Potiphar's Wife.* Minneapolis: Fortress, 1990.

Jeffers, Ann. *Magic and Divination in Ancient Palestine and Syria.* SHCANE 8. Leiden: Brill, 1996.

Jefferson, Andrew M. "Performances of Victimhood, Allegation, and Disavowal in Sierra Leone." In *Histories of Victimhood,* edited by Steffen Jensen and Henrik Ronsbo, 218–38. Ethnography of Political Violence. Philadelphia: University of Pennsylvania Press, 2014.

Jemielity, Thomas. *Satire and the Hebrew Prophets.* LCBI. Louisville: Westminster John Knox, 1992.

Jenson, Philip P. Review of *Pilgrimage Pattern in Exodus,* by Mark S. Smith. *JTS* 52 (2001) 149–51.

Jiang, Zhenshuai. *Critical Spatiality in Genesis 1–11.* FAT 99. Tübingen: Mohr Siebeck, 2018.

Johnson, William H. "Law or Lawlessness?" *NAR* 202 (1915) 621–22.

Joines, Karen Randolph. "The Bronze Serpent in the Israelite Cult." *JBL* 57 (1965) 245–56.

Josephus, Flavius. *Judean Antiquities 1–4.* Edited and translated by Louis H. Feldman. Leiden: Brill Academic, 2004.

Kaiser, Otto. *Introduction to the Old Testament: A Presentation of Its Results and Problems.* Translated by John Sturdy. Minneapolis: Augsburg, 1975.

Kaminsky, Joel. "Reclaiming a Theology of Election: Favoritism and the Joseph Story." *PRSt* 31 (2004) 135–52.

Kaufmann, Yeḥezkel. *The Religion of Israel.* New York: Schocken, 1972.

Kelly, David E. Review of the *Ancient Egyptian "Tale of Two Brothers": The Oldest Fairy Tale in the World,* by Susan T. Hollis. *Classical World* 85 (1992) 740.

Kikawada, Isaac. "The Double Creation of Mankind in Enki and Ninma⌧, Atra⌧asis 1.1–351, and Genesis 1–2." *Iraq* 45 (1983) 43–45.

Kikawada, Isaac, and Arthur Quinn. *Before Abraham Was: The Unity of Genesis 1–11.* Nashville: Abingdon, 1985.

Kilmer, Anne D. "Speculations on Umul, the First Baby." In *Kramer Anniversary Volume: Cuneiform Studies in Honor of Samuel Noah Kramer,* edited by Barry L. Eichler, 265–70. AOAT 25. Kevalaer: Butzon & Burcker, 1976.

King, Marcus Dubois. "A Watershed Moment: Assessing the Hydropolitics of Iraqi Kurdistan." In *Water and Conflict in the Middle East,* edited by Marcus Dubois King, 71–100. Oxford: Oxford University Press, 2020.

Kinnier-Wilson, J. V. "Medicine in the Land and Times of the Old Testament." In *Studies in the Period of David and Solomon and Other Essays: Papers Read at the International Symposium for Biblical Studies, Tokyo, 5–7 December, 1979,* edited by Tomoo Ishida, 337–65. Winona Lake, IN: Eisenbrauns, 1982.

Kislev, Itamar. "The Cities of Refuge Law in Numbers 35:9–34: A Study of Its Sources, Textual Unity, and Relationship to Deuteronomy 19:1–13." *ZABR* 26 (2020) 249–63.

Kissane, Edward J. *The Book of Job*. Dublin: Browne & Nolan, 1939.

Kitchen, Kenneth A. "The Desert Tabernacle." *BRev* 16 (2000) 14–23.

Klawans, Jonathan. *Impurity and Sin in Ancient Judaism*. Oxford: Oxford University Press, 2000.

———. *Purity, Sacrifice and the Temple: Symbolism and Supersessionism in the Study of Ancient Judaism*. Oxford: Oxford University Press, 2006.

Klein, Ralph. "Back to the Future: The Tabernacle in the Book of Exodus." *Int* 50 (1996) 264–76.

Klingbeil, Gerald A. *Bridging the Gap: Ritual and Ritual Texts in the Bible*. BBRSup 1. Winona Lake, IN: Eisenbrauns, 2007.

Klinger, Jörg. *Untersuchungen zur Rekonstruktion des hattischen Kultschicht*. Wiesbaden: Harrassowitz, 1996.

Knohl, Israel. *The Sanctuary of Silence: The Priestly Torah and the Holiness School*. Minneapolis: Fortress, 1995.

Knoppers, Gary N. *Jews and Samaritans: The Origins and History of their Early Relations*. Oxford: Oxford University Press, 2013.

Knudtzon, Johannes A. *Die El Amarna Tafeln*. Repr., Aalen: Zeller, 1964. First published 1915.

Koch, Klaus. *Was ist Formgeschichte?* Neukirchen-Vluyn, Germ.: Neukirchen, 1964.

Komoróczy, Géza. "Work and Strike of Gods: New Light on the Divine Society in the Sumero-Akkadian Mythology." *Oikumene* 1 (1976) 9–37.

König, Eduard. *Die Genesis*. Gütersloh: Bertelsman, 1925.

Korson, Gerald. "The Problem with Dishonoring Christopher Columbus." In *Presentism: Examining Historical Figures through Today's Lens*, edited by Sabine Cherenfant, 90–96. New York: Greenhaven, 2019.

Köstenberger, Andreas J., and David A. Croteau. "'Will a Man Rob God (Malachi 3:8)?' A Study of Tithing in the Old and New Testaments." *BBR* 16 (2006) 53–77.

Kowalzig, Barbara. *Singing for the Gods: Performances of Myth and Ritual in Archaic and Classical Greece*. OCM. Oxford: Oxford University Press, 2007.

Kratz, Reinhard G. *Die Komposition der erzählenden Bücher der Alten Testaments: Grundwissen der Bibelkritik*. UTB 2157. Göttingen: Vandenhoeck & Ruprecht, 2000.

———. "The Pentateuch in Current Research: Consensus and Debate." In *The Pentateuch: International Perspectives on Current Research*, edited by Thomas B. Dozeman et al., 31–61. FAT 78. Tübingen: Mohr Siebeck, 2011.

Kuemmerlin-McLean, Joanne. "Magic." *AYBD* 4:468–71.

Kugel, James. "The Descent of the Wicked Angels and the Persistence of Evil." In *The Call of Abraham: Essays on the Election of Israel in Honor of Jon D. Levenson*, edited by Gary A. Anderson and Joel S. Kaminsky, 210–35. CJA 19. Notre Dame, IN: University of Notre Dame Press, 2013.

Kugler, Gili. "Egypt without Slavery—Tracing the Tradition of Israel's Residence in Egypt." *SJOT* 35 (2021) 111–25.

Kunin, Seth Daniel. *The Logic of Incest: A Structuralist Analysis of Hebrew Mythology*. LHBOTS. Sheffield: Academic, 1995.

Lack, Rémi. "Les origines de `Elyôn, le Très-Haut, dans la tradition cultuelle d'Israël." *CBQ* 24 (1962) 44–64.

Laffey, Alice L. *The Pentateuch: A Liberation-Critical Reading*. Minneapolis: Fortress, 1998.
Lambert, Wilfrid G. *Babylonian Creation Myths*. MC 16. Winona Lake, IN: Eisenbrauns, 2013.
———. "A Catalogue of Texts and Authors." *JCS* 16 (1962) 59–77.
Lambert, Wilfrid G., and Alan R. Millard. *Atra-Ḫasīs: The Babylonian Story of the Flood*. Repr., Winona Lake, IN: Eisenbrauns, 1999.
LaSor, William Sanford, et al. *Old Testament Survey: The Message, Form, and Background of the Old Testament*. 2nd ed. Grand Rapids: Eerdmans, 1996.
Lauinger, Jacob. "Esarhaddon's Succession Treaty at Tell Tayinat: Text and Commentary." *JCS* 64 (2012) 87–123.
Law, David R. *The Historical-Critical Method: A Guide for the Perplexed*. Guides for the Perplexed. New York: Oxford University Press, 2012.
Leach, Edmund R. *Genesis as Myth and Other Essays*. London: Cape, 1969.
Leach, Edmund R., and D. Alan Aycock. *Structuralist Interpretations of Biblical Myth*. Cambridge: Cambridge University Press, 1983.
Leach, John. *Survival Psychology*. New York: Macmillan, 1994.
Le Grys, Alan. "Difficult Texts: 1 Samuel 2:25." *Th* 117 (2014) 116–19.
Leibowitz, Nehama. *Studies in Shemot: The Book of Exodus*. Translated by Aryeh Newman. Jerusalem: World Zionist Organization, 1976.
Lemke, Niels. "Ḫabiru." *AYBD* 3:6–10.
Lennox, John. *Joseph: A Story of Love, Hate, Slavery, Power and Forgiveness*. Wheaton, IL: Crossway, 2019.
Lenzi, Alan. "Moses as Israelite *apkallu*." In *Secrecy and the Gods: Secret Knowledge in Ancient Mesopotamia and Biblical Israel*, 362–73. SAAS 19. Helsinki: Neo-Assyrian Text Corpus Project, 2008.
Leveen, Adriane B. "Falling in the Wilderness: Death Reports in the Book of Numbers." *Proof* 22 (2002) 245–72.
Levenson, Jon. *Creation and the Persistence of Evil: The Jewish Drama of Divine Omnipotence*. San Francisco: Harper and Row, 1988.
———. *Inheriting Abraham: The Legacy of the Patriarch in Judaism, Christianity, and Islam*. Library of Jewish Ideas 3. Princeton: Princeton University Press, 2012.
———. *Sinai and Zion: An Entry into the Jewish Bible*. San Francisco: HarperCollins, 1985.
Levinson, Bernard M. *Deuteronomy and the Hermeneutics of Legal Innovation*. New York: Oxford University Press, 1997.
Levine, Baruch A. "Foreword." In *WealthWatch: A Study of Socioeconomic Conflict in the Bible*, by Michael S. Moore, vi–ix. Eugene, OR: Pickwick, 2011.
———. *In the Presence of the Lord: A Study of Cult and Some Cultic Terms in Ancient Israel*. SJLA 5. Leiden: Brill, 1974.
———. "Leviticus." *AYBD* 4:311–21.
———. *Leviticus: The JPS Torah Commentary*. New York: Jewish Publication Society, 2003.
———. *Numbers: A New Translation with Introduction and Commentary*. 2 vols. AYBC 4A, 4B. New Haven, CT: Yale University Press, 1993, 2000.
Lévy-Bruhl, Lucien. *La mentalité primitive*. Paris: Alcan, 1922.
———. *Primitive Mentality*. Translated by L. A. Clare. London: Allen and Unwin, 1923.
Lewis, Jack P. "Flood." *AYBD* 2.798–803.

———. *A Study of the Interpretation of Noah and the Flood in Jewish and Christian Literature*. Leiden: Brill, 1968.
Lewis, Theodore J. *Cults of the Dead in Ancient Israel and Ugarit*. HSM 39. Atlanta: Scholars, 1989.
———. *The Origin and Character of God: Ancient Israelite Religion through the Lens of Divinity*. New York: Oxford University Press, 2020.
Lewis-Williams, J. David, and Thomas A. Dowson. "The Signs of All Times: Entoptic Phenomena in Upper Paleolithic Art." *CA* 29 (1988) 201–45.
Lieu, Judith M. *Marcion and the Making of a Heretic: God and Scripture in the Second Century*. Cambridge: University of Cambridge Press, 2015.
Liverani, Mario. *International Relations in the Ancient Near East*. New York: Palgrave, 2001.
Lohfink, Norbert. *Theology of the Pentateuch: Themes of the Priestly Narrative and Deuteronomy*. Translated by Linda M. Maloney. London: T&T Clark, 1994.
Lonergan, Bernard. *Insight: A Study of Human Understanding*. New York: Longmans, Green, and Co., 1957.
Longman, Tremper, III. *Literary Approaches to Biblical Interpretation*. Grand Rapids: Zondervan, 1987.
Longman, Tremper, III, and John H. Walton. *The Lost World of the Flood: Mythology, Theology, and the Deluge Debate*. Lost World 5. Downers Grove, IL: IVP Academic, 2018.
Lossow, Tobias von. "Weaponizing Water in the Middle East." In *Water and Conflict in the Middle East*, edited by Marcus Dubois King, 151–70. Oxford: Oxford University Press, 2020.
Luckenbill, Daniel D. "The Temples of Babylonia and Assyria." *AJSL* 24 (1908) 291–322.
Luhrmann, T. M. *Persuasions of the Witch's Craft: Ritual Magic in Contemporary England*. Cambridge, MA: Harvard University Press, 1989.
Lurquin, Paul F., and Linda Stone. *Evolution and Religious Creation Myths: How Scientists Respond*. Oxford: Oxford University Press, 2007.
Luther, Martin. *Die Bibel*. Repr., Berlin: Königliche Geheime Ober-Hofbuchdruckerei, 1863. First published 1534.
MacIntosh, Andrew A. *A Critical and Exegetical Commentary on Hosea*. ICC. Edinburgh: T&T Clark, 1997.
Maidman, Maynard P. *Nuzi Texts and Their Uses as Historical Evidence*. WAW 18. Atlanta: Society of Biblical Literature, 2010.
Mailloux, Steven. *Interpretive Conventions: The Reader in the Study of American Fiction*. Ithaca, NY: Cornell University Press, 1982.
Maimonides, Moses. *The Guide of the Perplexed*. Translated by Shlomo Pines. Chicago: University of Chicago Press, 1963.
Malul, Meir. "'āqeb 'Heel' and 'āqab 'To Supplant' and the Concept of Succession in the Jacob-Esau Narratives." *VT* 46 (1996) 190–212.
———. Review of *Inventing God's Law: How the Covenant Code of the Bible Used and Revised the Laws of Hammurabi*, by David P. Wright. *Strata* 29 (2011) 155–59.
Mann, Thomas W. *The Book of the Torah: The Narrative Integrity of the Pentateuch*. 2nd ed. Eugene, OR: Cascade, 2013.
Ma'oz, Moshe. *The Meeting of Civilizations: Muslim, Christian, and Jewish*. East Sussex, UK: Sussex Academic, 2009.

Marcus, David. "The Practical Use of the Masorah for the Elucidation of the Story of Samuel's Birth." In *The Text of the Hebrew Bible: From the Rabbis to the Masoretes*, edited by Elvira Martín-Contreras and Lorena Miralles-Maciá, 215–22. JAJSup 13. Göttingen: Vandenhoeck & Ruprecht, 2014.

Margueron, Jean-Claude. "Ur." *AYBD* 6:766–67.

Maritain, Jacques. *Christianisme et democratie*. New York: Maison française, 1943.

Marshall, I. Howard. *Biblical Inspiration*. London: Hodder & Stoughton, 1982.

Martin, Dale B. *Pedagogy of the Bible: An Analysis and Proposal*. Louisville: Westminster John Knox, 2008.

Marx, Karl, and Frederick Engels. *The Communist Manifesto*. Repr., London: Verso, 2012.

Mathews, Kenneth A. *Genesis 1—11:26*. NAC 1A. Nashville: B&H, 1996.

McCarter, P. Kyle. "When the Gods Lose Their Temper: Divine Rage in Ugaritic Myth and the Hypostasis of Anger in Iron Age Religion." In *Divine Wrath and Divine Mercy in the World of Antiquity*, edited by Reinhard G. Kratz and Hermann Spieckermann, 78–91. FAT, 2nd ser., 3. Tübingen: Mohr Siebeck, 2008.

McCarthy, Dennis J. *Treaty and Covenant: A Study in Form in the Ancient Oriental Documents and in the Old Testament*. AnBib 21. Rome: Pontifical Biblical Institute, 1963.

McConville, J. Gordon. *Law and Theology in Deuteronomy*. JSOTSup 33. Sheffield: JSOT, 1984.

McCoy, Bowen H. "The Parable of the *sadhû*." *HBR* 75 (1983) 103–8.

McDermott, Gerald R. *Famous Stutterers: Twelve Inspiring People Who Achieved Great Things while Struggling with an Impediment*. Eugene, OR: Cascade, 2016.

McEvenue, Seán. *Interpreting the Pentateuch*. OTS. Collegeville, MN: Liturgical, 1990.

McKnight, Edgar V. *Post-Modern Use of the Bible: The Emergence of Reader-Oriented Criticism*. Nashville: Abingdon, 1988.

Mendelsohn, Isaac. "Slavery in the Ancient Near East." *BA* 9 (1946) 74–88.

Mendenhall, George E. *Law and Covenant in Israel and the Ancient Near East*. Pittsburgh: Biblical Colloquium, 1955.

———. *The Tenth Generation: The Origins of the Biblical Tradition*. Baltimore: Johns Hopkins University Press, 1973.

Menéndez, Ramón, dir. *Stand and Deliver*. Burbank, CA: Warner Bros., 1988.

Middleton, J. Richard. *The Liberating Image: The* Imago Dei *in Genesis 1*. Grand Rapids: Brazos, 2005.

Milgrom, Jacob. *Leviticus 1–16: A New Translation with Introduction and Commentary*. AYBC 3A. New Haven, CT: Yale University Press, 1991.

———. "Magic, Monotheism, and the Sin of Moses." In *The Quest for the Kingdom of God: Studies in Honor of George E. Mendenhall*, edited by H. B. Huffmon et al., 251–65. Winona Lake, IN: Eisenbrauns, 1983.

Miller, Patrick D. *Genesis 1–11: Studies in Structure and Theme*. JSOTSup 8. Sheffield: University of Sheffield, 1978.

Miller, Robert D. "What Are the Nations Doing in the *Chaoskampf*?" In *Creation and Chaos: A Reconsideration of Hermann Gunkel's* Chaoskampf *Hypothesis*, edited by JoAnn Scurlock and Richard H. Beal, 206–15. Winona Lake, IN: Eisenbrauns, 2013.

Miller, Robert H. *Campus Confidential: The Complete Guide to the College Experience by Students for Students*. San Francisco: Jossey Bass, 2006.

Miller, Thomas, et al. *Promoting Reasonable Expectations: Aligning Student and Institutional Views of the College Experience*. San Francisco: Jossey Bass, 2005.

Milstein, Sara J. *Making a Case: The Practical Roots of Biblical Law*. Oxford: Oxford University Press, 2021.

Milton, Sybil. "The Expulsion of Polish Jews from Germany October 1938 to July 1939: A Documentation." In *The Nazi Holocaust*, edited by Michael R. Marrus, 2:518–52. Berlin: de Gruyter, 1989.

Mirguet, Francoise. *La représentation du divin dans les récits du Pentateuque*. VTSup 123. Leiden: Brill, 2009.

Moberly, Robert L. W. *The Old Testament of the Old Testament: Patriarchal Narratives and Mosaic Yahwism*. OBT. Minneapolis: Fortress, 1992.

———. "What Is Theological Interpretation of Scripture?" *JTI* 3 (2009) 161–78.

Mobley, Gregory. *The Empty Men: The Heroic Tradition of Ancient Israel*. New York: Doubleday, 2005.

———. "The Wild Man in the Bible and the Ancient Near East." *JBL* 116 (1997) 217–33.

Momigliano, Arnaldo. "Biblical Studies and Classical Studies: Simple Reflections on Historical Method." In *On Pagans, Jews, and Christians*, 3–9. Repr., Middletown, CT: Wesley University Press, 1987.

Monroe, Lauren A. S. *Josiah's Reform and the Dynamics of Defilement: Israelite Rites of Violence and the Making of a Biblical Text*. New York: Oxford University Press, 2011.

Moore, Michael S. "1 and 2 Maccabees." In *The Old Testament and Apocrypha*, edited by Gale A. Yee et al., 1055–71. Fortress Commentary on the Bible. Minneapolis: Fortress, 2014.

———. "Abraham's Temptation." In *Reconciliation: A Study of Biblical Families in Conflict*, 35–48. Joplin, MO: College Press, 1994.

———. *The Balaam Traditions: Their Character and Development*. SBLDS 113. Atlanta: Scholars, 1990.

———. "Bathsheba's Silence." In *Inspired Speech: Prophecy in the Ancient Near East: Essays Presented to Herbert B. Huffmon*, edited by John Kaltner and Louis Stulman, 336–46. LHBOTS 378. New York: Continuum, 2004.

———. "Divine Presence." *DOTPr* 166–70.

———. *Faith under Pressure: A Study of Biblical Leaders in Conflict*. Siloam Springs, AR: Leafwood, 2003.

———. "הגאל: The Cultural Gyroscope of Ancient Hebrew Society." *ResQ* 23 (1980) 27–35.

———. "Jehu's Coronation and Purge of Israel." *VT* 53 (2003) 97–114.

———. "Jesus Christ: 'Superstar.'" *NovT* 24 (1982) 82–91.

———. "Miriam's Error." In *Reconciliation: A Study of Biblical Families in Conflict*, 61–72. Joplin, MO: College Press, 1994.

———. "Numbers." In *The Transforming Word: A One-Volume Commentary on the Bible*, edited by Mark W. Hamilton, 185–202. Abilene: ACU Press, 2009.

———. "Obduracy, Hardness of Heart." *EHJ* 428–29.

———. *Reconciliation: A Study of Biblical Families in Conflict*. Joplin, MO: College, 1994.

———. *Retribution or Reality? A Short Theological Introduction to the Book of Job*. Eugene, OR: Pickwick, 2023.

———. Review of *Abiding Astonishment*, by Walter Brueggemann, *CBQ* 54 (1992) 740–41.

———. Review of *Deuteronomium 28 und die adê zur Thronfolgeregelung Asarhaddons: Segen und Fluch im Alten Orient und in Israel*, by Hans Ulrich Steymans. *JBL* 116 (1997) 729–30.

———. Review of *The Bridling of the Tongue and and the Opening of the Mouth in Biblical Prophecy*, by Gregory Yuri Glazov. *JBL* 122 (2003) 558–60.

———. Review of *The Jehu Revolution: A Royal Tradition of the Northern Kingdom and Its Ramifications*, by Jonathan Miles Robker. *CBQ* 77 (2015) 151–53.

———. Review of *Theology of the Old Testament: Testimony, Dispute, Advocacy*, by Walter Brueggemann. *PSB* 19 (1998) 212–15.

———. Review of *Welcoming but Not Affirming*, by Stanley J. Grenz. *BBR* 10 (2000) 143–53.

———. "Role Preemption in the Israelite Priesthood." *VT* 46 (1996) 316–29.

———. "Ruth." In *Joshua, Judges, Ruth*, 291–373. UBCS. Grand Rapids: Baker, 2000.

———. "Sacrifice, Tithes, Offerings." *EHJ* 533–36.

———. *WeathWarn: A Study of Socioeconomic Conflict in Hebrew Prophecy*. Eugene, OR: Pickwick, 2019.

———. *WealthWatch: A Study of Socioeconomic Conflict in the Bible*. Eugene, OR: Pickwick, 2011.

———. *WealthWise: A Study of Socioeconomic Conflict in Hebrew Wisdom*. Eugene, OR: Pickwick, 2021.

———. *What Is This Babbler Trying to Say? Essays on Biblical Interpretation*. Eugene, OR: Pickwick, 2016.

Moore, Michael S., and Marlene Klunzinger. "Codependency and Pastoral Care: A Report from the Trenches." *ResQ* 38 (1996) 159–74.

Morales, L. Michael. *Who Shall Ascend the Mountain of the Lord? A Biblical Theology of the Book of Leviticus*. NSBT 37. Downers Grove, IL: Apollos, 2015.

Moran, William. *The Amarna Letters*. Baltimore: Johns Hopkins University Press, 1992.

———. "Ancient Near Eastern Background to the Love of God in Deuteronomy." *CBQ* 25 (1963) 77–87.

———. "Some Considerations of Form and Interpretation in Atrahasis." In *Language, Literature, and History: Philological and Historical Studies Presented to Erica Reiner*, edited by Francesca Rochberg-Halton, 245–55. New Haven, CT: American Oriental Society, 1987.

Moss, Candida R., and Joel S. Baden. *Reconceiving Infertility: Biblical Perspectives on Procreation and Childlessness*. Princeton: Princeton University Press, 2015.

Mouton, Alice. *Rêves hittites: Contribution a une histoire et une anthropologie du rêve en Anatolie ancienne*. CHANE 28. Leiden: Brill, 2007.

Mowinckel, Sigmund. *Erwägungen zur Pentateuch Quellenfrage*. Oslo: Universitetsvorlaget, 1964.

———. *Zur Komposition des Buches Jeremia*. Kristiana, Nor.: Dybwad, 1914.

Mugerauer, Robert. "Literature as Reconciliation: The Art of Hypothetical Vision." *Soundings* 58 (1975) 407–15.

Muilenburg, James. "The Biblical View of Time." *HTR* 54 (1961) 225–52.

Murnane, William J. "The History of Ancient Egypt: An Overview." *CANE* 2:691–717.

Nathan, Emmanuel, and Anya Topolski. "The Myth of a Judeo-Christian Tradition: Introducing a European Perspective." In *Is There a Judeo-Christian Tradition? A European Perspective*, edited by Emmanuel Nathan and Anya Topolski, 1–14. Perspectives on Jewish Texts and Contexts 4. Berlin: de Gruyter, 2016.

Nicholson, Ernest. *The Pentateuch in the Twentieth Century: The Legacy of Julius Wellhausen*. Oxford: Oxford University Press, 1998.

Niditch, Susan. *A Prelude to Biblical Folklore: Underdogs and Tricksters*. Urbana: University of Illinois Press, 2000.

Nixon, Jon. *Erich Auerbach and the Secular World: Literary Criticism, Historiography, Post-Colonial Theory and Beyond*. Literary Criticism and Cultural Theory. New York: Routledge, 2022.

Nogalski, James. *Literary Precursors to the Book of the Twelve*. BZAW 217. Berlin: de Gruyter, 1993.

Noonan, Benjamin. "On the Efficacy of the Atoning Sacrifices: A Biblical Theology of Sacrifice from Leviticus." *BBR* 31 (2021) 285–318.

Nordheim, Eckhard von. *Die Selbstbehauptung Israels in der Welt des Alten Orients: Religionsgeschichtlicher Vergleich anhand von Gen 15/22/28, dem Aufenthalt Israels in Ägypten, 2 Sam 7, 1 Kön 19 und Psalm 104*. OBO 115. Göttingen: Vandenhoeck & Ruprecht, 1992.

Noth, Martin. *A History of Pentateuchal Traditions*. Translated by Bernard W. Anderson. Englewood Cliffs, NJ: Prentice-Hall, 1972.

———. *The Laws in the Pentateuch and Other Studies*. Translated by D. R. Ap-Thomas. London: SCM, 1984.

———. *Numbers*. OTL. Philadelphia: Westminster, 1968.

———. *Überlieferungsgeschichtliche Studien*. Schriften der Königsberger Gelehrten Gesellschaft: Geisteswissenschaftliche Klasse 18. Wiesbaden: Harrassowitz, 1943.

Nozick, Robert. *Anarchy, State, and Utopia*. London: Blackwell, 1974.

O'Brien, Julia. *Priest and Levite in Malachi*. SBLDS 121. Atlanta: Scholars, 1990.

Ollenburger, Ben C. *God the Creator: The Old Testament and the World God Is Making*. Grand Rapids: Baker Academic, 2023.

Olson, Dennis T. *The Death of the Old and the Birth of the New: The Framework of the Book of Numbers and the Pentateuch*. BJS 71. Chico, CA: Scholars, 1985.

Olyan, Saul M. *Social Inequality in the World of the Text: The Significance of Ritual and Social Distinctions in the Hebrew Bible*. Göttingen: Vandenhoeck & Ruprecht, 2011.

O'Neill, John C. "Biblical Criticism." *AYBD* 1:725–30.

Oppenheim, A. Leo. *The Interpretation of Dreams in the Ancient Near East*. Philadelphia: American Philosophical Society, 1956.

Otto, Eckart. "Neue Aspekte zum keilschriftlichen Prozessrecht in Babylonien und Assyrien." *ZABR* 4 (1998) 263–83.

Otto, Rudolf. *The Idea of the Holy*. Oxford: Oxford University Press, 1946.

Parkinson, Richard B. "The Tale of Sinuhe." In *The Tale of Sinuhe and Other Egyptian Poems 1940–640 BC*, 21–53. Oxford: Oxford University Press, 1997.

———. "The Tale of the Eloquent Peasant." In *The Tale of Sinuhe and Other Egyptian Poems 1940–640 BC*, 54–88. Oxford: Oxford University Press, 1997.

Parpola, Simo. *Assyrian Prophecies*. SAA 9. Helsinki: Helsinki University Press, 1997.

Parunak, Henry van Dyke. "Transitional Techniques in the Bible." *JBL* 102 (1983) 525–48.

Pavlac, Brian A. "The Chosen People: Hebrews and Jews, 2000 BC to AD 125." In *A Concise Survey of Western Civilization: Supremacies and Diversities throughout History*, 53–68. 3rd ed. London: Rowman and Littlefield, 2019.

Peake, Harold. *The Flood*. London: Kegan Paul, Trench, Trubner and Co., 1930.

Pelham, Abigail. *Contested Creations in the Book of Job: The-World-as-It-Ought-and-Ought-Not-to-Be*. BI 113. Leiden: Brill, 2012.
Pemberton, Glenn D. "Leviticus." In *The Transforming Word: A One-Volume Commentary on the Bible*, edited by Mark W. Hamilton, 167–84. Abilene: ACU Press, 2009.
Perdue, Leo. *Reconstructing Old Testament Theology: After the Collapse of History*. Minneapolis: Fortress, 2005.
———. *Wisdom and Creation: The Theology of Wisdom Literature*. Repr., Eugene, OR: Wipf & Stock, 2009.
Perrin, Norman. *What Is Redaction Criticism?* Philadelphia: Fortress, 1973.
Petersen, David L. *The Roles of Israel's Prophets*. JSOTSup 17. Sheffield: JSOT, 1981.
Peterson, Ryan S. *The Imago Dei as Human Identity*. JTISup 14. Winona Lake, IN: Eisenbrauns, 2016.
Petrie, William Matthew Flinders. *Six Temples at Thebes*. London: Quaritch, 1897.
Picirilli, Robert E. *Free Will Revisited: A Respectful Response to Luther, Calvin, and Edwards*. Eugene, OR: Wipf and Stock, 2017.
Polzin, Robert. "The Framework of the Book of Job." *Int* 28 (1974) 182–200.
Porter, James I. "Erich Auerbach and the Judaizing of Philology." *CI* 35 (2008) 115–47.
Propp, Vladimir. *Morphology of the Folktale*. Edited by Louis A. Wagner. Translated by Laurence Scott. 2nd ed. American Folklore Society Bibliographical and Special Series. Austin: University of Texas Press, 1968.
Propp, William H. C. *Exodus 1–18: A New Translation with Introduction and Commentary*. AYBC 2. New Haven, CT: Yale University Press, 1999.
———. *Water in the Wilderness: A Biblical Motif and Its Mythological Background*. HSM 40. Atlanta: Scholars, 1987.
Provan, Iain. "Knowing and Believing: Faith in the Past." In *"Behind" the Text: History and Biblical Interpretation*, edited by Craig Bartholomew et al., 229–66. Grand Rapids: Zondervan, 2003.
Pury, Albert de. *Promesse divine et légende cultuelle dans le cycle de Jacob: Gen 28 et les traditions patriarcales*. EBib. Paris: Gabalda, 1975.
Rabinowitz, Louis I. "Famine and Drought." *EncJud* 6:707–8.
Radcliffe-Brown, Alfred. *Structure and Function in Primitive Society*. London: Cohen & West, 1952.
Radday, Y. "Chiasm in Tora." *LB* 19 (1972) 21–23.
Räisänen, Heikki. *Paul and the Law*. 2nd ed. WUNT 29. Tübingen: Mohr Siebeck, 1983.
Redford, Donald B. "Amarna, Tell-El." *AYBD* 1:181–82.
———. "Ancient Egyptian Literature: An Overview." *CANE* 2223–41.
Reidy, Richard J. *Everlasting Egypt: Kemetic Rituals for the Gods*. Bloomington, IN: iUniverse, 2018.
Reiner, Erica. "Die akkadische Literatur." In *Neues Handbuch der Literatur-Wissenschaft*, edited by Wolfgang Röllig, 1:151–210. Wiesbaden: Athenaion, 1978.
Rendsburg, Gary A. *The Redaction of Genesis*. Winona Lake, IN: Eisenbrauns, 1986.
Rendtorff, Rolf. "Is It Possible to Read Leviticus as a Separate Book?" In *Reading Leviticus: Responses to Mary Douglas*, edited by John F. A. Sawyer, 22–35. LHBOTS 227. Sheffield: Academic, 1996.
———. *Das überlieferungsgeschichtliche Problem des Pentateuch*. BZAW 147. Berlin: de Gruyter, 1977.
Renger, Johannes. "Untersuchungen zum Priestertum in der altbabylonischen Zeit." *ZA* 58 (1967) 110–88; 59 (1969) 104–230.

Richter, Sandra L. *Deuteronomistic History and the Name Theology:* לשכן שמו שם *in the Bible and the Ancient Near East*. BZAW 319. Berlin: de Gruyter, 2002.
Rickett, Dan. *Separating Abram and Lot: The Narrative Role and Early Reception of Genesis 13*. TBN 26. Leiden: Brill, 2020.
Roberts, Jimmy Jack McBee. "The Ancient Near Eastern Environment." In *The Hebrew Bible and Its Modern Interpreters*, edited by Douglas A. Knight and G. M. Tucker, 75–121. Chico, CA: Scholars, 1985.
Rofé, Alexander. ספר בלעם [The book of Balaam]. Jerusalem: Simor, 1979.
Römer, Thomas. "La Construction du Pentateuque, de l'Hexateuque et de l'Ennéateuque: Investigations préliminaires sur la formation des grands ensembles littéraires de la Bible hébraïque." In *Les Dernières Rédactions du Pentateuque, de l'Hexateuque et de l'Ennéateuque*, edited by T. Römer and K. Schmid, 9–34. BETL 203. Leuven: Leuven University Press, 2007.
———. "Israel's Sojourn in the Wilderness and the Construction of the Book of Numbers." In *Reflection and Refraction: Studies in Biblical Historiography in Honour of A. Graeme Auld*, edited by Robert Rezetko et al., 419–46. VTSup 113. Leiden: Brill, 2006.
———. "Os papeis papéis de Moisés no Pentateuco." In *Pentateuco: da formação à recepção*, edited by Marcelo de Silva Carneiro et al., 89–108. São Paulo: Paulinas, 2016.
Rooker, Mark F. *Leviticus*. NAC 3. Nashville: B&H, 2000.
Ross, Allen P. *Creation and Blessing: A Guide to the Study and Exposition of the Book of Genesis*. Grand Rapids: Baker, 1988.
Rost, Leonhard. "Ein hethitisches Ritual gegen Familienzwist." *MIO* 1 (1953) 345–79.
Rothenberg, Benno. *Timna*. London: Thames and Hudson, 1972.
Rubio, Gonzalo. "Time before Time: Primeval Narratives in Early Mesopotamian Literature." In *Time and History in the Ancient Near East: Proceedings of the 56th Rencontre Assyriologique International at Barcelona 26–30 July 2010*, edited by Lluis Feliu et al., 3–18. Winona Lake, IN: Eisenbrauns, 2013.
Sailhamer, John H. *The Pentateuch as Narrative: A Biblical-Theological Commentary*. Library of Biblical Interpretation. Grand Rapids: Zondervan, 1992.
Sakenfeld, Katharine D. "The Problem of Divine Forgiveness in Numbers 14." *CBQ* 37 (1975) 317–30.
Salkin, Jeffrey. "The Frankists and the Reformers: A Hidden Link." *JRJ* 35 (1988) 25–30.
Sanders, John. *The God Who Risks: A Theology of Divine Providence*. 2nd ed. Downers Grove, IL: IVP Academic, 2007.
Sarisky, Darren. "What Is Theological Interpretation? The Example of Robert W. Jenson." *IJST* 12 (2010) 201–16.
Sarna, Nahum M. "Exodus, Book of." *AYBD* 2:689–700.
Schlimm, Matthew R. *From Fratricide to Forgiveness: The Language and Ethics of Anger in Genesis*. SiLTHS 7. Winona Lake, IN: Eisenbrauns, 2011.
Schmid, Hans Heinrich. *Der sogenannte Jahwist: Beobachtungen und Fragen zur Pentateuchforschung*. Zurich: Theologisch, 1976.
Schmid, Konrad. "Genesis and Exodus as Two Formerly Independent Traditions of Origins for Ancient Israel." *Bib* 93 (2012) 187–208.
———. *Genesis and the Moses Story: Israel's Dual Origins in the Hebrew Bible*. Translated by James D. Nogalski. SiLTHS 3. Winona Lake, IN: Eisenbrauns, 2010.
———. *Gibt es Theologie im Alten Testament? Zum Theologiebegriff in der alttestamentlichen Wissenschaft*. ThSt 7. Zurich: Theologisch, 2017.

———. "Der Pentateuch und seine Theologiegeschichte." *ZTK* 111 (2014) 239–70.

———. *The Scribes of the Torah: The Formation of the Pentateuch in Its Literary and Historical Contexts*. AIL 45. Atlanta: SBL, 2023.

Schmidt, Ludwig. *Gesammelte Aufsätze zum Pentateuch*. BZAW 263. Berlin: de Gruyter, 1998.

Schneider, Tammi J. *An Introduction to Ancient Mesopotamian Religion*. Grand Rapids: Eerdmans, 2011.

Schniedewind, William. *The Word of God in Transition: From Prophet to Exegete in the Second Temple Period*. JSOTSup 197. Sheffield: Academic, 1995.

Schnittjer, Gary E. *Torah Story: An Apprenticeship on the Pentateuch*. 2nd ed. Grand Rapids: Zondervan Academic, 2023.

Scholer, John M. *Proleptic Priests: Priesthood in the Epistle to the Hebrews*. JSNTSup 49. Sheffield: Academic, 1991.

Scurlock, JoAnn. "Chaos and (Re)Creation: *Chaoskampf* Lost—*Chaoskampf* Regained." In *Creation and Chaos: A Reconsideration of Hermann Gunkel's* Chaoskampf *Hypothesis*, edited by JoAnn Scurlock and Richard H. Beal, 257–68. Winona Lake, IN: Eisenbrauns, 2013.

———. "Introduction." In *Creation and Chaos: A Reconsideration of Hermann Gunkel's* Chaoskampf *Hypothesis*, edited by JoAnn Scurlock and Richard H. Beal, ix–xiv. Winona Lake, IN: Eisenbrauns, 2013.

———. "Searching for Meaning in Genesis 1:2: Purposeful Creation out of *Chaos* without *Kampf*." In *Creation and Chaos: A Reconsideration of Hermann Gunkel's* Chaoskampf *Hypothesis*, edited by JoAnn Scurlock and Richard H. Beal, 48–61. Winona Lake, IN: Eisenbrauns, 2013.

Segal, Michael. "Between Bible and Rewritten Bible." In *Biblical Interpretation at Qumran*, edited by Matthias Henze, 10–28. Grand Rapids: Eerdmans, 2005.

———. "The Literary Relationship between the Genesis Apocryphon and Jubilees: The Chronology of Abram and Sarai's Descent into Egypt." *AS* 8 (2010) 71–88.

Sellin, Ernst, and Georg Fohrer. *Introduction to the Old Testament*. Translated by David Green. Nashville: Abingdon, 1968.

Shapiro, Aharon H. "Moses: Henry George's Inspiration." *AJES* 47 (1988) 493–501.

Sharp, Carolyn J. *Prophecy and Ideology in Jeremiah: Struggles for Authority in the Deutero-Jeremianic Prose*. New York: Continuum, 2003.

Shectman, Sarah. "Themes and Perspectives in Torah: Creation, Kinship, and Covenant." In *The Old Testament and Apocrypha*, edited by Gale A. Yee et al., 67–87. Fortress Commentary on the Bible. Minneapolis: Fortress, 2014.

———. *Women in the Pentateuch: A Feminist and Source-Critical Analysis*. HBM 23. Sheffield: Sheffield Phoenix, 2009.

Schifferdecker, Kathryn M. *Out of the Whirlwind: Creation Theology in the Book of Job*. HTS 61. Cambridge, MA: Harvard University Press, 2008.

Shuval, Hillel. "Meeting Vital Human Needs: Equitable Resolution of Conflicts over Shared Water Resources of Israelis and Palestinians." In *Water Resources in the Middle East: Israel-Palestinian Water Issues—From Conflict to Cooperation*, edited by Hillel Shuval and Hassan Dweick, 3–16. Hexagon Series on Human and Environmental Security and Peace 2. New York: Springer, 2007.

Sibler, Earle. *Helping Students Adapt to Graduate School: Making the Grade*. New York: Routledge, 2021.

Silva, Moisés. *Has the Church Misread the Bible? The History of Interpretation in the Light of Current Issues*. Grand Rapids: Zondervan, 1987.

Ska, Jean-Louis. *Introduction to Reading the Pentateuch*. Winona Lake, IN: Eisenbrauns, 2006.

Skeel, David A. *Debt's Dominion: A History of Bankruptcy Law in America*. Princeton: Princeton University Press, 2001.

Skinner, John. *A Critical and Exegetical Commentary on Genesis*. Edinburgh: T&T Clark, 1930.

Smith, Geoffrey S. *Valentinian Christianity: Texts and Translations*. Berkeley: University of California Press, 2019.

Smith, Mark S. *The Pilgrimage Pattern in Exodus*. JSOTSup 239. Sheffield: Sheffield Academic, 1997.

Smith, William Cantwell. *What Is Scripture? A Comparative Approach*. Philadelphia: Fortress, 1993.

Snell, Daniel C. *Flight and Freedom in the Ancient Near East*. CHANE 8. Leiden: Brill, 2001.

Snyman, Gerrie F. "Reader's Disgust in the Case of Rebekah, Jacob, Isaac, and Esau: Perverters of Justice?" *OTE* (2020) 445–72.

Sofer, Arnon. *Rivers of Fire: The Conflict over Water in the Middle East*. Lanham, MD: Rowman and Littlefield, 1999.

Sommer, Benjamin D. "Dating Texts and the Peril of Pseudo-Historicism: Some Remarks on a Depressingly Pervasive Fallacy in Biblical Studies." In *The Pentateuch: International Perspectives on Current Research*, edited by Thomas B. Dozeman et al., 85–108. FAT 78. Tübingen: Mohr Siebeck, 2011.

Sonik, Karen. "From Hesiod's Abyss to Ovid's *rudis indigestaque moles*: Chaos and Cosmos in the Babylonian 'Epic of Creation.'" In *Creation and Chaos: A Reconsideration of Hermann Gunkel's* Chaoskampf *Hypothesis*, edited by JoAnn Scurlock and Richard H. Beal, 1–25. Winona Lake, IN: Eisenbrauns, 2013.

Spalinger, Anthony. "Orientations on Sinuhe." *SAK* 25 (1998) 311–39.

Sparks, Kenton L. "*Enūma eliš* and Priestly Mimesis: Elite Emulation in Nascent Judaism." *JBL* 126 (2007) 625–48.

Speiser, Ephraim A. *Genesis*. AYB 1. New Haven, CT: Yale University Press, 2021.

Spencer, Herbert. *Principles of Sociology*. London: Williams & Norgate, 1871.

Spero, Shubert. "Jacob's Growing Understanding of his Experience at Beth-El." *JBQ* 26 (1998) 211–15.

Spicq, C., OB. *Agapè: Prolégomènes à une étude de théologie néo-testamentaire*. SH 10. Leiden: Brill, 1955.

Spier, Hedwige. "The Motive for the Suppliants' Flight." *CJ* 57 (1962) 315–17.

Stackert, Jeffrey. *Deuteronomy and the Pentateuch*. AYBRL. New Haven, CT: Yale University Press, 2022.

———. *Rewriting the Torah: Literary Revision in Deuteronomy and the Holiness Legislation*. FAT 52. Tübingen: Mohr Siebeck, 2007.

Staubli, Thomas. "Cultural and Religious Impacts of Long-Term Cross-Cultural Migration between Egypt and the Levant." *JAEI* 12 (2016) 50–88.

Steinmann, Andrew E. *Genesis: An Introduction and Commentary*. TOTC. Downers Grove, IL: IVP Academic, 2019.

Steinmetz, Devorah. *From Father to Son: Kinship, Conflict, and Continuity in Genesis*. LCBI. Louisville: Westminster John Knox, 1991.

Steinsaltz, Adin. *The Essential Talmud*. London: Weidenfeld and Nicholson, 1976.

Sternberg, Meir. *The Poetics of Biblical Narrative: Ideological Literature and the Drama of Reading*. Biblical Literature. Bloomington: University of Indiana Press, 1985.

Steymans, Hans Ulrich. *Deuteronomium 28 und die adê zur Thronfolgeregelung Asarhaddons: Segen und Fluch im Alten Orient und Israel.* OBO 145. Göttingen: Vandenhoeck & Ruprecht, 1996.

Stökl, Jonathan. *Prophecy in the Ancient Near East: A Philological and Sociological Comparison.* CHANE 56. Leiden: Brill, 2012.

Strauss, Barry. *The Spartacus War.* New York: Simon & Schuster, 2009.

Stuart, Douglas K. *Exodus.* NAC 2. Nashville: B&H, 2006.

Sturtevant, Edgar H. "A Hittite Text on the Duties of Priests and Temple Servants." *JAOS* 54 (1934) 363–406.

Surls, Austin D. "Making Sense of the Divine Name in the Book of Exodus: From Etymology to Literary Onomastics." PhD diss., Wheaton College, 2015.

Syrén, Roger. *The Forsaken Firstborn: A Study of a Recurrent Motif in the Patriarchal Narratives.* JSOTSup 133. Sheffield: Academic, 1993.

Taggar-Cohen, Ada. "Law and Family in the Book of Numbers: The Levites and the *tidennutu* Documents from Nuzi." *VT* 48 (1998) 74–94.

Thompson, Thomas L. "'He Is Yhwh: He Does What Is Right in His Own Eyes': The Old Testament as Theological Discipline." In *Patronage in Ancient Palestine and in the Hebrew Bible: A Reader*, edited by Emanuel Pfoh, 342–58. SWBA, 2nd ser., 12. Sheffield: Sheffield Phoenix, 2022.

Throntveit, Mark A. "Things We Never Preach About, Part IV: The Dark Side of Abraham and Sarah." *LF* 47 (2013) 24–26.

Tigay, Jeffrey H. *The Evolution of the Gilgamesh Epic.* Philadelphia: University of Pennsylvania Press, 1982.

Tomlinson, F. Alan. "Cohesion and Structure in the Pastoral Epistles." In *Entrusted with the Gospel: Paul's Theology in the Pastoral Epistles*, edited by Andreas J. Köstenberger and Terry L. Wilder, 84–104. Nashville: B&H Academic, 2010.

Tov, Emanuel. "Rewritten Bible Compositions and Biblical Manuscripts, with Special Attention to the Samaritan Pentateuch." *DSD* 5 (1998) 334–54.

Töyräänvuori, Joanna. "The Northwest Semitic Conflict Myth and Egyptian Sources from the Middle and New Kingdoms." In *Creation and Chaos: A Reconsideration of Hermann Gunkel's* Chaoskampf *Hypothesis*, edited by JoAnn Scurlock and Richard H. Beal, 112–26. Winona Lake, IN: Eisenbrauns, 2013.

Trible, Phyllis. *Texts of Terror: Literary-Feminist Readings of Biblical Narratives.* OBT. Minneapolis: Fortress, 1984.

Tsumuraya, Katsuko. "A Canonical Reading of Genesis 1–3." PhD diss., Catholic University of America, 1994.

Tutt, Trevor D. "Sibling Rivalry: Sibling Relationships in World Mythology." MA thesis, Northwest Missouri State University, 2015.

Tylor, Edward B. *Primitive Culture: Researches into the Development of Mythology, Philosophy, Religion, Art and Custom.* London: Murray, 1871.

Ulanowski, Krzysztof. *Neo-Assyrian and Greek Divination in War.* CHANE 118. Leiden: Brill, 2021.

Urbainczyk, Theresa. *Slave Revolts in Antiquity.* New York: Routledge, 2014.

Van de Mieroop, Marc. "A History of Near Eastern Debt?" In *Debt and Economic Renewal in the Ancient Near East*, edited by Michael Hudson and Marc van de Mieroop, 59–94. International Scholars Conference on Ancient Near Eastern Economics 3. Bethesda, MD: CDL, 2002.

VanderKam, James C. *From Joshua to Caiaphas: High Priests after the Exile.* Minneapolis: Fortress, 2004.

Van der Toorn, Karel. *Becoming Diaspora Jews: Behind the Story of Elephantine*. AYBRL. New Haven, CT: Yale University Press, 2019.

———. "Before the Decalogue: In Search of the Oldest Written Torah." *CBQ* 85 (2023) 385–401.

———. "Did Jeremiah See Aaron's Staff?" *JSOT* 43 (1989) 83–94.

———. "Ordeal." *AYBD* 5:40–42.

———. *Scribal Culture and the Making of the Hebrew Bible*. Cambridge, MA: Harvard University Press, 2007.

Van Dijk, Jacobus. "Myth and Mythmaking in Ancient Egypt." *CANE* 3:1697–1709.

Vanhoozer, Kevin J. *Is There a Meaning in This Text? The Bible, the Reader, and the Morality of Literary Knowledge*. Landmarks in Christian Scholarship. Grand Rapids: Zondervan Academic, 1998.

Van Inwagen, Peter. "Do You Want Us to Listen to You?" In *"Behind" the Text: History and Biblical Interpretation*, edited by Craig Bartholomew et al., 101–30. Grand Rapids: Zondervan Academic, 2003.

Van Seters, John. *Abraham in History and Tradition*. New Haven, CT: Yale University Press, 1975.

———. *The Pentateuch: A Social-Science Commentary*. T&T Clark Cornerstones. Repr., London: Bloomsbury T&T Clark, 2004.

———. *Prologue to History: The Yahwist as Historian in Genesis*. Louisville: Westminster John Knox, 1992.

Veidlinger, Jeffrey. *In the Midst of Civilized Europe: The 1918–1921 Pogroms in Ukraine and the Onset of the Holocaust*. New York: Holt, 2021.

Vermès, Géza. *Scripture and Tradition in Judaism: Haggadic Studies*. StPB. Leiden: Brill, 1973.

Vermeylen, Jacques. *Job, ses amis, et son Dieu: La légende de Job et ses relectures postexiliques*. StudBib 2. Leiden: Brill, 1986.

Vieyra, M. "Le sorcier hittite." In *Le monde du sorcier*, edited by Denise Bernot et al., 101–25. SO 7. Paris: Seuil, 1966.

Vita, Juan-Pablo. "The Society of Ugarit." In *Handbook of Ugaritic Studies*, edited by Wilfred G. E. Watson and Nicolas Wyatt, 455–98. HdO 39. Leiden: Brill, 1999.

Vogt, Peter T. *Deuteronomic Theology and the Significance of Torah: A Reappraisal*. Winona Lake, IN: Eisenbrauns, 2006.

Von Rad, Gerhard. *Deuteronomium-Studien*. FRLANT 58. Göttingen: Vandenhoeck & Ruprecht, 1947.

———. *Das erste Buch Mose (Genesis)*. Altes Testament Deutsch Neubearbeitungen 2–4. Göttingen: Vandenhoeck & Ruprecht, 1958.

———. "The Form-Critical Problem of the Hexateuch." In *The Problem of the Hexateuch and Other Essays*, 1–78. Edinburgh: Oliver & Boyd, 1966.

———. "Josephsgeschichte und die ältere Chokma." VTSup 3 (1953) 120–27.

———. *Old Testament Theology*. 2 vols. New York: Harper and Row, 1962.

Wahlde, Urban C. von. *The Earliest Version of John's Gospel: Recovering the Gospel of Signs*. Wilmington, DE: Glazier, 1989.

Walker, Christopher, and Michael Dick. *The Induction of the Cult Image in Ancient Mesopotamia: The Mesopotamian Mīs Pî Ritual*. SAALT 1. Helsinki: Neo-Assyrian Corpus Project, 2001.

Walsh, George. *The Role of Religion in History*. New York: Routledge, 2017.

Walsh, Jerome T. *Style and Structure in Biblical Hebrew Narrative*. Collegeville, MN: Liturgical, 2017.

Walton, John. "Babel's Invitation." *CT* 67 (2023) 73–77.
Walzer, Michael. *Exodus and Revolution*. New York: Basic, 1985.
Wang, Xianhua. *The Metamorphosis of Enlil in Early Mesopotamia*. Münster: Ugarit, 2011.
Washburn, Jennifer. *University, Inc.: The Corporate Corruption of American Higher Education*. New York: Basic, 2005.
Watson, Paul. "The Death of 'Death' in the Ugaritic Texts." *JAOS* 92 (1972) 60–64.
Watson, Rebecca S. *Chaos Uncreated*. BZAW 341. Berlin: de Gruyter, 2005.
Watts, James W. Review of *The Pilgrimage Pattern in Exodus*, by Mark S. Smith. *JBL* 118 (1999) 128–29.
———. *Understanding the Pentateuch as a Scripture*. Oxford: Wiley and Sons, 2017.
Wefing, Sabina. "Beobachtungen zum Ritual mit der roten Kuh (Num 19.1–10a)." *ZAW* 93 (1981) 341–64.
Weinfeld, Moshe. "Deuteronomy." *AYBD* 2:168–83.
———. *Deuteronomy 1–11: A New Translation with Introduction and Commentary*. AYBC. New Haven, CT: Yale University Press, 1974.
———. *Deuteronomy and the Deuteronomic School*. Oxford: Oxford University Press, 1972.
———. "Sarah and Abimelech against the Background of Assyrian Law and the Genesis Apocryphon." In *Mélanges bibliques et orientaux en l'honneur de M. Mathias Delcor*, edited by André Caquot et al., 431–36. AOAT. Neukirchen-Vluyn, Germ.: Neukirchen, 1985.
———. "Traces of Assyrian Treaty Formulae in Deuteronomy." *Bib* 46 (1965) 417–27.
Weiss, Shira. "The Ethics of Price Gouging: Jacob's Purchase of Esau's Birthright." *JRE* 45 (2017) 142–63.
Wellek, René. "Auerbach's Special Realism." *KR* 16 (1954) 299–307.
Wellhausen, Julius. *Die Composition des Hexateuchs und der historischen Bücher des alten Testaments*. Berlin: Goschen'sche, 1899.
———. *Israelitische und jüdische Geschichte*. 9th ed. Berlin: de Gruyter, 1958.
———. *Prolegomena zur Geschichte Israels*. Berlin: Reimer, 1883.
———. *Reste Arabischen Heidentums*. Berlin: de Gruyter, 1961.
Wells, Bruce. "Conditional Verdicts in Neo-Assyrian and Neo-Babylonian Legal Texts." In *"Gerechtigkeit und Recht zu üben" (Gen 18,19): Studien zur altorientalischen und biblischen Rechtsgeschichte, zur Religionsgeschichte Israels und zur Religionssoziologie; Festschrift für Eckart Otto zum 65. Geburtstag*, edited by Reinhard Achenbach and Martin Arneth, 34–44. BZAR 13. Wiesbaden: Harrassowitz, 2009.
———. Review of *Inventing God's Law: How the Covenant Code of the Bible Used and Revised the Laws of Hammurabi*, by David P. Wright. *JR* 90 (2010) 558–60.
———. "What Is Biblical Law? A Look at Pentateuchal Rules and Near Eastern Practice." *CBQ* 70 (2008) 223–43.
Wenham, Gordon J. *The Book of Leviticus*. NICOT. Grand Rapids: Eerdmans, 1979.
———. *Exploring the Old Testament: A Guide to the Pentateuch*. Exploring the Bible. Downers Grove, IL: IVP Academic, 2003.
———. *Genesis 1–15*. WBC 1.1. Repr., Grand Rapids: Zondervan, 2017.
Westbrook, Raymond. *A History of Ancient Near Eastern Law*. 2 vols. HdO 72. Leiden: Brill, 2003.
———. "Punishments and Crimes." *AYBD* 5:546–56.

Westermann, Claus. *Genesis 1–11: A Continental Commentary*. Translated by John J. Scullion, SJ. Minneapolis: Fortress, 1994.

———. *Genesis 12–36*. Neukirchen-Vluyn, Germ.: Neukirchen, 1981.

———. *The Promises to the Fathers: Studies on the Patriarchal Narratives*. Translated by David E. Green. Philadelphia: Fortress, 1980.

Wette, Wilhelm Martin Leberecht de. *Kritischer Versuch über die Glaubwürdigkeit der Bücher der Chronik mit Hinsicht auf die Geschichte der Mosaischen Bücher und Gesetzgebung*. Vol. 1 of *Beiträge zur Einleitung in das Alte Testament*. Repr., Darmstadt: Wissenschaftliche, 1971.

Wettengel, Wolfgang. *Die Erzählung von den beiden Brüdern: Der Papyrus d'Orbiney und die Königsideologie der Ramessiden*. OBO 195. Göttingen: Vandenhoeck & Ruprecht, 2003.

Wheeler, Brannon M. *Moses in the Qur'an and Islamic Exegesis*. Routledge Studies in the Qur'an. New York: Routledge Curzon, 2002.

White, Hugh C. *Narration and Discourse in the Book of Genesis*. Cambridge: Cambridge University Press, 1991.

Whybray, R. Norman. *Introduction to the Pentateuch*. Grand Rapids: Eerdmans, 1995.

———. *The Making of the Pentateuch: A Methodological Study*. JSOTSup 53. Sheffield: Academic, 1987.

Wilcke, Claus. *Early Ancient Near Eastern Law: A History of Its Beginnings*. 2nd ed. Winona Lake, IN: Eisenbrauns, 2007.

Willis, John T. "The Repentance of God in the Books of Samuel, Jeremiah, and Jonah." *HBT* 16 (1994) 156–75.

Wilson, Ian. *Out of the Midst of Fire: Divine Presence in Deuteronomy*. SBLDS 151. Atlanta: Scholars, 1995.

Wilson, Robert R. *Prophecy and Society in Ancient Israel*. Philadelphia: Fortress, 1980.

Wise, Michael, et al. *The Dead Sea Scrolls: A New Translation*. San Francisco: HarperCollins, 2005.

Wiseman, Donald J. "The Vassal-Treaties of Esarhaddon." *Iraq* 20 (1958) 1–99.

Wolkstein, Diane, and Samuel Noah Kramer. *Inanna: Queen of Heaven and Earth*. New York: Harper and Row, 1983.

Woolley, Paul. "Downward Trends at Modern Princeton." *PresG* 12 (1943) 17–18, 27–29.

Wright, David P. "Ancient Near Eastern Literature and the Pentateuch." In *The Oxford Handbook of the Pentateuch*, edited by Joel S. Baden and Jeffrey Stackert, 379–98. Oxford Handbooks. Oxford: Oxford University Press, 2021.

———. "Azazel." *AYBD* 1:536–37.

———. *The Disposal of Impurity: Elimination Rites in the Bible and in Hittite and Mesopotamian Literature*. Atlanta: Scholars, 1987.

———. *Inventing God's Law: How the Covenant Code of the Bible Used and Revised the Laws of Hammurabi*. Oxford: Oxford University Press, 2009.

———. "Purification from Corpse Contamination in Numbers XXXI 19–24." *VT* 35 (1985) 213–23.

———. "The Spectrum of Priestly Impurity." In *Priesthood and Cult in Ancient Israel*, edited by Saul M. Olyan and Gary A. Anderson, 150–81. LHBOTS 125. Sheffield: Academic, 1991.

Wyschogrod, Michael. *The Body of Faith: God in the People Israel*. London: Aronson Inc., 1996.

Yadin, Yigael. *Bar Kokhba*. London: Weidenfeld and Nicholson, 1971.
Yavin, Zipora. "'Wife-Sister' Stories: The Art of Storytelling in Three Parshas in the Book of Genesis—Gen 12:10–20; 20:1–18; 26:1–12 (The Status of Chapter 12:1–20 as a Typological Narrative in Biblical Literature)" [in Hebrew]. PhD diss., University of Haifa, 2005.
Zellentin, Holger M. *Law beyond Israel: From the Bible to the Qur'an*. Oxford Studies in the Abrahamic Religions. Oxford: Oxford University Press, 2022.
Zenger, Erich, and C. Frevel. "Die Bücher Levitikus und Numeri als Teile der Pentateuchkomposition." In *The Books of Leviticus and Numbers*, edited by Thomas Römer, 35–74. BETL 215. Leuven: Peeters, 2008.
Zevit, Ziony. *The Religions of Ancient Israel*. New York: Continuum, 2001.
———. *What Really Happened in the Garden of Eden?* New Haven, CT: Yale University Press, 2013.
Zucker, David J. *The Torah: An Introduction for Christians and Jews*. New York: Paulist, 2005.

Subject Index

Aaron(id), 9, 53, 57, 59, 60, 61, 64, 68, 71, 78, 80, 81, 82, 84, 87, 89, 91, 92, 96, 97, 98, 100, 104, 107, 111, 112
Abel, 14, 20, 21, 37, 40, 42
Abraham, 8, 13, 23, 26–36, 39, 41, 46–49, 57, 58, 93, 110, 120, 124
Adam, 14, 19, 20–25
Anatolia(n), 15, 30, 59, 68, 74, 104
Atrahasis, 15–18, 21, 22, 53–55

Babel, 14, 23–25, 58
Balaam, 4, 48, 59, 74, 78, 100–103, 105, 109, 110

Cain, 14, 20, 21, 31, 37, 40, 42, 49
Canaan(ite), 15, 28, 33, 45, 46, 52, 61–64, 78, 86, 92, 94, 99, 109, 110, 118, 119, 123, 126
Christ(ianity), 1, 2, 35, 64, 94, 103

Dumuzi, 20, 21

Egypt(ian), 8–10, 15, 21, 28–31, 34, 37, 42, 43, 46–52, 54, 56, 60, 61, 63, 66, 77–79, 88, 89, 92, 94, 95, 110, 117, 125, 127, 129
Enki, 16, 22, 24
Enlil, 17, 22, 24, 54, 55
Enmerkar, 24, 25

Ephraim, 48, 128
Erra, 36, 37
Esau, 37–39, 41, 42, 48, 49, 61, 99
Eve, 14, 19, 20, 25
Ezekiel, 20, 58

Gilgamesh, 11, 20, 24, 37
Greek, 2, 15, 34

Hosea, 104, 122, 129
Hurrian, 15, 82

Inanna, 16, 21, 24
Isaac, 28, 31, 34, 35, 38, 42, 47, 49, 120
Isaiah, 57, 112
Ishmael, 34, 35, 42, 49
Islam, 1, 2, 35

Jacob, 13, 14, 33, 36–45, 47–49, 54, 61, 120
Jeremiah, 59, 89, 91, 115, 118, 129
Joseph, 13, 36, 40, 42, 43, 45–49, 54, 55, 126, 128
Joshua, 78, 90, 92, 93, 98, 100, 104, 107, 110, 111, 128
Judeo-Christian, 2, 75, 130

Laban, 41, 44, 49, 54
law, 1, 2, 83, 107, 125, 126

SUBJECT INDEX

Leah, 41–43, 45, 49
Levite, 1, 80, 81, 84, 85, 96, 97, 100, 104, 108, 111, 124
Lot, 31–34, 49, 54

Manasseh, 48, 105, 109, 128
Marduk, 15, 110
Mesopotamia(n), 10, 15, 18, 26, 30, 62, 64, 70, 84
Miriam, 89–93, 98, 100, 107, 111
monotheism, 1, 4, 15, 77
Moses, 2, 3, 9, 13, 22, 35, 45, 52, 53, 55–59, 61, 62, 64, 76, 77, 78, 82, 86–96, 98, 100–103, 105, 109, 111, 112, 116, 118–22, 124, 125, 128, 129

Noah, 14, 22, 23, 24, 27, 49, 124
Nazarene, 2, 59, 83, 86, 101, 103, 118

Passover, 52, 53, 61, 85, 125
Pharaoh, 22, 28, 29, 31, 46, 47, 50, 54, 55, 56, 57, 59, 60, 61, 77, 79, 96, 121, 129
priest(hood), 1, 6, 63, 64, 70, 71, 72, 77, 80–83, 86, 87, 91, 92, 94, 96, 97, 98, 100, 105, 108, 111, 115

Psalter, 15–17

Qur'an, 2, 15, 20–22, 24, 26, 35, 43, 45–47, 54, 56–61, 69, 70, 84, 85, 90, 119, 123, 124, 130

Rachel, 41–43, 45, 49
Rebekah, 28, 34, 37–39, 48
Reuben(ite), 43–46, 49, 96, 104, 105, 109, 121

Sabbath, 64, 65, 72, 86, 95, 117, 122, 125
Sarah, 28–32, 34, 35, 46, 49, 54
Sinuhe, 46, 56
slave(ry), 12, 18, 43, 46, 48, 50, 51, 54, 57, 62, 64, 65, 66, 72, 79, 85, 88, 89, 124, 126, 130
Sodom(ite), 33, 34, 49

tabernacle, 64, 72, 80–82, 86, 97, 101, 107, 110, 112, 123, 125

Yahw(istic), 4, 7, 25, 26

Zaphenath-Paneah, 41, 42, 45, 48

Author Index

Abba, R., 71
Abrahams, I., 29
Abusch, T., 18, 63
Aeschylus, 3, 30
Alexander, D., 7, 8, 29, 53
Alster, B., 21
Alter, R., 6, 9, 11, 38
Anderson, B., 7
Anderson, J., 35
Apollodorus, 23
Aquinas, T., 8
Aristotle, 3
Arnold, B., 114
Artapanus, 47
Assmann, J., 78
Astruc, J., 7
Atran, S., 70
Auerbach, E., 35, 36
Augustine, 20
Auld, G., 75
Avruch, K., 29
Aycock, D., 9

Baden, J., 5, 7, 34, 66
Bailey, R., 5, 7, 8
Balberg, M., 69
Baltzer, K., 57
Bandstra, B., 26
Baptist, E. E., 55
Barrett, R., 128

Barth, K., 8
Batto, B., 24, 52
Baumgarten, J., 69
Beckert, S., 55
Berg, H., 2
Berlin, A., 9
Bernstein, M., 31
Betlyon, J., 124
Biggs, R. D., 80
Bildstein, M., 68
Bleich, D., 6
Blenkinsopp, J., 10, 17, 22, 64, 71
Bloch, R., 47
Boehm, O., 36
Bowler, K., 8
Boyd, G., 94
Braulik, G., 118
Brickell, H., 4
Brown, R., 116
Browning, D., 98
Brueggemann, W., 90, 92, 114
Bryan, B., 30
Bryce, T., 68
Burchard, C., 47
Byron, J., 21

Campbell, D. R. E., 15
Carimokam, S., 2
Carr, D., 4, 5, 18, 26
Carroll, M. P., 20

Cassuto, U., 29
Cazelles, H., 7
Chalier, C., 7, 8
Chaloupka, L., 23
Chepey, S., 85
Childs, B., 1, 5, 7, 51
Chirichigno, G., 54
Christensen, D., 13, 118, 122
Christensen, W., 51
Clifford, R. C., 17
Clines, D. J. A., 6
Coats, G. W., 8, 51, 56, 88
Cody, A., 70, 71
Cohen, A., 2
Collins, C., 23
Collins, J., 2, 5, 52, 103, 115, 116
Collins, S., 33
Cornell, V., 70
Crenshaw, J., 95
Cross, F. M., 7, 52, 58, 64, 71
Crouch, C., 116
Crouteau, D., 97
Crüsemann, F., 10
Cryer, F., 70
Curtiss, S., 71

Davidson, R., 26
Davies, E., 5, 6
Davies, G., 8, 116
Day, J., 15, 26
Dein, S., 103
de Geus, C. H. J., 128
de Pury, A., 40
Dershowitz, A., 35
Dever, W., 109
de Wette, W. M. L., 115
Dick, M., 25
Dillard, R., 5
Dillmann, A., 29
Doedens, J., 23
Douglas, M., 8, 63, 68–70, 72, 83, 97, 102
Dowson, T. A., 70
Dozeman, T., 9, 10, 53, 56, 57, 60, 61, 64, 65
Driver, G. R., 73
Duhm, B., 115
Dumbrell, W., 40

Edelman, D., 4, 116
Eichrodt, W., 8
Eissfeldt, O., 4
Eliade, M., 107
Elledge, C. D., 31
Elrefaie, A., 115
Engel, B., 44
Engnell, I., 9
Epiphanius, 3
Espak, P., 19
Euripides, 3
Exum, J. C., 6

Farber, W., 43
Fee, G., 8, 69, 119
Feinman, P., 18
Feldman, L., 34
Firestone, R., 28, 29
Fishbane, M., 15, 95
Fleming, D., 61
Flury-Scolch, A., 27
Fohrer, G., 4
Fokkelman, J., 4, 37
Ford, W. A., 53
Fortna, R., 59
Foster, B., 3
Fowler, F., 27
Fowler, H., 27
Fowler, R., 5
França, R., 57
Frankena, R., 116
Frei, P., 10
Fretheim, T., 5, 8, 28, 93
Frick, F., 29
Friedman, R. E., 7, 64
Frymer-Kensky, T., 15, 16, 84

Gadamer, H., 6
Gaiser, F., 32
Gammie, J., 105, 112
García Martínez, F., 69
Gerstenberger, E., 9
Gertoux, G., 33
Gese, H., 33
Gilan, A., 15
Glazov, G. Y., 57, 58
Goldin, J., 69
Goldingay, J., 31, 44, 45

Good, E. S., 26
Gooder, P., 7
Goodnick, B., 96
Gordon, C., 39
Gorman, F., 70
Gossai, H., 34, 42
Gottwald, N., 7, 16, 70
Grabbe, L., 4, 9, 69, 76
Graetz, N., 92
Gray, J., 101
Graybill, R., 34
Grenz, S., 34
Gröger, M., 9
Gross, W., 4
Guinan, M., 7, 8, 15, 18
Gunkel, H., 7, 14, 42
Gurney, O. R., 74
Guthrie, S. E., 70
Gutiérrez, G., 66

Haag, E., 65
Habel, N., 58
Haberman, B., 84
Hackett, J., 102
Hallo, W. W., 75
Hamilton, M., 5, 63, 114
Hamilton, V., 8, 9
Haran, M., 70, 71
Hardmeier, C., 6
Harrington, H. K., 69, 75
Harris, P., 61
Harris, R., 98
Hays, R., 69
Healey, J., 78
Heard, R. C., 6, 14, 18, 20
Heller, B., 2
Helyer, L., 32
Hendel, R., 8, 26, 32
Hepner, G., 30
Herrmann, S., 114
Herrmann, W., 86
Heschel, A., 65
Heschel, S., 70
Hillers, D., 116
Hoffmeier, J., 51
Holladay, C., 47
Hollis, S., 21, 37, 46, 56
Holtz, S. E., 62

Homan, M., 80
Homer, 3, 11, 35
Hopper, S., 47
Houston, W., 7
Hughes, A., 1
Hummel, H., 8
Humphreys, W. L., 40
Hundley, M., 123
Hunt, L., 6
Hurowitz, V., 64, 65, 123

Jacobs, M. R., 45
Janowski, B., 74
Janzen, W., 57
Jeansonne, S. P., 38
Jeffers, A., 48
Jefferson, A., 19
Jemielity, T., 102
Jenson, P., 52
Jiang, Z., 26
Joines, K., 101
Josephus, 28, 29, 33, 34

Kaiser, O., 4
Kaminsky, J., 40
Kaufmann, Y., 14, 71, 115
Kelly, D., 46
Kikawada, I., 8, 9, 19
Kilmer, A. D., 19
King, M. D., 32
Kinnier-Wilson, J., 83
Kislev, I., 126
Kissane, E. J., 120
Kitchen, K., 81
Klawans, J., 68, 69, 71
Klein, R., 64
Klingbeil, G., 68, 70
Klinger, J., 70
Knohl, I., 71
Knoppers, G., 2
Koch, K., 29
Komoroczy, G., 15
König, E., 29
Korson, G., 6
Köstenberger, A., 97
Kowalzig, B., 38
Kramer, S. N., 21
Kratz, R., 4, 14

AUTHOR INDEX

Kuemmerlin-McLean, J., 125
Kugel, J., 23
Kugler, G., 52
Kunin, S., 8, 30

Lack, R., 33
Laffey, A., 7
Lambert, W. G., 11, 15
Lane, E., 23
LaSor, W., 5, 7
Lauinger, J., 116
Law, D. R., 5
Leach, E., 9, 20
Leach, J., 80
Le Grys, A., 31
Leibowitz, N., 57
Lemke, W., 99
Lennox, J., 44
Leveen, A., 89
Levenson, J., 2, 3, 14, 17, 27, 63
Levine, B. A., 8, 12, 70, 71, 91, 104, 108
Levinson, B., 62
Levy-Bruhl, C., 70
Lewis, J. P., 21
Lewis, T., 15, 98, 124
Lewis-Williams, J., 70
Lichtheim, M., 46
Lieu, J., 3
Liverani, M., 30
Lohfink, N., 121
Lonergan, B., 6
Longman, T., 5, 21
Lucian, 27
Luckenbill, D., 65
Luhrmann, T., 70
Lurquin, P., 26

MacIntosh, A., 1
Mailloux, S., 6
Maimonides, 36
Malul, M., 37, 62
Mann, T., 10, 11
Marcus, D., 27
Margueron, J. C., 26
Marshall, I. H., 3
Maritain, J., 2
Martin, D. B., 6
Ma'oz, M., 2

Mathews, K., 26
McCarthy, D., 116
McCarter, P. K., 68
McConville, J., 8
McCoy, B., 20
McDermott, G., 59
McEvenue, S., 6, 7, 10
McKnight, E., 5
Mendelsohn, I., 54
Mendenhall, G., 7, 104
Middleton, J. R., 8
Milgrom, J., 70, 71, 98
Millard, A., 15
Miller, R. D., 15
Miller, R. H., 4
Miller, T., 4
Milstein, S., 43
Milton, S., 35
Moberly, R., 2, 11
Mobley, G., 20, 37, 38
Momigliano, A., 6
Monroe, L., 115
Moore, M. S., 3, 5, 6, 8, 10, 14–16, 18,
    20–22, 24, 25, 28, 30, 32, 34, 35,
    38, 47, 48, 54, 55, 58, 59, 61–63,
    67, 72, 74, 75, 77, 88, 89, 99,
    101–3, 105, 107, 115, 116, 119,
    121, 122, 125, 126, 129
Morales, L. M., 67, 68
Moran, W., 15, 92, 99, 121
Moss, C., 34
Mouton, A., 30
Mowinckel, S., 9, 115
Mugerauer, R., 11
Muilenburg, J., 17
Murnane, W. J., 43

Narucki, M., 13
Nathan, E., 2
Nicholson, E., 7
Niditch, S., 40, 43
Nixon, J., 35
Nogalski, J., 27
Noonan, B. J., 71
Noth, M., 6, 8, 36, 91, 115
Nozick, R., 62

O'Brien, J., 71

Ollenburger, B., 15
Olson, D., 78, 105
Olyan, S., 70
O'Neill, J., 4
Oppenheim, A. L., 30
Otto, E., 84
Otto, R., 86

Parkinson, R., 46, 56
Parpola, S., 34
Parunak, H., 26
Paul, R., 4
Pavlac, B., 2
Peake, H., 21
Pelham, A., 16
Pemberton, G., 73
Perdue, L., 5, 16
Perrin, N., 5
Petersen, D., 125
Peterson, R. S., 8, 16
Petrie, W. M. F., 76
Philo, 29, 31, 33, 56, 57
Picirilli, R. E., 19
Plato, 62
Polzin, R., 5
Porter, J. I., 36
Propp, V., 38
Propp, W., 52, 98
Provan, I., 7
Ptolemaeus, 3

Quinn, A., 8, 9

Rabinowitz, L., 28
Radcliffe-Brown, A., 70
Radday, Y., 68
Räisänen, H., 63
Redford, D., 47, 77
Reidy, R. J., 61
Reiner, E., 3
Rendsburg, G., 9
Rendtorff, R., 7, 75
Renger, J., 70
Richter, S. L., 123
Rickett, D., 30, 32
Roberts, J. J. M., 70
Rockman, S., 55
Rofe, A., 102

Römer, T., 5, 57
Rooker, M., 71
Ross, A. P., 22
Rost, L., 74
Roth, C., 29
Rothenberg, B., 80, 81, 101
Rubio, G., 14

Sailhamer, J., 7
Sakenfeld, K., 94
Salkin, J., 103
Sanders, J., 22
Sarna, N., 51, 57
S/Paul of Tarsus, 1, 20, 59, 63, 69, 103
Schifferdecker, K., 16
Schlimm, M., 21
Schmid, H., 7
Schmid, K., 7, 52
Schmidt, L., 7
Schneider, T. J., 17
Schniedewind, W., 107
Schnittjer, G., 59
Scholer, J. M., 69
Scott, L. T., 33
Scurlock, J., 14, 15
Segal, M., 31
Sellin, R., 4
Shapiro, A., 28
Spencer, H., 70
Sharp, C., 115
Shectman, S., 2, 7
Shuval, H., 33
Sibler, E., 4
Silva, M., 5
Ska, J. L., 7, 10
Skeel, D., 75
Skinner, J., 29
Smith, G., 3
Smith, M., 51, 53, 63
Smith, W., 1
Snell, D., 52, 99, 108
Snyman, G. F., 39
Sofer, A., 2
Sommer, B., 5
Sonik, K., 15, 17
Spalinger, A., 46
Sparks, K., 15
Speiser, E., 27, 29, 33

AUTHOR INDEX

Spicq, C., 121
Spier, H., 30
Stackert, J., 5, 7, 62
Staubli, T., 46
Steinmann, A., 39
Steinmetz, D., 39
Sternberg, M., 44
Steymans, U., 115, 116
Stökl, J., 125
Stone, L., 26
Strauss, B., 55
Stuart, D., 52
Sturtevant, E. H., 70
Surls, A. D., 58
Syrén, R., 44

Taggar-Cohen, A., 82
Talon, P., 16
Tertullian,, 3
Thompson, T., 2
Throntveit, M., 28
Tigay, J., 10
Tomlinson, F. A., 26
Topolski, A., 2
Tov, E., 31
Töyräänvuori, J., 15
Trible, P., 34
Tsumuraya, K., 14
Tutt, T. D, 37
Tylor, E. B., 70

Ulanowski, K., 48
Urbainczyk, T., 54

Valentinus, 3
van de Mieroop, M., 83
VanderKam, J., 107
van der Toorn, K., 1, 13, 47, 84, 97
van Inwagen, P., 7
van Seters, J., 7, 9, 29
Veidlinger, J., 35
Vergil, 11
Vermès, G., 31
Vermeylen, J., 5
Vieyra, M., 74
Vita, J.-P., 80
Vogt, P. T., 8

von Lossow, T., 32
von Nordheim, E., 11
von Rad, G., 20, 29, 42, 117, 123
von Wahlde, U., 59

Walker, C., 25
Walsh, G., 2
Walsh, J., 27
Walton, J., 21, 25
Walzer, M., 57
Wang, X., 17
Warfield, B., 4
Washburn, J., 4
Watson, P., 78
Watson, R., 17
Watts, J. W., 7, 51
Wefing, S., 98
Wehr, H., 23
Weinfeld, M., 7, 29, 40, 114–118, 123
Weiss, S., 39
Wellek, R., 35
Wellhausen, J., 6, 7, 70, 71, 115
Wells, B., 29, 62, 84
Wenham, G., 7, 19, 71
Westbrook, R., 2, 68
Westermann, C., 18, 26, 27, 29
Wettengel, W., 21
Wheeler, B., 70
White, H., 38, 61
Whybray, R., 9, 11
Wilcke, C., 68
Willis, J., 94
Wilson, I., 123
Wilson, R. R., 125
Wise, M., 29
Wiseman, D. J., 115
Wolkstein, D., 21
Woolley, P., 4
Wright, D., 7, 62, 67, 70, 74, 97

Xenophon, 3

Yadin, T., 103

Zellentin, H. M., 69
Zevit, Z., 6, 77
Zucker, D., 2

www.ingramcontent.com/pod-product-compliance
Lightning Source LLC
Chambersburg PA
CBHW050807160426
43192CB00010B/1672